The Redeemed Good Defense

The Redeemed Good Defense

The Great Controversy as a Theodicy Response
to the Evidential Problem of Evil

ANTHONY MacPHERSON

WIPF & STOCK · Eugene, Oregon

THE REDEEMED GOOD DEFENSE
The Great Controversy as a Theodicy Response to the Evidential Problem of Evil

Copyright © 2021 Anthony MacPherson. All rights reserved. Except for brief quotations in critical publications or reviews, no part of this book may be reproduced in any manner without prior written permission from the publisher. Write: Permissions, Wipf and Stock Publishers, 199 W. 8th Ave., Suite 3, Eugene, OR 97401.

Wipf & Stock
An Imprint of Wipf and Stock Publishers
199 W. 8th Ave., Suite 3
Eugene, OR 97401

www.wipfandstock.com

PAPERBACK ISBN: 978-1-6667-0982-7
HARDCOVER ISBN: 978-1-6667-0983-4
EBOOK ISBN: 978-1-6667-0984-1

07/05/21

Contents

List of Tables		vii
Preface		ix
Acknowledgments		xi
Abbreviations		xiii
Introduction		1
Chapter 1	Mapping Theodicies	11
Chapter 2	Gregory Boyd's Trinitarian Warfare Theodicy	50
Chapter 3	Initial Construction of a Great Controversy Theodicy	88
Chapter 4	Comparative Analysis of Boyd's TWT and the Great Controversy Theodicy	128
Chapter 5	Modelling the Great Controversy as a Theodicy	167
Conclusion		205
Bibliography		213

List of Tables

Table 1: The Transformation of the Problem of Evil into its Evidential Form	5
Table 2: Two Kinds of Greater Good Approaches	38
Table 3: Justificatory Patterns and Theodicy Solutions	46
Table 4: Theodicy and Doctrines of God and Providence	47
Table 5: Theodicies and the Problem of Evil	48
Table 6: Elements in the Problem of Risk-Associated Freedom	132
Table 7: Boyd's TWT Resolution of Risk and the Problem of Evil	136
Table 8: The Great Controversy Theodicy Resolution of Risk and the Problem of Evil	137
Table 10: Hick's Soul-Making Theodicy and the Doctrine of Double Effect	181
Table 11: Plantinga's Felix Culpa Theodicy and the Doctrine of Double Effect	181
Table 12: The Divine Glory Defense and the Doctrine of Double Effect	182
Table 13: The Free Will Defense and the Doctrine of Double Effect	182
Table 14: Pruss's Felix Culpa as a Triple Effect	186
Table 15: The Great Controversy Theodicy as a Triple Effect	187
Table 16: Great Controversy Theodicy "Good's" and Triple Effect	187
Table 17: The Deontological (non-Consequentialist) Ethical Structure of the Great Controversy Theodicy	191
Table 19: The Four Stages and Six States of Freedom	196
Table 20: Comparing the Eras/Stages of Freedom in Shenk and the Great Controversy Theodicy	197

Preface

WHY GOD?

In the presence of pain and evil, the question is instinctual, unrelenting, universal. In the past believers asked this question with sorrow and bewilderment. Today it is often asked with hostility and accusation. Answering this emotionally-charged question is the theological task of theodicy.

This question of theodicy, of why God allows, permits, causes, or does not stop evil, is one of the greatest modern stumbling blocks to belief in God. If we are honest as theologians, theodicy has been a struggle. Many responses have been abstract, technical, and impersonal. Some responses even appear to exasperate the problem. I do not want to add to any exasperation but to better understand the problem of evil and why some theological solutions struggle with or even intensify the problem.

I believe there is promise in the cosmic warfare version of theodicy, in which God fights and defeats evil at its deepest level and seeks to draw us into this holy resistance. This form of theodicy foregrounds the necessity of recognizing the supernatural element in evil. It has deep scriptural roots and an ancient theological pedigree. Unfortunately, in modern times this supernatural element has been ignored or rejected. But if it is a necessary part of theodicy then its loss or neglect can only distort or truncate our efforts. Fortunately, there are hopeful signs in a small but significant resurgence of interest in cosmic warfare theodicy and it is again taking its place at the discussion.[1]

---

1. Of note are the works of Gregory A. Boyd which I extensively interact with. Just as I had completed my study, John Peckham's *Theodicy of Love: Cosmic Conflict and the Problem of Evil* came out. Peckham's work makes a significant contribution. I hope to address the topic again in the future and do so by utilizing and building upon some of Peckham's insights.

This study positions itself as part of this resurgence and further explores how a cosmic warfare approach may better deal with the great issues of theodicy. It is largely based on my PhD thesis but has undergone some minor changes. It represents a foundational introduction to the topic from a believing and cosmic warfare perspective. I hope people will come to see greater value in the warfare model with my articulation of a "redeemed good defense" based in a *felix soter* theodicy.

Acknowledgments

This thesis was a long time in the making, and I am deeply indebted to all who helped or encouraged me. Above all, I give my deepest thanks to Father, Son, and Holy Spirit. For the first half of my life, I would have never imagined I would or could complete a PhD. Now I cannot imagine otherwise. Living God, you placed in my heart an ever-growing quest to know you and your ways. Your beauty, glory, character, and actions have motivated me and I hope I've captured, by your grace, a little of it in this study. Thank you for who you are to us (and to me!).

Thank you to all my church members and fellow Pastors who encouraged me to pursue further study. Of special note are fellow theological nerds Andrew Skeggs, Grenville Kent, Christopher Stanley, and Stephen Ferguson. Thank you also to co-supervisors Dr. Rob McIver and Dr. Wendy Jackson who offered many helpful corrections and suggestions.

A special thank you to my principal supervisor Dr. Ray Roennfeldt for your encouragement and both the positive and necessarily critical feedback. The path to a PhD in theology all started with an essay I wrote for one of your systematic classes that I later published as my first journal article. I remember asking tentatively, "Do you think this could turn into an article one day?" "Yes," you replied but added with a smile, "with some more work."

Last but not least I want to thank my beautiful and intelligent wife, Sheree. You have always been my biggest supporter. When I wasn't sure if I could, you were cheerfully optimistic that indeed I could. I did not, however, take all your advice. When desperately needing to edit out thousands of words, your 'helpful' advice to "just delete every third page" was not followed. Your humor is priceless! I love you so much and am blessed to be with you.

Abbreviations

CW	Cosmic Warfare
CWT	Cosmic Warfare Theodicy
EDF	Exhaustive Divine Foreknowledge
EPOE	Evidential Problem of Evil
DDE	Doctrine of Double Effect
DTE	Doctrine of Triple Effect
FWD	Free Will Defense
GCT	Great Controversy Theodicy
GG	Greater Good
POE	Problem of Evil
SDA	Seventh-day Adventist
TWT	Trinitarian Warfare Theodicy

Introduction

THEODICY AND THE PROBLEM OF EVIL

The first formal statement of the problem of evil appears to be made by Epicurus (341–270 BC) who framed it as a logical dilemma.[1] It was put into more concise and memorable form by David Hume (1711–1776). Speaking of God, Hume asks, "Is he willing to prevent evil, but not able? Then is he impotent. Is he able, but not willing? Then he is malevolent. Is he both able and willing? Whence then is evil?"[2] The logical thrust of the problem comes in the form of a syllogistic trilemma involving a perceived incompatibility between a simultaneous affirmation of God's goodness, God's power, and the reality of evil. Evil here is usually understood to be both moral evil and natural evil. *Moral evil* is evil expressed in wrong acts (e.g., lying, murdering) or bad character traits (e.g., greed, cowardice). These are the things for which we hold people morally responsible.[3] *Natural evils* are events of physical pain and suffering (e.g., natural disasters, disease, and physical defects) for which people are not morally responsible.[4] The crux of Hume's argument is that it is impossible to hold all three propositions together, and so one of them must be logically untenable. The prime target for skeptics is the proposition of God's existence. Both atheists and theists consider the problem of evil to be the foremost barrier to belief in God.[5] One of the tasks for theologians has been to offer responses to the problem of evil that have

---

1. Epicurus is quoted by Lactantius, "A Treatise on the Anger of God," 271.
2. David Hume, *Dialogues*, 88.
3. Peterson et al., *Reason and Religious Belief*, 93.
4. Peterson et al., *Reason and Religious Belief*, 93.
5. Erickson, *Christian Theology*, 436.

become known as theodicies. The word "theodicy" was coined by Gottfried Wilhelm Leibniz (1646–1716) for his work by the same title.[6] It combines two Greek words, *theos* (God) and *dike* (justice), and implies a justification of God in the face of the problem of evil. All such attempts by theologians, both before and after Leibniz, are now termed theodicies. Mark Scott believes there are five questions essential to theodicy. These are "1. Origin of evil: How does evil originate? Who is responsible? 2. Nature of evil: What is the ontology of evil? How does it exist? 3. Problem of evil: How does evil pose a problem for theology? 4. Reason for evil: Why does God permit evil? What is the morality sufficient reason? 5. End of evil: How will God end evil and/or ultimately bring good out of evil?"[7] Scott suggests that "a complete theodicy will respond to all five questions."[8] These questions will lie in the background of this study, although they will not control it.

Logical Form of the Problem of Evil

The problem of evil commonly exists in a generic, ill-defined, everyday form—"Why does a good God allow suffering and evil?" The problem is instinctive but imprecise. Among academics the problem of evil takes on more technical formulations. Hume's articulation is more precise than its generic cousin yet even his formulation never demonstrates a contradiction. It only advances that one exists. There is a surprising lack of rigor. Australian philosopher J. L. Mackie (1917–1981) understood this and put forward the most rigorous version of the logical problem of evil. To do so Mackie had to add another proposition, without which the argument does not work. The addition is that "a good thing always eliminates evil as far as it can, and that there are no limits to what an omnipotent thing can do."[9] The key is "always" and "as far as it can." That evil still exists leaves the impression that the propositions about God must be false. Mackie argued that this was a fatal contradiction.[10]

---

6. Leibniz, *Theodicy: Essays on the Goodness of God*. Leibniz is (in)famous for his "best of all possible worlds" theodicy in which "if the smallest evil that comes to pass in the world were missing in it, it would no longer be this world; which, with nothing omitted and all allowance made, was found the best by the Creator who choice it." Leibniz, 128.

7. Scott, *Pathways*, 64.

8. Scott, *Pathways*, 65.

9. Mackie, "Evil and Omnipotence," 200. Or "a being who is wholly good eliminates evil as far as he can, and that there are no limits to what an omnipotent being can do." Mackie, *The Miracle of Theism*, 150.

10. Stewart calls it the "inconsistency strategy" on the part of the skeptic. Stewart, *The Greater-Good Defence*, 5.

Hume's and Mackie's specific formulations are no longer presented with the same confidence, nor do they command the focus in contemporary discussions. The reason for this is the belief that effective theistic defenses have been put forward in response.[11] A number of writers, both atheists and theists, claim that Alvin Plantinga's *free will defense*, in particular, provided an adequate logical response.[12] It is not that Plantinga has resolved the wider problem of evil but he has shown that it is not illogical to hold that God can be good and all-powerful and that evil exists. Plantinga succeeded in showing that no disproof of God had been established by presenting a defense rather than a theodicy. The difference between them is that a theodicy seeks to explain the reason why God permits evil, whereas a defense only attempts to explain what God's reason might possibly be.[13] The burden of proof is thus lowered. Plantinga's response was to show clearly that there is nothing about Mackie's additions which are necessarily true (necessity not possibility is needed for the logical problem of evil to succeed). In simple terms, Plantinga did this by the addition of a missing premise, that of free will.[14] If God creates creatures with free will then he cannot "*cause* or *determine* them to do only what is right. For if He does so, then they aren't significantly free after all; they do not do what is right *freely*."[15] God cannot logically give freedom and withhold it at the same time. Sadly, some of God's free creatures choose evil. But this "counts neither against God's omnipotence nor against His goodness; for He could have forestalled the occurrence of moral evil only by removing the possibility of moral good."[16] The use of free will in theodicy

---

11. "Few atheologians still maintain that the existence of evil is logically incompatible with the existence of an omnipotent, omniscient, wholly good God." Basinger, "Evil as Evidence against God's Existence," 141.

12. For many Plantinga "was an instance of philosophical victory being snatched from the jaws of final defeat. At the very least, there can be no denying that the tide turned." Timpe and Speak, eds., "Introduction," 5.

13. Plantinga, *God, Freedom and Evil*, 28. A defense need not even be correct, as long as it suffices to meet the logical objection.

14. For a detailed discussion of how Plantinga's argument works, see Davis, "Free Will and Evil," 76.

15. Plantinga, *God, Freedom and Evil*, 30. Italics in original.

16. Plantinga, *God, Freedom and Evil*, 30. Critics asked why God could not create a world in which creatures are free and yet always do what is right. This criticism only works if the form of freedom is compatibilist, however, Plantinga's concept of freedom is libertarian. "A person is free with respect to an action A at a time t only if no causal laws and antecedent conditions determine either that he performs A at t or that he refrains from doing so." Plantinga, *The Nature of Necessity*, 170–71. Mackie countered that it is not logically impossible for libertarian free creatures to be good in one, many, or even every occasion. He asks why God didn't actualize a world in which everyone always performs what is right (see Mackie, "Evil and Omnipotence," 209). Plantinga's

is not new to Plantinga. It was and is the most common approach to the problem of evil. Timpe and Speak note that "[n]early every recent systematic effort to address the shifting problem of evil rests significantly on robust (and, indeed, quite frequently libertarian) freedom."[17]

Evidential Form of the Problem of Evil

With the failure of the logical problem of evil, critics of theism have shifted the debate to what is called the evidential problem of evil.[18] This is now the most common form of the problem of evil.[19] The evidential argument is an inductive one that looks at the scale, magnitude, and intensity of evil. Some forms argue probabilistically that given the scale and scheme of things it is highly unlikely that the God of theism exists.[20] Other forms argue that given theistic assumptions about the world, evil (especially horrendous evils) should not be present. In this case it is not that theism is logically inconsistent with itself but that it is inconsistent with what we would expect the world to be like if theism were true.[21] Theism is not inconsistent but implausible. Skeptics agree that theists can give a reasonable explanation for some forms of evil but there are other instances of evil for which no good explanation exists; these are pointless or gratuitous evils and they "constitute *prima facie* evidence against the existence of God."[22] The best-known advocate of the evidential argument is William Rowe (1931–2015).[23] Rowe's argument will be discussed in more depth later, but a version of it will be given here:

1. There exist instances of intense suffering which an omnipotent, omniscient being could have prevented without thereby preventing the occurrence of any greater good.

---

response was to introduce the concept of "transworld depravity." This is the idea that is it possible that in whatever world God actualizes there will be people who will do at least one wrong act. Plantinga even suggests "it is possible that *everybody* suffers from it." Plantinga, *God, Freedom and Evil*, 48.

17. Timpe and Speak, "Introduction," 9.
18. Peterson, "Christian Theism and the Evidential Argument from Evil," 175.
19. Little, *A Creation-Order Theodicy*, 2.
20. Stewart terms this the probabilistic strategy in contrast to the inconsistency strategy. Stewart, *The Greater-Good Defence*, 7.
21. Madden and Hare, *Evil and the Concept of God*.
22. Peterson et al., *Reason and Religious Belief*, 98.
23. Rowe, *Philosophy of Religion*.

2. An omniscient, wholly good being would prevent the occurrence of any intense suffering it could unless it could not do so without thereby losing some greater good.[24]

Therefore,

3. There does not exist an omnipotent, omniscient, wholly good being.[25]

The first premise argues that genuine gratuitous or pointless evil exists (the *factual premise*).[26] The second premise is a statement about God and how he would act (the *theological premise*). Connecting the two premises is what has been called the "noseeum" inference.[27] This is the argument that we "no see um" the greater goods, that is, we cannot see any of these greater goods that morally justify God's permission of evil. This is undergirded by the assumption that it is likely that we could discern such goods.[28]

Table 1: The Transformation of the Problem of Evil into its Evidential Form

Basic problem of evil Trilemma:	Evil exists +	God is All-powerful +	God is All-loving	= Logical Contradiction
Changes to POE by EPOE	Relevant category of evil is specified as gratuitous evil	Divine Attributes (& Divine Providence) are understood in a more specific way		Shift from deductive logic to inductive inference
Evidential formulation	Gratuitous Evil exists (which an Omni-God could prevent without losing some greater good or permitting a worse evil)	An Omni-God *would prevent* gratuitous evils (unless it could not do so without losing some greater good or permitting a worse evil)		Therefore, an Omni-God does not exist (is not likely to exist)
	Factual Premise: Gratuitous evil exists	Theological Premises: Meticulous Providence & Restricted Standard Theism		

24. Rowe adds the following for completeness in his footnotes "or permitting some evil equally bad or worse" Rowe, *Philosophy of Religion*, 109, fn. 3.

25. Rowe, *Philosophy of Religion*, 99. Rowe has gone through a number of different formulations of the argument.

26. Rowe usually illustrates this with two paradigmatic examples of gratuitous evil. The first case illustrates natural evil. It is a fawn (termed "Bambi') trapped in a forest fire and undergoing days of terrible agony before dying. The second is the morally evil case of a five-year-old girl Sue who was raped, beaten, and murdered by strangulation. These two illustrations occur throughout Rowe's work. See, Rowe, *Selected Writings*, 195.

27. "No-see-ums" is an American colloquialism referring to small, hard-to-see biting midges or sandflies.

28. Trakakis and Nagasawa, "Skeptical Theism and Moral Skepticism," para. 1.

THE TOPIC OF STUDY: THE GREAT CONTROVERSY

The preceding discussion will prove an all-important context for this study. But first, there is a need to clarify what is the purpose of this study. It will look at the Seventh-day Adventist concept of the "Great Controversy" and its relationship to the problem of evil. In Adventist thinking, all of history and existence is understood under a theme known simply as the "Great Controversy."[29] It is one of the 28 fundamental beliefs of the Seventh-day Adventist church and affirms that "All humanity is now involved in a great controversy between Christ and Satan regarding the character of God, His law, and His sovereignty over the universe."[30] But more than a belief, the Great Controversy functions as the central organizing principle, worldview, and metanarrative of Adventism.[31] It is the big picture idea within which Adventist thought places all doctrine, beliefs, mission, and practice. This Great Controversy idea or narrative naturally and necessarily gives rise to a Great Controversy theodicy. Ellen White (1827–1915) is explicit about the link between the Great Controversy and the problem of evil.[32]

The significance of this opening discussion of theodicy is in providing an introduction and context for this investigation. It shows what is the problem of evil and the recent shift from the logical to evidential forms. This highlights what a Great Controversy theodicy must respond to. Of special note is that the evidential argument is something the logically-orientated free will defense is inadequate to answer. Any trouble for the free will approach will mean trouble for the Great Controversy as it is heavily dependent on the concept of free will. The key challenge the evidential argument makes against free will (and therefore the Great Controversy) is based on the amount of evil in the world. Even if free will is an inherent good it does

---

29. The phrase is shorthand for the fuller idea which is captured in the book title by Ellen G. White, *The Great Controversy between Christ and Satan*.

30. *Seventh-day Adventists Believe*, 113.

31. Davidson, "Cosmic Metanarrative," 102–19; Gulley, "The Cosmic Controversy," 82–124; and Douglas, "The Great Controversy Theme," 2000.

32. Ellen White writes that the Great Controversy is given "to present a satisfactory solution of the great problem of evil, shedding such a light upon the origin and the final disposition of sin as to make fully manifest the justice and benevolence of God in all His dealings with His creatures." White, *The Great Controversy*, xii. White's problem of evil is generic and does not distinguish between logical or evidential forms. Evil calls into question God's character, not his existence. The approach takes a narrative, historical form instead of a theoretical or syllogistic one.

not outweigh the amount of evil in the world nor especially extreme or gratuitous evils.[33] Is free will itself even worth it?[34]

The Thesis Question

The question which drives this study is: How does the Great Controversy resolve the problem of evil? How does the Great Controversy function as a theodicy? The goal is to uncover the inner workings of a *Great Controversy Theodicy*. This study is warranted on the grounds that while the issue of theodicy lies at heart of the Great Controversy, very little attempt has been made to articulate it as a theodicy in dialogue with the modern discussion of theodicy. The exceptions to this are some short works by Richard Rice and Martha Duah's PhD thesis comparing Gregory Boyd and Ellen White's Warfare Theodicies.[35] Rice's discussion, while limited in size (an article and a chapter), offers a penetrating look at the Great Controversy as a theodicy and raises a number of challenges that will be addressed in this study. Duah's thesis is substantial and shares some organizational similarities to this work.[36] Her goal is to ascertain the viability or feasibility of Boyd's and White's models in comparison to others and to see if they are "contradictory, unrelated, or complementary" to each other.[37] She concludes that the models are distinct and that White's warfare theodicy is a more satisfactory response to the problem of evil.[38] Despite some overlap, a reading of both studies reveals striking differences. This study's thesis question is focused on the Great Controversy, while Duah's is also on Gregory Boyd. This study does use Boyd but in an analogical and instrumental manner in order to more closely analyze the Great Controversy as a theodicy. Duah focuses on

---

33. Inwagen, "The Argument from Evil," 64.

34. There are other objections to free will that we will also consider: If freedom entails risk, and freedom is essential to intelligent beings, then risk is eternal; how could evil arise in a perfect environment in the first place? Pini, "What Lucifer Wanted," 3; How can free will explain natural evils such as earthquakes, diseases etc? See Inwagen, "The Argument from Evil," 64.

35. Rice, "The Great Controversy," 46–55; Rice, *Suffering and the Search for Meaning*, 75–90; Duah, "A Study of Warfare Theodicy."

36. Duah surveys the wider field of theodicy (howbeit only three theodicies: Augustine; Hick; Griffith), and compares Boyd and Ellen White as I do in a similar progression of chapters.

37. Duah, "A Study of Warfare Theodicy," 14.

38. She outlines four reasons for this, 1) explanatory adequacy and coherence, 2) comparative uses of sources (Scripture, science, philosophy), 3) contrasting models of divine foreknowledge, and 4) long-term viability or obsolescence of models. Duah, "A Study of Warfare Theodicy," 370–88.

the relationship between science and theodicy, critiquing Boyd's view of origins/creation (which have since changed) and natural evil. This study does not. Duah critiques Boyd's earlier views on hell. He has since changed to an annihilationist view. This work recognizes this. Duah's work is descriptive, analytical, comparative, and evaluative. This study is all of these but also constructive. It seeks to uncover the inner workings of the Great Controversy as a theodicy and construct a working model of it that is in dialogue with the wider contemporary field of theodicy. The survey of theodicies (including anti-theodicy), in the light of the evidential problem, is much more extensive in this study than Duah's and makes clearer how diverse theodicies work. Discussion of ethical assumptions is central to this study but not Duah's (although she shows awareness of such). The discussion of libertarian freedom in this study is a more distinct and radically constructive one. The degree of overlap between the studies is eclipsed by different goals, discussions, and conclusions.

This examination of the Great Controversy will focus on Ellen White's articulation. White's version is paradigmatic for Adventism and, while not widely known in theological or theodicy discussions, it is the most integrated warfare perspective on the problem of evil in Christian history.[39] At the same time, some other more recent representative Adventist sources that share the same paradigm will be referenced. Focusing on White will give unity to the study, and supplementing White with others in the paradigm will give greater depth and breadth.

Delimitations

The field of theodicy is vast, and so delimitations are essential.[40] Virtually all the major theologians, whether ancient or modern, address the topics of pain, suffering, and evil in some way. This means theodicy, whether explicit or implicit, is also ubiquitous. This study will restrict itself to a limited number of representative and explicit models of theodicy.[41] To provide clarity this

---

39. So says Boyd, *God at War*, 307, endnote 44. Although, after his contribution, Boyd somewhat rivals White.

40. For example, Barry Whitney documented over 4200 works on the problem of evil just between the years 1960–1991. See Whitney, *Theodicy*.

41. Potential theodicies not covered in our analysis abound and include Origen's theodicy, aptly explored in Scott, *Journey Back to God*. For the view of Thomas Aquinas, see Aquinas, *On Evil*. For a more recent interpretation of Aquinas, see McCabe, *God and Evil*. Barth's controversial and paradoxical idea of evil as *das Nichtige* (evil as nothingness), see Barth, *Church Dogmatics*, vol. III/3, §50. For a discussion of Barth's theodicy see Rodin, *Evil and Theodicy*. There are several significant modern approaches that

study will limit itself to the evidential problem of evil. Further, it will focus on the question of moral evil, not natural evil. This study will also assume the viability of a warfare perspective and will not engage in apologetic questions.

Methodology

This study will proceed along the following methodological lines. Chapter 1 is descriptive and analytical in nature. It reviews and surveys the literature on major theodicies, as well as anti-theodicy, in the light of the evidential problem of evil. The goal is to provide a map that situates theodicies, anti-theodicy, and the evidential problem in the wider discussion. Before understanding how the Great Controversy works as a theodicy there needs to be a study of how other theodicies work and what problems they face. This will all help in the ongoing analysis and construction of a Great Controversy theodicy.

Chapters 2 and 3 examine two cosmic warfare theodicies.[42] Chapter 2 is an examination of Gregory Boyd's Trinitarian Warfare Theodicy. This chapter is analytical and descriptive. Boyd's view is examined because it is a highly-developed warfare theodicy similar to the Great Controversy. This is something both fortuitous and rare. The similarity will enable a closer inner-category analysis of the Great Controversy not possible with dissimilar theodicies.

Chapter 3 is an examination of the Great Controversy metanarrative to discern and articulate its latent theodicy. This examination will be descriptive and analytical, but it will also begin synthetic and constructive work. This is necessary because much of its theodicy is implicit or pre-systemized. The goal of this study is to uncover and make explicit the inner logic of the Great Controversy narrative as a theodicy. This chapter is preliminary to further constructive and comparative work in chapters 4 and 5.

Chapter 4 involves an inner-cosmic warfare category comparison between Boyd's warfare theodicy and the Great Controversy. This chapter is

---

articulate a practical theodicy emphasising divine suffering. Preeminent among them is Jürgen Moltmann. see his *The Trinity and the Kingdom of God*, 21–60. For an introduction and evaluation of Moltmann's theodicy see Bauckham, *The Theology of Jürgen Moltmann*, 71–98. For a concise introduction that looks at both the German-speaking and English-speaking discussions of theodicy, see Klaus Von Stosch, *Theodizee*. There are also the person-centered theodicies, for example, see Armin Kreiner, *Gott Im Leid*, and Marilyn McCord Adams, *Horrendous Evils*.

42. Boyd defines warfare worldviews as the "perspective on reality which centres on the conviction that the good and evil, fortunate or unfortunate, aspects of life are to be interpreted largely as the result of good and evil, friendly or hostile, spirits warring against each other and against us." Boyd, *God at War*, 13.

comparative and critical. It identifies the major challenges specific to cosmic warfare theodicies and how they respond. This will reveal any areas of weakness within this approach that the Great Controversy must resolve and how it does so.

Chapter 5 is the final stage where the key ideas are brought together in order to construct a model which reveals how the Great Controversy functions as a theodicy in resolving the issues surrounding the evidential problem of evil. This chapter is comparative (comparing the discoveries of chapters 3 and 4 in the light of chapter 1), critical, and constructive. A working model of the Great Controversy theodicy will be provided to demonstrate how it works. The final section offers a conclusion to the entire work.

Chapter 1

Mapping Theodicies

THEODICIES AND THE EVIDENTIAL PROBLEM OF EVIL

The failure of the logical problem of evil led critics of theism to shift the debate to the evidential problem of evil. This chapter will look at the wider field of theodicy and its response to the evidential problem. This survey will highlight the predominant usage of the greater good defense. This defense argues in essence that evil is permitted and justified because it helps produce some greater good. This survey will also show the more recent discontent with the greater good defense in the form of protests against the whole theodicy enterprise (anti-theodicy) or a quest for an alternative approach. This chapter will map out the field of theodicy and finish by articulating how different theodicies attempt to resolve the problem of evil. This map will later help to situate the Great Controversy theodicy resolution to the problem of evil in awareness of other theodicies.

Preliminary Responses: Skeptical Theism

This study focuses on theodicy responses to the evidential problem of evil. There are other less ambitious responses tailored to the evidential argument that do not attempt to construct global theodicies. Due to its relevance to later discussions, this study will briefly consider the response of *Skeptical Theism*. Many Christian theologians and philosophers accept the narrow confines of the evidential framework and offer, from within it, a type of response that is known as "skeptical theism."[1] This refers to a theism that is skeptical of our human ability to know whether any given set of events are justified or unjustified by some set of divinely intended greater goods. Instead of denying Rowe's first premise, they argue that we must be skeptical about our ability to evaluate, let alone affirm, the first premise. Stephen Wykstra[2] has offered his well-known CORNEA (Conditions of Reasonable Epistemic Access) critique. "The heart of Wykstra's critique is that, given our cognitive limitations, we are in no position to judge as improbable the statement that there are goods beyond our ken secured by God's permission of many evils we find in the world."[3] Wykstra emphasizes the difference between our finite intellectual powers and God's infinity and thus our inability to know that something could not be justified by a greater good. "We are not entitled to move from a claim about what appears to be the case to a claim about what probably is the case."[4] Rowe cannot meet the conditions needed for his first premise. William Alston lists some of our cognitive limitations which justify the skeptical theism posture such as lack of data; complexity greater than we can handle; ignorance of full range of possibilities; ignorance of full range of values; and limits to our capacity to make well-considered value judgments.[5] Ganssle and Lee summarise skeptical theism as advancing two basic claims:

- (ST1) We do not know whether the good and evil we know of are representative of all the good and evil that exist.
- (ST2) We do not know whether the connections between a case of evil and various goods that we know of are representative of all the connections between good and evil that exist.[6]

Skeptical theism is controversial and has garnered a range of responses from both non-theists and fellow theists.[7] For many, including theists, skep-

---

1. See one such attempt by Michael Bergmann and Daniel Howard-Snyder, "Grounds for Belief in God Aside," 140–55.
2. Wykstra, "The Humean Obstacle," 73–93.
3. Trakakis, *The God Beyond Belief*, 77.
4. Ganssle and Lee, "Evidential Problems of Evil," 19.
5. Alston, "The Inductive Argument from Evil and the Human Cognitive Condition," 59–60.
6. Ganssle and Lee, "Evidential Problems of Evil," 23.
7. For an extensive survey, see McBrayer, "Skeptical Theism," 611–23.

tical theism is too skeptical and its price is too high.[8] Critics argue that it advances a skepticism concerning human epistemic limits that undermines theistic claims about God's goodness (e.g., can we ascribe any good events to God), a large portion of theological knowledge (e.g., the design argument), and leads to moral skepticism, as much as it undercuts the evidential problem of evil.[9] Several defenses have been offered in return.[10] This is an ongoing debate that currently sits at a stalemate. It should be remembered that the conversation between skeptical theists and non-theists operates in an exclusively philosophical domain in which faith claims and arguments from authority (i.e., Scripture) lack philosophical validity.[11] This study will now turn to actual full-scale theodicies.

AUGUSTINE'S FREE WILL THEODICY

St Augustine (374–430) is generally credited with producing the first fully-formed Christian theodicy.[12] The problem of evil was a lifelong interest for Augustine.[13] Because so many theodicies and critics proceed in reference to Augustine, it is essential to examine his position. At this point, it is helpful to mention the now widely recognized distinction between Augustinian and Irenaean theodicies. This distinction is due to the work of John Hick (1922–2012) who will be examined later. Hick argues that Augustine is the fountainhead for the majority report within Western theodicies. Hick seeks to retrieve the lesser-known minority report which he terms Irenaean.[14]

In much of his early thinking about evil Augustine is responding to his previous belief in Manichaean dualism. The Manichaean belief that two equal but morally opposite cosmic powers are eternally at war in the universe offers an obvious answer to the problem of evil. Having become a Christian, Augustine saw his previous Manichaean beliefs as shocking, detestable, and

---

8. Hasker, "All Too Skeptical Theism," 15–29.

9. Piper, "Why Theists Cannot Accept Skeptical Theism," 13.

10. Snapper, "Paying the Cost of Skeptical Theism," 45–56; McBrayer, "Are Skeptical Theists Really Skeptics?" 3–16.

11. Piper, "Why Theists Cannot Accept Skeptical Theism," 146.

12. Peterson, *God and Evil*, 85.

13. Hick, *Evil and the God of Love*, 37. The Irenaean theodicy purportedly goes back to Irenaeus. It suggests that humans begin immature or imperfect (they don't fall from perfection) and must progress toward perfection in a process that requires a struggle with suffering and evil. See the discussion below on pages 21–26.

14. Hick, *Evil and the God of Love*, 21–26.

profane.¹⁵ He now needed to account for evil within his new framework and demonstrate its superior coherence and plausibility. A central means to this was Augustine's denial that evil is the work of God and his deeply biblical affirmation that everything God has created is good. How then does evil exist? Augustine, drawing on Plotinus's Neo-Platonism, develops his idea of *privatio boni* or the "privation of the good" theory of evil.¹⁶ This theory is a metaphysical explanation for evil which accounts for its possibility based in the nature of being (or in regards to evil, its sheer nonbeing). Evil is not a thing that has been made. It has no positive or substantive existence. Evil is the absence of good.¹⁷ A ready analogy is that of darkness and light. Darkness is not a "thing" but the absence of light.¹⁸

Privatio boni exists alongside several other metaphysical claims such as the great chain of being (or hierarchy of being), the principle of plenitude,¹⁹ and the principle of harmony or the aesthetic theme. The "great chain of being" is the mature neo-platonic view of the world in which the whole of reality is ordered from the highest forms of life to the lowest. Within this chain or ladder every level is filled with innumerable forms of existence or being. This is the outworking of the principle of plenitude, and this vast array of higher and lower, greater and lesser, superior and inferior forms, taken together as a whole, make up a harmony. The seemingly ugly or comparatively horrible, serve the higher and more beautiful by way of their contrast with the higher.²⁰ Augustine explicitly denies that there is any "natural evil."²¹ By being what they are, they contribute to the greater good of the whole. Augustine even extends this aesthetic theme to cover moral evil and sinners.²²

15. Augustine, "Against the Epistle of Manichæus," chapter 24, 140.

16. Hick, *Evil and the God of Love*, 40–43.

17. "What is called Evil in the Universe is but the Absence of the Good," Augustine, "The Enchiridion," chapter 11, 240.

18. Evans, *Augustine on Evil*, 1,2.

19. This principle states "that the richest and most desirable universe contains every possible kind of existence: lower and higher, imperfect and (relatively) perfect, ugly and beautiful, cholera germs and humming-birds." Nichols, *The Shape of Catholic Theology* 69. Augustine explicitly references Plato as a source, see, "The City of God," Book XII, chapter 26, 243.

20. God only creates what can be part of "an exquisite poem set off with antitheses . . . [where] the beauty of the course of this world is achieved by the opposition of contraries arranged, as it were, by an eloquence not of words, but of things." Augustine, "The City of God," Book XI, chapter 18, 214–15.

21. Augustine, Book XI, chapter 22, 217.

22. "According to Augustine, the totality of things is better and more beautiful than any individual thing. Even evil, if it is considered within the universal order of things, does not disturb the beauty of the whole, since it makes the good stand out by contrast."

While sin provides the contrast to righteousness it also enables the display of God's justice to be seen in punishing sin. The retributive penalty on sin corrects the dishonour of sin and maintains the harmony of the whole.[23] In this way even hell can be incorporated into Augustine's theodicy.

Aesthetics explains the place of evil in Augustine's thought from a wider framework while privation explains that evil doesn't come from anything God created because creation is good.[24] But how did evil emerge from a good creation? Augustine explains that evil may emerge due to creation's inherent finite mutability. He states that because creatures "are not, like their Creator, supremely and unchangeably good, their good may be diminished and increased."[25] The good creation is liable to corruption due to the relative nature, or changeableness, of its being.[26] So evil is a privation but it is also parasitic. Because evil has no substance of its own, it doesn't exist of its own; rather it requires the good. "Accordingly, there is nothing of what we call evil, if there be nothing good . . . Nothing, then, can be evil except something which is good . . . Therefore every being, even if it be a defective one, in so far as it is a being is good, and in so far as it is defective is evil."[27] Evil is spoiled or corrupted goodness.

Augustine's account is not yet finished. Evil is not only a privation (absence of good) and parasitic (needing the good in order to be), it is also a perversion or corruption or turning or falling away from the good.[28] "This remained the fundamental paradox of evil for him. *Deprivatio* is one thing—a mere absence; but *depravatio* is something altogether more fearsome in its positive potential for doing damage."[29] This perversion can only come about by the power of personhood. Augustine finds the source of corruption or evil

---

In this way God is capable of putting even evil things to good use." Bychkov, *Aesthetic Revelation*, 233.

23. Middleton, "Why the 'Greater Good,'" 82.

24. "All things that exist, therefore, seeing that the Creator of them all is supremely good, are themselves good."; "All Beings were made Good, but not being made Perfectly Good, are liable to Corruption," Augustine, "The Enchiridion," chapter 12, 240. Hick, *Evil and the God of Love*, 44–45.

25. Augustine, "The Enchiridion," chapter 12, 240.

26. This relative nature is due to everything, except God, being made out of nothing, and thus mutable. Hick, *Evil and the God of Love*, 46–47.

27. Chapter 13 "There can be no Evil where there is no Good; and an Evil Man is an Evil Good," Augustine, "The Enchiridion," chapter 13, 241.

28. "Much of Augustine's vocabulary for describing the ways in which evil manifests itself has to do with turning away or falling away or movement from the good: *perversys, perversitas, aversion, defection, lapsus, deformitas, deviare, infirmare*." Evans, *Augustine on Evil*, 95.

29. Evans, *Augustine on Evil*, 3.

in "the rational will, which is free to choose between good or evil."[30] This is because inanimate objects cannot turn from the good. "It is in this sense that every evil event may be said to have a mind behind it."[31] In keeping with his ontology, Augustine describes how the will can decide for evil within a good order. Augustine argues that humans possess goods that fall into three levels. At the lowest level are those of bodily existence, in the middle (intermediate goods or *medium bonum*) are the will, and the highest goods are virtues. Sin happens, and therefore evil, when the will turns either to itself or to the lower good, instead of attaching itself to God and virtue. "The evil lies in the *aversio*, the turning away (*De Lib, Arb.* II.xix.53.199), not in the nature of the will or its objects, since they are the creation of a good God."[32] By use of privation theory and locating evil in the will Augustine can show that evil does not originate with God or his works; instead, it arises from creatures.

It has not been possible to do justice to Augustine's vast work on the problem of evil. But even what has been examined reveals tensions. The gains of Augustine's free will defense in securing God's innocence for evil are in danger of being lost in other elements of his theodicy. These include his aesthetic theme, the divine incorporation of evil and hell[33] into a greater good, and Augustine's increasing soteriological determinism.[34] All of these tend to make evil a necessity and thus shift the cause for evil back toward God. While the free will defense helped the early Augustine in his dispute with Manichaeism, he appears to have backtracked somewhat embarrassingly from it in his later disputes with the teachings of Pelagius.[35] It is helpful to be aware of both the overlap and the potential difference between Augustine's version of a free will theodicy and how the free will defense is used by others.

---

30. Evans, *Augustine on Evil*, 95. If evil is nothing then how can it apparently cause so much damage? "In the will of rational beings who have turned from goodness there is power and substance, that which makes the 'nothing' of evil a 'something.'" Evans, *Augustine on Evil*, 99. See also Augustine, "The Confessions of St. Augustin," Book VII; chapter XVI, 111.

31. Evans, *Augustine on Evil*, 95.

32. Evans, *Augustine on Evil*, 116.

33. Hick, *Evil and the God of Love*, 177. Hick notes that hell means "sin will continue without end, accompanied by unending punishment." Evil is not defeated.

34. What a theodicy might look like that more fully reflects Augustine's determinism is examined later in this chapter. This is the "Divine Glory Defense."

35. Evans, *Augustine on Evil*, 113. Griffin says that Augustine changed his earlier libertarian sounding view of freedom for a compatibilist one in harmony with divine determinism, and this undermines his free will defense. Griffin, "Creation out of Nothing," 94.

JOHN HICK: EVIL AND THE LOVE OF GOD

One of the most influential recent theodicies is the soul-making theodicy of John Hick. Hick's book *Evil and the Love of God* is now considered a classic in the field. Hick claims there are two predominant theodicies in the Christian tradition, which he terms the Augustinian and the Irenaean. Hick attempts to recover and adapt a modern, credible version of the Irenaean. Hick's theodicy belongs in the large grouping designated as greater good theodicies. While Hick believes in free will he rejects a free will theodicy because he claims that no one now believes in an angelic or human fall by perfect beings (or demonic influence).[36] For Hick, these ideas are pre-scientific and implausible. Rather, evolution has shown us that suffering has been present from the beginning.[37] Hick grounds this theologically by adapting the Eastern Orthodox distinction between the *image* of God and the *likeness* of God. In Hick's view, the "image of God" refers to the appearance of rationality and the capacity for relationship with God in humans.[38] It comes as a result of God working in the evolutionary process to produce such a creature. These creatures are spiritually and morally immature beings. The next stage is the "likeness of God" which is a goal to be reached and obtained. This goal is for creatures to love God of their own free volition. Hick sees coerced love and worship as oxymoronic.[39] This goal cannot be reached in the same way as the first stage. "It cannot be perfected by divine fiat, but through the uncompelled responses and willing co-operation of human individuals in their actions and reactions in the world in which God has placed them."[40] Perfection lies in the future as a result of a present process. "The reality is not a perfect creation which has gone tragically wrong, but a still continuing creative process whose completion lies in the eschaton."[41]

Central to the growth from the "image" to the "likeness" of God is humanity's experience within a world in which there is suffering and struggle, where a being must meet and overcome temptations, and where character is developed. Hence the designation "soul-making theodicy."[42] This soul built through suffering is considered superior to undeveloped beings created innocent. The worldly conditions of suffering and evil are necessary for the

---

36. "The notion of a fall is not basic to this picture." Griffin, "Creation out of Chaos," 41.

37. Hick, *Evil and the God of Love*, 245–50. Moral evil arises out of "humankind's basic self-regarding animality." Griffin, "Creation out of Chaos," 45.

38. Hick, *Evil and the God of Love*, 254–55.

39. Little, *A Creation-Order Theodicy*, 66.

40. Hick, *Evil and the God of Love*, 255.

41. Griffin, "Creation out of chaos," 42.

42. Hick, *Evil and the God of Love*, 253. Or as Hick puts it "vale of soul-making."

realization of the beings God desires. Thus, the perfected soul is the greater good that justifies and necessitates the existence of suffering and evil.[43]

For Hick not only does humankind need an environment in which there is pain and suffering but in order for the love of God to be unconstrained there is need for epistemic distance between God and humanity. This is so that finite beings will sense no pressure from an overwhelming and infinite God. God must endow humans with a certain relative autonomy over and against God.[44] The world must be "as if there is no God" and "God must be a hidden deity veiled by His creation."[45] This is needed for morally immature but free beings to attain goodness.[46]

An Eschatological Solution

It becomes clear that Hick's theodicy is eschatological in nature.[47] Appeal is not made to a perfection lost in the past (as in Augustine) but to a perfection yet to be obtained in the future. Thus, "our theodicy must find the meaning of evil in the part that it is to play in the eventual outworking of that purpose; and must find the justification of the whole process in the magnitude of the good to which it leads."[48] We have seen that Hick is quite willing to leave aside major orthodox beliefs (i.e., rejecting the fall). This change in beginnings is matched by a comparable departure in endings. Hick's eschatological orientation means the notion of an afterlife is of supreme importance.[49] Hick sees the traditional notion of eternal suffering in hell as in tension with his soul-making theodicy.[50] Indeed it would be the supreme example of "dysteleological" suffering in which no constructive purpose is served. Hick believes hell makes theodicy essentially impossible.[51] As a result, he considers other eschatological alternatives. He acknowledges that annihilation does not have "eternally useless and unredeemed suffering" and a theodicy would

---

43. Little, *A Creation-Order Theodicy Evil*, 63.
44. Hick, *Evil and the God of Love*, 281.
45. Hick, *Evil and the God of Love*, 281.
46. Griffin, "Creation out of Chaos," 44.
47. Hick, *Evil and the God of Love*, 261.
48. Hick, *Evil and the God of Love*, 261.
49. "The notion of an after-life is no less crucial for theodicy." Hick, *Evil and the God of Love*, 338.
50. Hick, *Evil and the God of Love*, 341–42.
51. Hick, *Evil and the God of Love*, 341–42. "Indeed misery which is eternal and therefore infinite would constitute the largest part of the problem of evil." "I believe therefore that the needs of Christian theodicy compel us to repudiate the idea of eternal punishment."

be possible but even here God's good purpose would fail for those souls who suffer extinction.[52] Instead, Hick turns to universalism because "God will eventually succeed in His purpose of winning all men to Himself in faith and love."[53] Hick realizes this is in tension with his acceptance of free will[54] and he has rejected any form of Augustinian or Calvinistic predestination. He therefore softens his approach, "The least we must say, surely, is that God will never cease to desire and actively work for the salvation of each created person. He will never abandon any as irredeemably evil."[55] This softening seems to be temporary and rhetorical as Hick continues by asking, "Can we go beyond this and affirm that somehow, sooner or later, God will succeed in His loving purpose? It seems to me that we can, and that the needs of theodicy compel us to do so."[56] For those who die in wickedness Hick draws upon the idea of a 'purgatory' in the after-life which will help bring about final and universal reconciliation.[57] In this way universal salvation ensures compensation for the difficulties and sufferings of soul-making.

Gratuitous Evil and Soul-Making

Suffering and evil are necessary in Hick's theodicy. What then of horrendous evils which serve no purpose? It is true that much suffering when properly faced does lead to maturity and development of character. But much suffering and evil can have the opposite effect. Some suffering is so excessive it is "dysteleological." Critics have pointed out that the world contains evil so great it can soul-destroy instead of soul-make. Hick is aware of this and admits to the problem of "dysteleological suffering" which is "unjust, inexplicable, haphazard and cruelly excessive."[58] On this point, Hick appeals

---

52. Hick, *Evil and the God of Love*, 342.

53. Hick, *Evil and the God of Love*, 342.

54. How can Hick know that everyone will accept God's way? Is it theoretically possible that everyone will reject God's way but are not both absolute positions extreme and unlikely?

55. Hick, *Evil and the God of Love*, 343. Yet what if the state of irredeemability is an objective condition? God would know this and when it has occurred. What then would God do with such beings?

56. Hick, *Evil and the God of Love*, 344. "It seems morally (although still not logically) impossible that the infinite resourcefulness of infinite love working in unlimited time should be eternally frustrated, and the creature reject its own good, presented to it in an endless range of ways."

57. Hick, *Evil and the God of Love*, 345–349., Hick's later reflections have evolved and incorporate some form of eastern-style reincarnation. See Hick, *The Fifth Dimension*, 159.

58. Hick, *Evil and the God of Love*, 335.

to mystery, confessing he has no current answer.[59] But then he tentatively attempts to pull even extreme evils into the soul-making scheme by suggesting that the very mysteriousness of evil may play a role in soul-making, as unjust suffering calls forth acts of great human mercy, sympathy, service, and love which are not done for reward.[60] And for souls seemingly destroyed by misery and evil in this life, Hick can always fall back on his afterlife progression and universalism.

PROCESS THEODICY

Another more recent but distinct theodicy is process theodicy.[61] This theory takes the process philosophy of A. N. Whitehead (1861–1947) and Charles Hartshorne (1897–2000) as basic.[62] Process theists, in common with the logical and evidential problems of evil, see an inevitable conflict between the affirmations of traditional omnipotence and the reality of genuine or gratuitous evil (evil without any point or divinely-allowed purpose) which process theists affirm.[63] Because genuine evil is real and God's goodness is non-negotiable, the "only possible way to solve the problem of evil is to modify the traditional doctrine of divine power. That modification lies at the heart of process theodicy."[64] The first element to the process solution to evil is defining God's power as persuasive and not controlling.[65] David Ray Griffin acknowledges that some traditional theodicies also say God's primary modus operandi is persuasion, "but they have regarded the reason for this to be moral rather than metaphysical."[66] In these traditional theodicies God's choice to persuade results from a divine self-limitation (e.g., God will not compel free will); in contrast, the process God cannot control creatures even if he wanted to. He lacks such power.

Process theodicy builds this understanding on a rejection of the doctrine of creation *ex nihilo* (out of nothing). In its place is the alternative

---

59. Hick, *Evil and the God of Love*, 333–34.

60. Hick, *Evil and the God of Love*, 334–35.

61. The most prominent advocate is Griffin, in his *God, Power and Evil*; *Evil Revisited*; and "Creation out of Chaos and the Problem of Evil."

62. Griffin, *God, Power and Evil*, 275.

63. Griffin, *Evil Revisited*, 3.

64. Griffin, *Evil Revisited*, 3. Griffin in another work states "Most of the problems of Christian theology, I contend, have been created by the traditional doctrine of divine omnipotence," Davis, *Encountering Evil*, 96.

65. Griffin, *God, Power and Evil*, 276.

66. Griffin, *God, Power and Evil*, 276.

conception of creation of order out of chaos.[67] This means there are some actualities that pre-exist God's ordering of them and these actualities must possess some level of power of their own. There is a power that is common to both God and all actualities and is foundational to both. "Process theism distinguishes between God and the aboriginal power of the universe, which it calls *creativity*. Creativity is not a thing, or a being. It is simply the ultimate activity that all concrete actualities embody."[68] Whitehead maintained that Creativity is the "ultimate metaphysical principle" which lies in "the nature of things," and this means that the world's actual entities having creative power is not a contingent feature of reality: "It is beyond all volition, even God's."[69] "Accordingly, it is impossible for God to have a monopoly on power."[70] The process of creation and the activity of creativity is not due to the sole power of God.[71] God has evocative power but he can't unilaterally control. Instead, he can take the long view and draw creatures over time to higher aims.

God "creates" by luring the creation. God can do this because all pure possibilities are contained in the unchanging primordial nature of God.[72] This gives the initial aim for creatures or actual occasions. But each actual occasion has its own "subjective aim" which is the aim the subjective agent actually chooses which can differ from the initial aim evoked by God. "The initial aim is given by God; the subjective aim is chosen by the subject."[73] This initial aim by God is not coercive and must itself elicit the freely given creativity of the subjective entity. This avoids determinism. At the same time, because God is active in attempting to lead creation in this manner, there is such a thing as divine providence at work.

The concept of an independent subjective aim not under the control of the divine initial aim opens the possibility of evil. But how and what is evil? Process theodicy has two criteria for an intrinsic good. Something is good

---

67. Griffin, *God, Power and Evil*, 279. Griffin, "Creation out of Chaos," 101–2.

68. Griffin, *Evil Revisited*, 22. "Creativity is the twofold power of an individual (1) to create or determine itself on the basis of creative influences received from others and (2) to be a creative influence on the self-creation or self-determination of subsequent individuals." Griffin, *Evil Resisted*, 22.

69. Griffin, *God, Power and Evil*, 279.

70. Griffin, *God, Power and Evil*, 279. "Because power is essentially shared, God's power cannot be thought to be unilateral power." Griffin, *Evil Revisited*, 23.

71. Process theism can speak of a cosmic semi-dualism (Creativity in God and in others) and "It is on this basis that process theology responds to the problem of evil." Griffin, *Evil Resisted*, 24.

72. "While all have creativity—God is the only primordial, omnipresent, all-inclusive embodiment of creativity. And God is the only one who characterizes creativity with perfect love." Griffin, *Evil Resisted*, 23.

73. Griffin, *God, Power and Evil*, 280–81.

to the extent that it is characterised by beauty, which consists of the aesthetic values of harmony and intensity. The criteria for evil is the opposite of these "values." In contrast to harmony is disharmony or discord, and the opposite of intensity is triviality or even "boredom."[74] How evil arises is due to the tension between harmony and intensity. Changes in one effect the other. An increase in intensity requires an increase in complexity to sustain the harmony. When this doesn't happen, discord results. The interesting feature is that as God lures subjects (in the evolutionary process) to greater complexity, to a higher aim, tension inevitably arises and evil can result. God's luring of creation to higher aims necessarily involves the emergence of evil. This is because there are necessary metaphysical correlations of value and power that exist within creation. For example, the capacity for intrinsic good (what affects oneself) correlates to that of intrinsic evil, the capacity for instrumental good (that which affects others) correlates to that of instrumental evil. "The correlations among these variables are positive—as one rises, the rest rise proportionately. They are also taken to be metaphysically necessary."[75] So as freedom increases so do all the other variables. Something with increased freedom can experience or cause more good or evil as a result. Like the free will defense, this doesn't mean all specific occurrences of suffering are necessary, only that "the *possibility* of all this evil is necessary *if* there was to be the possibility of all the good that has occurred and may occur in the future."[76] There could have been less suffering.

How then does process theism alleviate the problem of evil and function as a theodicy? Process theism advocates a metaphysical state of affairs in which evil is unavoidable in whatever world God creates. The process theologian doesn't need to justify God's establishment of these things.[77] God "creates" or lures this world to higher forms but he does not create the underlying metaphysical characteristics of the world. God finds himself in a universe in which these are givens he is powerless to change. Any horrors that occur are the responsibility of agents who possess a self-determination over which God has no control. In order to achieve higher forms of experience God has persuasively led the finite realm out of a state of trivial chaos, and as a result discord has appeared as "the half-way house between

---

74. Griffin, *God, Power and Evil*, 282.

75. Griffin, *God, Power and Evil*, 291. These are implicit in Whitehead's philosophy and drawn out by Griffin.

76. Griffin, *God, Power and Evil*, 294.

77. Griffin, *God, Power and Evil*, 296. There is a direct correlation between creation out of chaos and the notion that there are metaphysical principles which are beyond divine decision. It is the nature of things. Griffin, *God, Power and Evil*, 297.

perfection and triviality."[78] God is responsible for bringing creation to the "place" where intense discord is possible but he is not responsible for the fact that this progress inevitably produces discord. God's purpose in engaging in this creative activity is "to maximize intrinsic good in the present in such a way as to provide the foundations for greater good in the future."[79] For Griffin, God is good in spite of evil, "because the conditions for the possibilities of greater good are necessarily the conditions for the possibilities of greater suffering; because God does not promote any new level of intensity without being willing to suffer the possible consequences" and because he is always seeking to overcome evil with good and enlisting us in the same.[80] From the perspective of classical theism, process theodicy, with its denial of creation *ex nihilo* and its rejection of divine omnipotence, resolves the problem of evil by positing a finite deity.[81]

NATURAL ORDER THEODICIES

Another important theistic response to the problem of evil is the natural order or natural law theodicy. Like the free will defense this approach can be incorporated into theodicies. There are some theologians or philosophers whose work is particularly centered on this argument, although each gives it their own shape.[82]

Richard Swinburne

Richard Swinburne's theodicy combines natural order, free will, open theism, and a version of soul-making. Swinburne argues that a world with evil and suffering is necessary to the development of certain goods, the most important being character and virtue. Suffering and evil thus serve a greater good and are essential to it. Moral character and virtues can only be developed in an environment in which people must face evils and learn by experience and induction of the consequences and causes of actions.[83] Having this,

---

78. Griffin, *God, Power and Evil*, 300; Whitehead, *Adventures of Ideas*, 355.
79. Griffin, *God, Power and Evil*, 291.
80. Griffin, *God, Power and Evil*, 310.
81. Mormon theology with its finite god constructs a theodicy strikingly similar to process theodicy. See Mosser, "Exaltation and Gods Who Can Fall," 45–67; Mosser, "Evil, Mormonism," 56–69; Potter, "Finitism," 83–95.
82. Swinburne, *Providence*; Reichenbach, *Evil and a Good God*; Hasker, *Providence*.
83. "Knowledge of the future is obtained by normal induction, that is by induction from patterns of similar events in the past." Swinburne, *The Existence of God*, 211.

people can then choose either good or evil. This requires a natural order, predictable and constant, in which there are cause and effect.[84] Natural evil is not gratuitous but purposeful. Swinburne illustrates his view in many ways. Humankind must see rabies in order to learn to prevent it, and must observe the effects of asbestosis to prevent it in the future. To learn to build earthquake-proof buildings they must first learn of the effects of earthquakes on buildings.[85] Swinburne even tries to show the greater good that comes from Rowe's example of a fawn (Bambi) dying from burns due to a forest fire. The fawn's suffering provides an opportunity for courage to rescue and help. Its death helps other deer and people learn to avoid or prevent fires. It is an opportunity to show compassion to the fawn.[86] Swinburne summarises his position by saying that the "fewer natural evils a God provides, the less opportunity he provides for man to exercise responsibility . . . the less natural evil, the less opportunity for the exercise of the higher virtues . . . for freedom and responsibility."[87] Any less would be a "toyworld."[88]

Bruce Reichenbach

Whereas for Swinburne there is a natural order in which moral evil is possible and natural evil is necessary for soul-making, in Bruce Reichenbach's theodicy, natural evil arises as an inevitable by-product of the natural order. Evils "are not willed by God, but are the consequences of the outworking upon sentient creatures of the natural laws according to which God's creation operates."[89] Reichenbach's theodicy combines free will defense with natural law. This natural order that makes free will human beings possible is also the same thing that makes possible disease, sickness, disasters, and birth defects. God is justified in doing this because these are by-products "made possible by that which is necessary for the greater good."[90] There is an inevitabil-

---

84. Swinburne, *The Existence of God*, 211.

85. Swinburne, *The Existence of God*, 208.

86. Swinburne, *Providence*, 217–18.

87. Swinburne, *The Existence of God*, 219–20. Swinburne extends this reasoning to things such as "Hiroshima, Belsen, the Lisbon earthquake, or the Black Death." Swinburne, *The Existence of God*, 219. Clearly, with Hiroshima and Belsen, this is not just natural evils. Swinburne even argues the slave trade "opened by innumerable opportunities for good or bad choices" in later centuries and other places. Swinburne, *Providence*, 245–46.

88. Swinburne, *The Existence of God*, 220.

89. Reichenbach, *Evil and a Good God*, 101.

90. Reichenbach, *Evil and a Good God*, 102. "Thus, his action of creation of a natural world and a natural order, along with the resulting pain and pleasure we experience,

ity to this state of affairs. God only had the option of either (a) this world with its natural laws or (b) a world which operates according to continuous miraculous intervention. But Reichenbach argues that (b) is not possible. In such a world, rational action would not be possible as there would be no cause and effect. One could not exercise freedom, God would be deciding all that comes to pass, and no one could will evil or observe its results.[91] It could be asked then why didn't God make a world in which the natural laws never lead to suffering. Reichenbach suggests that for the skeptic to plausibly outline such a world system, which also contains moral free will, is impossible.[92]

ALVIN PLANTINGA'S FELIX CULPA

Alvin Plantinga is best known for his free will defense response to the logical problem of evil. However, when Plantinga responds to the evidential problem he offers not the free will defense but something different, the *felix culpa* theodicy.[93] In many respects this is Plantinga's real thinking behind the problem of evil.[94] Felix Culpa means "happy fault" and refers to the fortunate benefits or greater goods that result from the fall into sin. Plantinga discusses good possible worlds God could create and the good-making qualities that make these good possible worlds, but notes that in Christian belief there is a contingent good-making characteristic of our world "that towers enormously above all the rest of the contingent states of affairs included in our world: the unthinkably great good of divine incarnation and atonement."[95]

These states are far greater and more valuable than worlds without them, however, you "can't have a world whose value exceeds L [L = Level of goodness] without sin and evil; sin and evil is a necessary condition of the value of every really good possible world."[96] Given this, the answer to the question of "why is there evil in the world?" is that God wanted the best of all possible worlds. All such worlds have incarnation and atonement, and therefore, all also have sin and evil. "So if a theodicy is an attempt to explain

---

is justified."

91. Reichenbach, *Evil and a Good God*, 103–7.
92. Reichenbach, *Evil and a Good God*, 116–17.
93. Plantinga, "Supralapsarianism, 'Felix Culpa,'" 1–25.
94. "Christian philosophers should also turn to a different task: that of understanding the evil our world displays from a Christian perspective. Granted, the atheological arguments are unsuccessful; but how should Christians think about evil?" Plantinga, "Supralapsarianism,' or 'Felix Culpa,'" 5.
95. Plantinga, "Supralapsarianism, or 'Felix Culpa,'" 7.
96. Plantinga, "Supralapsarianism, or 'Felix Culpa,'" 12.

why God permits evil, what we have here is a theodicy—and, if I'm right, a successful theodicy."[97]

Plantinga anticipates three main objections. The first objection is: "Why does God permit suffering as well as sin and evil?" To explain moral evil Plantinga uses the free will defense (significantly free and rational creatures are a good-making feature of a world and yet they also may and do commit evil). In response to natural evil he plays with a Natural Law Defense, "perhaps . . . this is the price God had to pay for a regular world."[98] But in the end appears to opt instead for collapsing natural evil into moral evil by means of a Satanic/angelic fall previous to humanity: "Much of the natural evil the world displays is due to the actions of Satan and his cohorts."[99] He also argues that suffering itself is instrumentally valuable, adapting the soul-making defenses of Hick and Swinburne, with the added Christian element that suffering enables believers to experience solidarity with Jesus Christ.[100] With the second objection, "why does God permit so much suffering and evil?" Plantinga eventually says we can't know how much is needed and finds this objection inconclusive. The third objection is more challenging. It asks, "If God permits human suffering and evil in order to achieve a world within incarnation and atonement, would that make him manipulative, calculating, treating his creatures like means instead of ends?" Does God suffer from "a sort of cosmic Munchausen syndrome by proxy"?[101] This is a telling objection, and it is hard to see how Plantinga convincingly responds to this objection. Plantinga toys with ideas that he does not necessarily commit to. He reasons that it is possible that God is right in allowing us to suffer if our suffering benefits someone else or achieves a great good if we consent to it. But, of course, we didn't consent to suffering. We were born into it. Plantinga argues that sometimes we make decisions involving other people and their suffering who don't have all the information (e.g., on behalf of children, or people in comas). These are decisions that the person would make if they were able to. Maybe God has done that for us. If we knew what God knows, we would freely make the same decision he makes, and it is only our ignorance that holds us back from seeing that (how could we ever know or substantiate this?). Additionally, God may know that if I didn't have a disordered disposition or affections then I would freely choose to undergo suffering (this appears to undercut the libertarian understanding of free will).

97. Plantinga, "Supralapsarianism, or 'Felix Culpa,'" 12.
98. Plantinga, "Supralapsarianism, or 'Felix Culpa,'" 15.
99. Plantinga, "Supralapsarianism, or 'Felix Culpa,'" 16.
100. Plantinga, "Supralapsarianism, or 'Felix Culpa,'" 17.
101. Plantinga, "Supralapsarianism, or 'Felix Culpa,'" 21.

In all these cases God is not simply treating people as means to an end.[102] Plantinga then pulls back from this specific individual-centered course of argumentation and resorts back to the broad greater good of incarnation and atonement. Here he says that a world with incarnation and atonement is a better world for human beings (he is no longer arguing for an individual benefit) within it than one without. So "his perfect love perhaps mandates that he actualize a world in which those who suffer are benefited in such a way that their condition is better than it is in those worlds in which they do not suffer."[103] In both his initial individual-centered musings and his latter greater good/better world argument the acclaimed benefits only apply to the redeemed. What of the lost? Are they not the means to an end that does not benefit them?

DETERMINISTIC THEODICY: THE DIVINE GLORY DEFENSE

Given the dominance of free will in historical discussions of the problem of evil one could be forgiven for thinking that all theodicies pivot on the question of free will.[104] But this is not the case. A powerful counterpoint to free will theodicies is found in the realms of theological determinism. This study will look at one important Calvinistic response called the *divine glory defense* that is found in the thought of Jonathan Edwards (1703–1758) and many modern-day influential Calvinists.[105] If Calvinists cannot appeal to libertarian concepts of freedom then what do they do? They appeal to a set of "demonstrative goods of uncertain size," that is, greater goods which justify the occurrence of evil, in this case goods connected to divine glory.[106] The central claim is that "there are certain excellences of God (justice and mercy, for example) that cannot be displayed or manifested in the creation unless there are evils to be punished or forgiven."[107] Evil has teleological and eschatological significance in providing the context for God displaying

---

102. Plantinga, "Supralapsarianism, or 'Felix Culpa,'" 24.

103. Plantinga, "Supralapsarianism, or 'Felix Culpa,'" 25.

104. The dominance of libertarian accounts has overshadowed Calvinistic responses, see, Alexander and Johnson, "Introduction," 2.

105. For example, evil "is ordained by an infinitely holy and all-wise God *to make* the glory of Christ shine more brightly." Piper, "Is God Less Glorious." See also Doug Erlandson who states that God ordained evil "in order to display . . . his glory in a way otherwise impossible," in Erlandson, "A New Perspective."

106. Green, "A Compatibicalvinist," 234.

107. Johnson, "Calvinism and the Problem of Evil: A Map of the Territory," 44.

his glory. For the divine glory defense to work it needs to show that glory requires two features. First, that it is such a profound good that it is "worth allowing the moral evil in our world for its sake," and, second, that it "cannot exist without the evil that exists, or at least that certain kinds or amounts of glory cannot exist without the evil that exists."[108] Advocates recognize that God's innate glory does not need evil's existence but the display of divine glory does need evil.[109]

Johnson notices the structural similarity to Plantinga's felix culpa theodicy and even claim that his theodicy is a version of the divine glory defense.[110] Others state that Edward's divine glory theodicy is a version of felix culpa.[111] Both are versions of the traditional greater good approach. But what makes the difference between Plantinga's felix culpa and the divine glory defense, is that in the divine glory view Plantinga's justifying greater goods, incarnation and atonement, do not exhaust or adequately fulfill the requirements for the full display of God's glory.[112] While Christ's work did reveal God's glory, it did not properly or fully reveal God's attributes of wrath and judgment.[113] This is for a number of reasons: because Jesus wasn't the actual object of God's wrath; Jesus' sufferings were only of a limited duration; and on the Cross we see a singular undifferentiated judgment, what we do not see is the different demands and punishments justice places on specific sins.[114] What all this adds up to is that evil is necessary, and with that an eternal, observable hell is necessary. God's "program of self-glorification in eternity necessitated the eternal, conscious experience of this wrath on the part of its objects, as well as the observation of the fruits of divine disfavour by the redeemed."[115] If evil or hell do not eventuate then the fullness of God's glory is not displayed. Bruce Davidson says that Edwards "aggressively recommends hell as an essential manifestation" of divine glory which is the "'chief end' of everything God does."[116] Without a hint of irony

---

108. Johnson, "Calvinism and the Problem of Evil: A Map of the Territory," 44.

109. Johnson, "Calvinism and the Problem of Evil: A Map of the Territory," 44.

110. Plantinga's Felix Culpa defense claims God's self-expressive actions (incarnation and atonement) couldn't happen without evil. "Plantinga's defense, then, is a version of the divine glory defense." Johnson, "Calvinism and the Problem of Evil," 47.

111. Hoon Woo, "Is God the Author of Sin?" 122.

112. Hart, "Calvinism and the Problem of Hell," 248–72.

113. Davidson, "Glorious Damnation," 809–22.

114. Hart, "Calvinism and the Problem of Hell," 256–57. Hart also adds, building on top of these points, "a greater perception of the majesty of God" and gratitude from the elect by an appreciation of the alternative outcomes for elect ad reprobate.

115. Davidson, "Glorious Damnation," 817.

116. Davidson, "Glorious Damnation," 814.

Davidson says for Edwards that "*Thanks to hell*, God is glorified much more profoundly and comprehensively than he would be otherwise."[117] The divine glory defense is thus used by Calvinists as a defense against the problem of evil and the problem of hell.

There are several obvious objections to the divine glory defense. One is the tension between the absolute divine control and the emergence of genuine opposition to God. Where did the first sin come from? How could evil arise without it being traceable to God's desire that it arise? This is usually where appeal to libertarian free will is made but of course this is not available to compatibilists. Green mentions Edwards's seeming side-step in he which claims God only withheld the grace needed for obedience but humanity chose to sin; therefore, humanity and not God is directly responsible for sin.[118] He recognizes this still has problems: "Even if God cannot be charged with evil person E's evil actions as such, he might still be charged with (a) making it the case that E has E's character, and (b) making it the case that E's evil actions affect others the way they do."[119] Green's follow-up is striking as it reveals a reasoning that non-determinists find highly objectionable. Green argues that God creates Hitler, in order that Hitler commits evil, in order that God might punish Hitler and show his hatred of such a character.[120] What is "positive" is that Hitler makes possible a mode of presentation of God's glory achievable in no other way.

What some non-determinists find so appalling is the implied ethics which brings us to another major objection to the divine glory defense. "The objection is that this defense seems to portray God as using human beings as mere means to his own ends rather than as ends in themselves."[121] In response Johnson argues that when God seeks the greatest good for himself it is also the greatest good for human beings (and vice versa). He gives the example of the elect, for whom God displaying his glory also means eternal life.[122] Of course, this argument works for the elect but not for the reprobate! God's glory means their eternal pain. Johnson's response to this is relegated to a footnote in which he *acknowledges that the lost do serve as a means to God's ends!*[123] How then does he avoid this defeater? He simply argues that

---

117. Davidson, "Glorious Damnation," 814. Italics mine.
118. Green, "A Compatibicalvinist," 237.
119. Green, "A Compatibicalvinist," 238.
120. Green, "A Compatibicalvinist," 240–41.
121. Johnson, "Calvinism and the Problem of Evil: A Map of the Territory," 48.
122. Johnson, "Calvinism and the Problem of Evil: A Map of the Territory," 48.
123. He states "Clearly, God does allow some to come to grief in order to achieve a greater good, and so treats the lost as a means to a further end." Johnson, "Calvinism and the Problem of Evil: A Map of the Territory," 48.

God's love does not require that God never treats someone as a means to an end. Here love is defined/redefined to allow for an instrumental use of another. This appears to amount to ethical consequentialism. Such an ethical stance occurs again in another objection concerning the scale of evil and the vast numbers who will be in hell.[124] Could not God achieve his goals with only a few hundred damned? Hart claims no. God could not achieve a number of "goods" for the elect unless vast numbers are condemned.[125] These are goods such as feelings of gratitude and appreciation for salvation by the elect in view of how rare and infrequent salvation is.[126] All this is for the greater good of the elect's observation of divine wrath on the reprobate.[127] It appears as if God has made the reprobate the instrumental means of the "good" of displaying his glory and the "good" of the elect observing it.[128] This is again ethical consequentialism. There are more arguments and defenses but this gives us a sense of how the divine glory defense is perceived to work or not.

THE GREATER GOOD DEFENSE AND GRATUITOUS EVIL

Earlier it was seen that theistic responses to the evidential problem of evil challenge Rowe's first premise, the factual premise, which affirmed the existence of gratuitous suffering/evil.[129] Traditional theodicy denies gratuitous evil (the exception being Process Theodicy) by offering both positive and

---

124. Hart highlights a tangential dilemma: "If Calvinism is true, it seems perfectly easy for God to create a world in which universalism is true—a world in which everyone accepts God's offer of salvation and goes to heaven. Why wouldn't God do this? What could stop him? 'Surely nothing' says the Arminian, 'and so Calvinism is false.'" Hart, "Calvinism and the Problem of Hell," 250.

125. So "important aspects of the divine majesty are not displayed if everyone is saved, so God decrees that many shall refuse his offer of salvation." Hart, "Calvinism and the Problem of Hell," 250.

126. For the full list of "goods" see Hart, "Calvinism and the Problem of Hell," 259–62.

127. Hart narrows down what is the key issue, "The issue therefore centers around this great and terrible decree of reprobation . . . " and, "It might therefore be said that I am not really offering a theodicy of hell, but a theodicy of reprobation. I am happy to accept this." Hart, "Calvinism and the Problem of Hell," 253–54.

128. "I suggest it is for the sake of the occupants of heaven that God creates people to occupy hell." Hart, "Calvinism and the Problem of Hell," 250. This is clearly instrumentalist.

129. "A gratuitous evil, in this sense, is a state of affairs that is not (logically) necessary to the attainment of a greater good or to the prevention of an evil at least as bad." Trakakis, *The God Beyond Belief*, 52. Rowe's definition is specifically defined and refined by his debate with theism.

negative responses to the factual premise. The positive response constructs a theodicy that defends the notion that God has a greater good which justifies his permission of all evil.[130] For every evil that occurs there is a corresponding good that justifies its occurrence. The negative response of skeptical theism denies that non-theists have the epistemic ability to declare that no such greater goods exist and thus no one can claim an evil is gratuitous. Both of these positive and negative approaches accept the second premise, and its idea of a greater good, and reject the first premise and its idea of gratuitous evil.

The Greater Good Theodicy or Defense

The greater good approach to evil is of immense significance. It has been the classical and predominant approach. Melville Y. Stewart states that "Most if not all theistic attempts to resolve the problem of evil make use in some way of the greater-good defense."[131] Stewart has offered what he sees as a defensible version of the greater good theodicy. His definition of a greater good defense is:

> GGD = "For every evil that God permits there is a good state of affairs which counterbalances and which logically requires the evil in question (or some other evil of at least equal negative value), and some evil is overbalanced by a good state of affairs (or good states of affairs) which logically require the evil in question (or some other evil of at least equal negative value)."[132]

Most of the theodicies examined employ the greater good defense in some form. For example, despite free will putting a distance between God and evil, Augustine's views on predestination and his aesthetic theme of overall harmony (involving the beauty of antitheses) make both evil and evils necessary.[133] Griffin sums up Augustine's position by saying "there is only one thing that is clearly evil intrinsically, and this is sin, or evil willing. But this *prima facie* evil is only apparently evil, for the universe is a better place with sin than it would have been without it."[134] Hick positioned his Irenaean soul-making

---

130. Obviously, many theodicies pre-date the evidential formulation and are not directly responding to it.

131. Stewart, *The Greater-Good Defence*, 56.

132. Stewart, *The Greater-Good Defence*, 144.

133. Peterson, "Religious Diversity," 159. There is an "aesthetic theme in Augustine that the evils we experience are parts of a greater whole that must still be seen as good, even as beautiful, under God's sovereignty."

134. Griffin, *God, Power and Evil*, 76–77. Apparently, gratuitous suffering is also either punishment for sin or an aid to achieving eternal life and is thus a good when

theodicy as the great alternative to Augustine. Yet he also employs a strong greater good theodicy. Souls created in the image of God cannot become like God unless they exist in the soul-making environment this world is. Evil and suffering are unavoidable and necessary features in order to bring about the eschatological greater good of matured souls who love God and are like him. Swinburne's views are similar to Hick's but with a much stronger emphasis on the greater good. He thinks the natural order necessarily brings about a world of good and evil in order for people to make choices between them and learn and grow. Natural evil is required and thus not gratuitous. Swinburne states strongly that "Every moral evil in the world is such that God allowing it to occur makes possible . . . the great good of a particular choice between good and bad . . . Every pain makes possible a courageous response . . . and normally the goods of compassion and sympathetic action . . . And all animal pain gives knowledge and opportunity for compassion to animals and humans if they know of it."[135] In the felix culpa and divine glory defenses, evil is necessary for the greater good, and for displaying the divine glory in incarnation and atonement or wrath and punishment.

The only exceptions to this are process theology and the concept of free will. If creatures are capable of free but evil decisions, neither ordained by God or metaphysically necessitated, then gratuitous evil is a genuine possibility. This realization, as well as concern at the moral and theological implications of the greater good defense, has led to alternative theodicies.

Problems with Greater Good Theodicies

Bruce Little has strongly criticized the greater good theodicy response to the evidential argument from evil. He argues that horrific evil is the greatest challenge to greater good theodicies.[136] Little believes that claiming that a greater good obtains for every evil, including horrific evils, places an unnecessary and impossible empirical burden of proof on the theist. The evidential argument becomes unanswerable and the retreat into skeptical theism unavoidable.[137]

A number of criticisms have been raised against the greater good approach. First, by suggesting that *evil is necessary to good* a new dilemma arises: "either evil is necessary for God to bring about greater good than

---

seen from the whole. "Accordingly, there is no genuine evil in reality." Griffin, *God, Power and Evil*, 77.

135. Swinburne, *Providence*, 217.

136. Little, *A Creation-Order Theodicy*, 100.

137. Little believes this is an unsuccessful move and skeptical theism fails to completely protect the greater good approach. Little, *A Creation-Order Theodicy*, 107–9.

would have otherwise transpired, or evil is morally unnecessary."[138] If evil is necessary then God's goodness is questioned, as he operates on an end-justifies-the-means principle,[139] and his omnipotence is questioned, as he is unable to achieve his aims without evil. This appears to undercut and nullify any of the gains made by the free will defense.[140] Second, the greater good approach raises ethical questions about God and the good. The *very concept of the good is relativized*.[141] Good is not understood in an intrinsic sense, but in relation to something thing else. Good then cannot be judged by itself but in relation to its consequences and outcomes. This is a consequentialist ethic. What appears to be a morally good action may in fact bring about evil or a lesser good, and conversely, an evil action may bring about a greater good. Good becomes relativized and equivocal, something that appears to be at odds with theism and perfect goodness. Third, a further difficult question is raised—*who receives the good*?[142] Is it God? The sufferer? The onlooker? Often a victim or sufferer of an evil receives no good. The good appears to go somewhere else. It seems questionable that suffering and evil is inflicted on one simply as a means for another's good. This reduces the person to an instrumental means. How is that good? Fourth, a greater good theodicy also appears to *lack objective criteria for good and evil*.[143] How does one calculate (quantitatively or qualitatively) the amount of good needed to outweigh an evil? What measure is used? For example, what resulting greater good justifies the rape and dismemberment of someone? And if horrendous evil necessitates an extreme greater good that means that mild evil produces only mild good, whereas extreme evil produces extreme good. The perverse result is that "it is better to be beaten and raped than only beaten since the good is greater (something no one actually believes)."[144] The greater good belief consistently applied produces a morally confusing world.[145] Fifth, the net effect of the greater good approach is that *evil ceases to be genuinely*

---

138. MacGregor, "The Existence and Irrelevance," 169.

139. Little, *A Creation-Order Theodicy*, 113.

140. Little, *A Creation-Order Theodicy*, 112. This "diminishes God and makes evil a necessary part of his plan, thus destroying the Free Will Defense used ever since Augustine."

141. Little, *A Creation-Order Theodicy*, 118–119. I would add that this also means the concept of evil is relativised.

142. Little, *A Creation-Order Theodicy*, 119–20.

143. Little, *A Creation-Order Theodicy*, 121–22.

144. Little, *A Creation-Order Theodicy*, 121.

145. Kirk R. MacGregor states, "The absurdity of the Greater-Good Defense is multiplied by its transformation of the universe into a philosophically overdetermined system, where hidden benefits are needlessly assigned to all instances of ostensibly pointless evil therein." MacGregor, "The Existence and Irrelevance," 168.

evil. J. Richard Middleton argues that "to claim that every evil in the world contributes to some equal or greater good which would be otherwise attainable means quite simply that there is no *genuine* evil."[146] Sixth, efforts at *social justice are undercut*. After all, why stop evils that are necessary to produce greater goods?[147] Seventh is the problem of purely mental evil. Little asks how the greater good defense deals with evil which is thought or imagined but never practiced or acted on. That appears to be a class of evil for which there is no greater good.[148] Eighth, on the theological front, Middleton claims that greater good theodicies *do not take the Bible seriously enough* nor the ruthlessly honest way it speaks of pain, evil, and suffering (especially Laments such as those in the Psalms). Theodicies take the form of apologetics, whereas the Bible takes the form of prayer or complaint to God about his justice (or delay of it). Theodicy discusses God abstractly as a third person, whereas biblical theology directly addresses God and wants to hear his answer. Classical theodicy can lead to passivity regarding the status quo, whereas biblical theology questions the present social arrangements.[149] Much of Scripture does not resolve the problem of evil as much as intensify it.[150] Middleton believes greater good theodicies take rationality far too seriously, that Scripture instead suggests the inscrutability of evil and hence the apparent impossibility of theodicy, and that this should turn our focus to the participation of God in our suffering and his eschatological work.[151]

Discarding the Greater Good Theodicy

These crushing criticisms have led to a search for alternative theodicies. Positions that reject the greater good approach accept the first premise that gratuitous evil/suffering exists, and instead question how the second premise, the theological premise, is understood. This is a radical inversion of the traditional greater good approach. For example, William Rowe took it as uncontroversial that the second premise "is held in common by many theists and nontheists" and that it expressed "basic moral principles, principles

---

146. Middleton, "Why the 'Greater Good' Isn't a Defense," 86.

147. Little, *A Creation-Order Theodicy*, 115. The same reasoning raises issues about petitionary prayer, see, Middleton, "Why the 'Greater Good' Isn't a Defense," 91.

148. Little, *A Creation-Order Theodicy*, 122.

149. Middleton, "Why the 'Greater Good' Isn't a Defense," 100–1.

150. Middleton, "Why the 'Greater Good' Isn't a Defense," 105.

151. Middleton, "Why the 'Greater Good' Isn't a Defense," 104–8. Elements of Middleton's thought here reflect the concerns of practical anti-theodicies.

shared by both theists and nontheists. If we are to fault this argument, therefore, we must find some fault with its first premise."[152]

But not all theists are so persuaded. Michael Peterson, William Hasker, Bruce Little, and others respond to the evidential argument by acknowledging gratuitous evil and questioning the second premise. Michael Peterson is important as he is an early exponent of this alternative approach. Peterson claims that the implied theological assumption underlying the second premise is that of "meticulous providence" and that it should be rejected.[153] Meticulous providence is the belief that God doesn't allow any gratuitous evil.[154] It is most well known in its Calvinist form, where every event, no matter how small, whether good or evil, has been ordained and meticulously rendered certain by the determination of God. We have encountered it in Augustine and the divine glory defense. Peterson rejects such a doctrine, as it makes the theist's position extremely difficult. In contrast to this Peterson's theodicy is a complex combination of a free will defense, natural-law theodicy, apparent open theism,[155] and a version of soul-making. Peterson claims the created world order makes possible freedom (stability and predictability are required for deliberation and free choice). And this freedom for great good entails the possibility that freedom could be used for gratuitous evil.[156] Trakakis comments that "in providing an environment in which free will can operate, a natural order makes possible the existence of gratuitous moral evil." And as regards gratuitous natural evil, "it is difficult to imagine that God would or could arrange all natural events so that they always realized some higher goods." This would require God to be always interfering and thereby eliminating the *natural* order.[157]

Issues with Alternatives to Greater Good Theodicies

This move to reject the greater good approach, meticulous providence, and acceptance of the reality of gratuitous evil is a very significant recent alternative to the majority of standard theodic approaches. Ronald Nash

152. Rowe, *Philosophy of Religion: An Introduction*, 99.

153. Peterson, *Evil and the Christian God*, 93–95, 124. We will see that meticulous providence is what Gregory Boyd calls the "Blueprint" model of the providence.

154. Hasker describes this providence as that in which "all events are carefully controlled and manipulated in such a way that no evils are permitted to occur except as they are necessary for the production of a greater good." Hasker, "Must God Do His Best?," 216.

155. See Bruce Little's discussion of this in *A Creation-Order Theodicy*, 86–88.

156. Peterson, *Evil and the Christian God*, 102–107.

157. Trakakis, *The God Beyond Belief*, 321.

(1936–2006) believes that, if successful, it would tip the balance of probability in the evidential problem of evil away from the skeptic and toward the theist![158] However, several thinkers such as Feinberg, Stewart, and Trakakis are less sanguine and have identified a major challenge to the current formulation of this alternative. Stewart claims Peterson's dismissal of the greater good defense is unsuccessful, and in the end he still remains within the greater good tradition. His main argument is that "Peterson's gratuitous evils are not really gratuitous, since they are subsumed under one or some combination of three general justificatory patterns."[159] The three justificatory patterns Stewart refers to are the free will defense, natural law theodicy, and soul-making theodicy. These are the greater goods that justify God allowing evil, including gratuitous evil. Given the definitions and frame of the debate, it appears that Peterson has not fully escaped the dilemma. John Feinberg is of a similar opinion. "If the evil is genuinely pointless, then why present the free will defense, for example, to explain its point? If it is genuinely pointless, nothing will explain it. On the other hand, if the free will defense does explain its point (which it seems to do), then why call it pointless?"[160] Trakakis concurs: "Peterson, then, finds himself in a quandary: he cannot reject the factual premise without the credibility of Christian theism being diminished in his eyes, and he cannot reject the theological premise without importing a non-standard definition of gratuitous evil."[161] Peterson seems to be both denying the greater good approach and utilizing it. He is caught on the horns of a new dilemma and his position appears inconsistent and possibly incoherent.

Retrieving Peterson's Alternative by Modification and Clarification

Peterson's position is not as hopeless as it may seem. It is possible to modify the argument, and, in fact, both Feinberg and Nash provide ways of doing so. Once modified, Peterson's formulation emerges as a genuine alternative.

---

158. Nash, *Faith and Reason*, 221.

159. Stewart, *The Greater-Good Defence*, 79. Trakakis criticises the idea of "necessary gratuitous evil" as an oxymoron and asks us to "consider the paradoxical nature of his claim that a given moral evil may be gratuitous even though God is justified in permitting that evil for the sake of preserving human freedom." Trakakis, *The God Beyond Belief*, 322.

160. Feinberg, *The Many Faces of Evil*, 270.

161. Trakakis, *The God Beyond Belief*, 324.

Nash notes the problem outlined above[162] but then offers the following clarification; a distinction can be made between general evil and specific particular evil. "When a theist says that he believes God's creation contains gratuitous evil, he means that it includes *specific instances* of moral and/or natural evil for which there is no specific reason or purpose in God's plan."[163] God has a reason and purpose for allowing evil in general (preserving the existence of the "good" of free will, sustaining the "necessity" of a stable natural order) but God does not have a specific reason or purpose for each and every specific evil. Specific evils are either the actions of individuals, and find their meaning in their choices, or the unfortunate outworking of natural law, and in neither case is God meticulously guiding these events in order that they happen for a specific purpose. These evils can be pointless in themselves. While free will may have meaning, not every exercise of it need be.

In addition to Nash's distinction between general and specific instances of evil, John Feinberg's offers a further and complementary distinction. Classic greater good theodicies claim that there is no evil for which God does not produce a greater good. The good is *subsequent* to the evil event, and either outweighs it or prevents a worse evil from coming, and this subsequent good is the higher reason justifying God's ordaining or allowing of it. The realization of the higher good required the evil to occur (think Augustine's antitheses). Peterson denies this and yet appeals to a greater good to give divine reason for allowing the evil. Feinberg helps clarify that Peterson is not contradicting himself, although he claims his argument and language is muddled. What Peterson is not denying is that an *antecedent* good (e.g., free will) may be what makes possible the evil event but does not require it. Peterson's argument does work if the good is antecedent, whereas the greater good theodicy sees the good as subsequent. For Peterson, the antecedent good is necessary, but the evil is not necessary, nor is there a point to it. There is a point to the antecedent good (free will). It is a "great good," but there is no divine purpose to the non-necessary evil event. And since God does not meticulously control all things, the explanation for the evil is with the agent, not God. God's purpose is the existence of free will and its proper exercise, not the commission of evil.

Instead of a simple division between greater good theodicies and those others that are not, it is more accurate to recognize a distinction between *full greater good theodicies* which deny gratuitous evil and *limited* or *partial*

162. Nash writes, "If evils that these theists are willing to regard as gratuitous end up serving a higher purpose such as free will, natural law, or soul-making, how can they be gratuitous? After all, a gratuitous evil is one for which there is no purpose or meaning." Nash, *Faith and Reason*, 219.

163. Nash, *Faith and Reason*, 219–20.

greater good defenses which allow for gratuitous evil. Theists who acknowledge gratuitous evil must still recognize some kind of greater good defense that seems unavoidable (God is not without purpose). The distinction between full and partial greater goods brings out more clearly Peterson's important discussion.[164] Table 2 below outlines a clearer picture of the alternative way the idea of a 'greater good' functions within theodicies.

Table 2: Two Kinds of Greater Good Approaches

Full Greater Good Theodicy	Partial Greater Good Defense
Every evil is linked to the accomplishment of a greater good or the prevention of a greater evil	Not every evil is linked to the accomplishment of a greater good or the prevention of a greater evil (although some evil can be so linked)
The greater good is *subsequent* to the evil (justifies the evils occurrence)	The greater good is *antecedent* to the evil (the evil itself is not justified, although its permission is)
No evil is truly gratuitous or pointless	
God's providence is meticulous and ensures the realization of a subsequent greater good from an evil act	Evil can be gratuitous and pointless
	God's providence is general, upholds the antecedent good, and can sometimes bring greater goods subsequent to an evil act
The allowance of evil (in general) is justified and all (particular) evil that is allowed is justified by God who ensures and renders certain all things and brings good from it	The allowance of evil's possibility (in general) is justified by a greater good—but the (particular) evil itself is not (responsibility rests with the causative agent) and may not bring any good

These distinctions are significant and make a considerable difference to how a theodicy responds to the problem of evil. The limited greater good defense avoids many of the criticisms leveled against the full greater good theodicies mentioned earlier. Because of this they deserve to be considered as distinct approaches.

ANTI-THEODICY

Bruce Little and Richard Middleton's comments have highlighted the ethical criticisms of the greater good approach. Such criticisms are at the heart

---

164. This alternative is important to the coherence of a number of Arminian-styled theodicies.

of another response to theodicy known as "anti-theodicy." Anti-theodicy rejects the whole attempt to construct theodicies.[165] This is not to be confused with the atheistic rejection of theodicy. These are theistic objections to theodicies. No modern discussion of the problem of evil can ignore this important stream of thinking. There are several kinds of anti-theodicies. *Protest* theodicies (such as John Roth), *practical* theodicies (advocated by Kenneth Surin), and, for clarification, atheistic or skeptical denials of theism will be termed *pure* anti-theodicies. This study's interest is in the first two, which share considerable overlap.

Protest Theodicy

Protest theodicy is a form of anti-theodicy that protests either God (esp. John Roth), or theodicies in defense of God (Terrence Tilley). Roth's protest draws on ancient dissenting Jewish voices that quarrel "with God over *his* use of power."[166] While many theodicies affirm God's eschatological ending of evil as an answer to the problem of evil, protest theodicy does not as "too much has been lost."[167] Protest theodicy "puts God on trial, and in that process the issue of God's *wasteful* complicity in evil takes center stage," and as a result "human repentance will have to be matched by God's."[168] Protest theodicy calls into question, but does not completely reject, the goodness of God.[169] Protest theodicy leads to activism on behalf of the suffering and thus overlaps with practical theodicy.[170] Roth does not want to lessen human responsibility for evil by scapegoating God. We must fight evil but Roth also hopes his protesting activism will shame or spur a morally ambiguous deity to act against evil and reduce his neglectful inaction and waste.[171] Critics draw attention to Roth's decision to reject God's goodness and yet hope that God will eventually do good. They ask how likely this is. If God has a demonic side then how can we hope?[172] Griffin notes that such a moral lack

165. See for example, Pinnock, *Beyond Theodicy*.
166. Roth, "A Theodicy of Protest," 8.
167. Roth, "A Theodicy of Protest," 8.
168. Roth, "A Theodicy of Protest," 10. "Such a wasteful God cannot be totally benevolent. History itself is God's indictment." Roth, "A Theodicy of Protest," 11.
169. The issue is that God is not using his power as he should; see Roth, "A Theodicy of Protest," 16. This is also a protest against all theodicies which "legitimate evil." A "theodicy of protest is an anti-theodicy. It has no desire to legitimate waste." Roth, "A Theodicy of Protest," 19.
170. Roth, "A Theodicy of Protest," 19.
171. Roth, "A Theodicy of Protest," 20.
172. Davis, *Encountering Evil*, 22.

in God would be as irreversible as an ontological limitation in God: "I see no basis for hope that a partly evil deity could be lead to repent."[173] There is no demonic in Roth's theodicy, or rather it seems to be partially incorporated into God. It may be that Roth needs to take seriously the biblical concept of Satan and evil as external to God. Middleton protests that Roth has taken the biblical supplicant's questioning of God's justice and reified it into a systemized foundation for constructing a doctrine of God. He sees this as inappropriate and isolates the complaint from the dialogue of prayer.[174] Roth's view is rare but interesting because, unlike the majority of theists, he questions God's goodness, not his power.

The Evils of Theodicy

Terrence W. Tilley's book *The Evils of Theodicy* is not a solution to the problem of evil but a book about "the problems such solutions create in their attempts to justify God's ways to those who think the problem of evil is solved by producing an explanation." Tilley lists the problems that theodicies create as (1) misportraying and effacing genuine evils, (2) warping the way traditional texts are read today, (3) consigning other "discourse about God and evil to philosophical and theological irrelevance," (4) silencing "powerful voices of insight and healing," and (5) contributing to "the power of the "classical" Humean problem of evil, the alleged incoherence of belief in an all-powerful, all-good, all-knowing God, and that there is genuine evil in the world."[175] Tilley traces theodicies back to the advent of the Enlightenment where attempts were made at constructing totalizing systems to answer philosophical questions. Previous answers to evil were pastorally-motivated and offered defenses of God but not global explanations. Tilley is disturbed by the academic nature of theodicy and how it offers little pastorally (i.e., comfort to those suffering) and marginalizes the concept of social evils in favor of natural or moral evils. Ultimately, Tilley goes too far. The problem of evil can be traced back to Epicurus, well before the enlightenment. While Tilley rejects theodicy he allows for a defense against the problem of evil. However, Phan has pointed out that all his complaints about theodicy can be charged against the "defense" to the problem of evil he allows.[176] In the end, Tilley's work functions as a warning about theodicy poorly practiced[177]

173. Griffin in Davis, *Encountering Evil*, 26.
174. Middleton, "Why the 'Greater Good' Isn't a Defense," 105–6.
175. Tilley, *The Evils of Theodicy*, 1.
176. Phan, "The Lesser Evil of Theodicy," 194–95.
177. Patrick, "Is Theodicy an Evil?," 201–4. Patrick observes that Tilley is arguing

but fails to sustain its case against theodicy by making absolute its claim that any attempted at theodicy is evil.

Practical Theodicy

Another version of anti-theodicy, only slightly friendlier to the exercise of theodicy, is that of "practical theodicy," exemplified in the writings of Kenneth Surin. He, like Tilley, believes theodicy is a modern enlightenment practice that is largely ahistorical and theoretical. He claims theodicies frustrate a historically-situated reflection on various forms of evil, but worse than this they militate "against a properly Christian response to the 'problem of evil.'"[178] Theory triumphs over practice and actual evil remains untouched.

Practical theodicy protests theodicy but also its equally theoretical nontheistic critics. Yet theologians come under greater criticism because they have allowed nontheistic critics the shifts from practice to theory; from a "problem of evil" to a "problem of God"; and from the God of Christian theology to the God of the philosophers.[179] Surin protests the "metaphysical theodicist."[180] This appears to be a protest against the radical reductionism that follows theodicy's polemic turn in the Enlightenment era. This reductionism led to an abstract concept of evil (no longer the particular evils of victims but an ahistorical, abstract category and its theoretical implications),[181] and as a result the attempted solution is found in "the application of reason to that which transcends rationality."[182] Surin observes that, ironically, this is itself irrational. "Evil and suffering in their innermost depths are fundamentally mysterious; they confound the human mind. And yet the goal of theodicy is, somehow, to render them comprehensible, explicable."[183] The effect of this is that the theodicist tries to "render the intractable tractable," trusts words to answer a "wordless abyss," and "promotes a non-tragic vision of the realities of evil and

---

that theologians have an ethical responsibility to not further evils.

178. Surin, *Theology and the Problem of Evil*, 3.

179. Surin, *Theology and the Problem of Evil*, 3,4. A prime example for Surin is Richard Swinburne, who advances a minimalistic deity where doctrines as the Trinity, Holy Spirit, incarnation are non-primary, ancillary hypotheses, Swinburne, *The Existence of God*, 221–222. Surin contends this is unchristian.

180. Surin, "Taking Suffering Seriously," 343.

181. Surin, *Theology and the Problem of Evil*, 52.

182. Surin, *Theology and the Problem of Evil*, 52–54.

183. Surin, *Theology and the Problem of Evil*, 52–53.

suffering."[184] They become Job's comforters, the "prototypical theodicists."[185] "Theodicy, it could be said, founders on the 'mystery of iniquity.'"[186]

For Surin, theodicy and theodicists are concerned with 3 main questions: (1) Can evil be rendered intelligible? (2) Is the existence of God logically compatible with the existence of evil (or with the varieties and profusion of evil)? And, (3) does the existence of evil constitute evidence that counts against (or reduces the possibility of the truth of) theism?[187] Two more questions can be added to these three. These are: (4) What does God do to overcome the evil and suffering that exist in his creation? And, (5) what do we (creatures of God) do to overcome evil and suffering?[188] Does the unintelligibility of evil, just discussed above, mean that all theodicy is impossible and the whole enterprise is broken and irreparable?[189] Theodicists may reply that they do not try or have to try to make evil intelligible but only to make theism intelligible. The rejoinder is that seeking to situate evil within a wider theological framework is still an attempt to rationalize evil by the principle that God permits evil.[190] Surin accepts this and argues that the theodicist needs to leave questions (1) to (3) and move to (4) and (5), or in other words, to "evacuate theodicy from the realm of theory in order to relocate it in the realm of practice."[191]

Before looking at practical theodicy it needs to be asked, What are the theoretical theodicies that Surin refers to? Not simply the more obvious culprits such as Leibniz and his "Best of all possible worlds," but Alvin Plantinga's free will defense, Swinburne's natural law theodicy, David Ray Griffin's process theodicy, and John Hick's soul-making theodicy, which for Surin all bear the unmistakable theoretical bent.[192] This does not mean that Surin opposes any intellectual response to evil but only a theoretical one. Surin instead advocates that the only allowable and needed theodicies are those which may be termed "practical theodicy." Surin's examples of this kind of theodicy include

184. Surin, *Theology and the Problem of Evil*, 53.
185. Surin, *Theology and the Problem of Evil*, 54.
186. Surin, *Theology and the Problem of Evil*, 54.
187. Surin, *Theology and the Problem of Evil*, 59.
188. Surin, *Theology and the Problem of Evil*, 60–67.
189. Surin, *Theology and the Problem of Evil*, 53–54.
190. Surin, *Theology and the Problem of Evil*, 66–67.
191. Surin, *Theology and the Problem of Evil*, 67. This proposal aligns with theologians who employ a practical theodicy based in a theology of the Cross in which "a God of salvation would be justified in creating a world which contained so much pain and suffering only if he were prepared to share the burden of pain and suffering with his creatures." Surin, *Theology and the Problem of Evil*, 67.
192. Surin, *Theology and the Problem of Evil*, 70–111.

the theological responses to evil and suffering in the works of Dorothee Soelle (1929–2003), Jürgen Moltmann, and P.T. Forsyth (1848–1921).[193] What is common to these theodicies, and what sets them apart from their theoretical cousins? Surin tells us they display the following commonalities:

1. They affirm the principle that God in some sense suffers with his creatures.
2. They maintain that the God who suffers in this world cannot be an immutable and impassible deity.
3. They insist that the question of overwhelming import to the sufferer is not "Is theism unintelligible because I am suffering?," but "Is this God a God of salvation—is this a God who can help?"
4. They claim that it is a corollary of (1) and (3) that a theological approach to the "problem of evil" from the standpoint of victims will necessarily lead to soteriology, or, more precisely (given the framework of the Christian mythos), into the doctrine of atonement.[194]

For Surin, what is wrong with theoretical theodicies is their immutable, impassable God incapable of suffering with us; their preference for intellectual solutions instead of practical soteriological solutions; and, finally, their resolution in theoretical theory rather than atonement. Theoretical theodicy discusses evil from the "tranquillity of the study." In contrast, practical theodicy discusses evil from the place of the victim, aiming to be in solidarity with the cross-revealed-God who is in solidarity with the victim, and working toward salvation. This highlights that questions are "interest relative"; the theorist's interest is in seeing if theories of "soul-making" or "free will" account for evil, whereas the victim and the praxis-orientated theodicist wants to answer the question "Why am I here imprisoned?," "Why am I being tortured?," or "Why is God an indifferent spectator?"[195] Thus, the "only theological discourse about Auschwitz which can be permitted is the one that could have been enunciated in Auschwitz."[196] Only a fellow sufferer can speak and bring answers to the situation of evil. Hence the crucial need for God to be a fellow sufferer and in that suffering to be working out salvation.[197]

---

193. Surin, *Theology and the Problem of Evil*, 112–41. Key works include Dorothee Soelle, *Suffering*; P. T. Forsyth, *The Justification of God*; Moltmann. *The Trinity*.

194. Surin, *Theology and the Problem of Evil*, 137.

195. Surin, *Theology and the Problem of Evil*, 137; Surin, "Taking Suffering Seriously," 341–42.

196. Surin, "Taking Suffering Seriously," 342.

197. Surin sees the "self-revelation of God in Christ on the cross as God's self-justification." God's answer renders human theoretical explanations superfluous: "What

Response to Surin

James Wetzel has responded to Surin and raised a number of issues. He notes the interesting progression in theodicy debates. From defending God against charges of a lack of justice in ancient times, to removing obstacles to belief in God in modern times, to the questioning of theodicy itself. Surin epitomizes this last stage.[198] Anti-theodicists are more concerned with "elimination of evil than with its explanation and gauge the success of their theodicies by their political and societal consequences."[199] But Wetzel argues that theodicy is unavoidable. And that Surin in fact engages in a kind of *ad hominem* argument against theodicists along the lines of "if you engage in theodicy then you are morally corrupt" and insensitive to people's suffering.[200] But theodicists are aware of this danger and are explicit that their theodicies are not meant to respond to people in the midst of suffering. That requires the work of a pastor, not a philosopher. Wetzel distinguishes between minimalist theodicy (concerned only to answer logical objections to theism) and speculative theodicy (to offer an explanation of evil and show how it fits within God's providence), a distinction that parallels that of Plantinga's defense versus theodicy. Accordingly, Wetzel uses Plantinga as the representative minimalist. Wetzel maintains that minimalism may satisfy conditions of logic but satisfies no person.[201] There is a need to go beyond it. This is what speculative theodicies aim to do. However, the "vice of speculative evil is that it cannot accept the possibility of irredeemable evil. Many theologians of course may not see this as a vice at all, but as a hopeful conclusion of religious faith."[202] Speculative theodicists give the impression that they are committed to a redescription of evil as a means to a greater good, and struggle to avoid appearing as an apologetic for evil.[203] This does not mean Wetzel sides with practical theodicy. Instead, he claims that evil fails to respect the theoretical/practical distinction and "neither side can

---

God reveals is that divinity itself, through the cross of the Son, endures the sufferings that afflict us." And "The Christian who takes atonement seriously has no real need for theodicy." Surin, "Taking Suffering Seriously," 339.

198. Wetzel, "Can Theodicy Be Avoided?," 351.

199. Wetzel, "Can Theodicy be Avoided?," 352.

200. Wetzel, "Can Theodicy be Avoided?," 352–53. A similar point is made by Barry Whitney, "Anti-Theodicy," 474.

201. Wetzel, "Can Theodicy Be Avoided?," 357.

202. Wetzel, "Can Theodicy Be Avoided?," 359. "In some way the impulse to theodicy must be reconciled with the tragic recognition that in the balance of history there are some losses which can never be recouped. Otherwise speculative theodicy will continually need to beg the indulgence of the victims of the system for its success."

203. Wetzel, "Can Theodicy Be Avoided?," 361.

avoid coming to terms with the possibility of irredeemable suffering" unless they sink into a total silence.[204] He argues that practical theodicy be seen as the tradition's loyal opposition.[205] "Neither the poles of theodicy nor tragedy seem to be acceptable standards for God's sovereignty, but the alternatives, if there are any, await articulation."[206]

OVERVIEW OF DIFFERENT KEY AREAS OF CHOICE IN THE PROBLEM OF EVIL

The investigation so far has revealed no singular way theodicies seek to resolve the problem of evil, instead a range of distinctly different approaches can be discerned. Each approach makes distinctive choices in the following three areas.

1. Choice of Overall Method of Response: Defense, Theodicy or Anti-theodicy

Theists respond to the evidential problem of evil with a variety of methods. One is the minimalistic approach of *defense*. As Plantinga used his free will defense in response to the logical problem of evil, so many theists utilize skeptical theism as a minimalistic defensive strategy. The majority of thinkers have undertaken the more ambitious task of trying to construct a *theodicy* in which actual reasons and explanations are offered to vindicate God in the face of evil. This is a theoretical approach but can have an eye on the practical. On the other end of the spectrum is the direction taken by *anti-theodicies*.[207] Anti-theodicies are marked by protest against an abstract and theoretical resolution of the intellectual problem of evil and argue for a shift to a practical response to evil by God and/or believers. God's practical response is in a work of atonement that overcomes evil, and in being a God capable of both suffering and entering the suffering of the world. Followers of God are called to practically oppose evil and suffering in the world.

---

204. Wetzel, "Can Theodicy Be Avoided?," 362. "When presented with this kind of evil, practical theodicists are not less evasive than their theoretical counterparts."

205. Wetzel, "Can Theodicy Be Avoided?," 363.

206. Wetzel, "Can Theodicy Be Avoided?," 363.

207. This is apart from what I call "pure" anti-theodicy which is the stance of atheists and skeptics who formulate the problem of evil as an objection to theism.

2. Choice of Justificatory Patterns and the Relationship between Evil and the Greater Good

Central to how theodicies answer the problem of evil is the use of major justificatory patterns which occur again and again in the literature of theodicy. For the theodicist these patterns act as missing premises which are added to the logical or evidential formulation of evil to diffuse the trilemma or render it solvable. There are many kinds of justificatory patterns (free will, soul-making, natural order, higher harmony, divine glory defense, felix culpa, etc.) which function within wider theological framework. It is common for a theodicy to incorporate a number of patterns. Usually, they underline some idea of a greater good which either denies gratuitous evil or accounts for it in a way that does not invalidate the theodicy. Usually, these responses do not focus on the theological premise (God is omnipotent and good) but seek to tackle the factual premise (evil and/or gratuitous evil exists). Table 3 below outlines three broad relationships between justificatory patterns, greater goods, and evil.

Table 3: Justificatory Patterns and Theodicy Solutions

A: Solutions that rely on justificatory patterns to demonstrate a full greater good theodicy and deny gratuitous evil (e.g., Leibniz/Augustine/divine glory defense)
B: Solutions that rely on justificatory patterns to demonstrate a partial greater good defense which allows for the possibility of gratuitous evil (e.g., Peterson/Little)
C: Solutions in which both gratuitous evil and justificatory patterns are inevitable features of natural reality which God cannot avoid. God achieves some greater goods despite gratuitous evil (e.g., Process theodicy)

3. Choice of How to Formulate the Doctrines of God and Providence

Lying behind the way justificatory patterns are used and the manner of how the greater good is advocated are the important and interrelated areas of the doctrine of God, his attributes, and his providence. Theodicies are the outworking of theological systems. The range of theodicies is closely linked to these areas or potential modifications in each of these areas.[208] Trakakis, for example, thinks Rowe is successful in his argument against theism and suggests that if theists cannot appeal to their own evidence in support of God's

---

208. The internal theistic debate between determinist and free will theisms is both a debate about providence and the doctrine and attributes of God. Trakakis, *The God Beyond Belief*, 342.

existence, then the only option is to abandon theism or alter one's conception of God.[209] The God debated within the logical and evidential arguments is always the threefold God who is *omnipotent, omniscient,* and *omnibenevolent* (fourfold if *creator* is added, which is usually entailed in omnipotence). Every one of these divine attributes is open to more exact definition or change. The different theodicy approaches can be mapped as follows:

- Goodness/Benevolence: This is denied by John Roth's protest theodicy.
- Omniscience: The traditional understanding is modified by open theism (e.g., Swinburne) and process theology (i.e., Griffin).
- Omnipotence: this is either denied (as in Process or Mormon theodicies) or refined as a voluntary self-limitation for the existence of genuine free will (as in free will or Arminian theologies).
- Creator: Process theology (and Mormon theology) denies creation from nothing as part of its denial of traditional omnipotence. This approach can be termed "finite theism."

Changes in divine attributes are directly related to views on providence and divine limitations. Table 4 below outlines the various groupings in the following manner:

Table 4: Theodicy and Doctrines of God and Providence

Doctrine of God	Limitations on God	Classical Attributes	Providence
Classical Full theism (Augustine, Divine Glory defense)	No limitations	Affirmed	Meticulous
Modified Full theism (Reichenbach)	Self-limitations on divine power	Affirmed/Revised	General
Modified Full theism (Swinburne, Peterson)	Self-limitations on divine power & limits on divine foreknowledge	Affirmed/Revised (some radically)	General
Process Finite theism (Griffin)	Divine power limited by external forces	Revised and/or Rejected	Externally Constrained

These three areas of choice help in understanding the way theodicies work. It should be remembered that any respective theodicy is usually more

---

209. Trakakis, *The God Beyond Belief*, 337. "The end result is that the theological premise, or some version of it, cannot be rejected without departing from the understanding of God common to the historically significant varieties of theism, viz., Judaism, Christianity, and Islam." Trakakis, *The God Beyond Belief*, 325.

complex and intricate than simply these areas and must be understood on its own terms. To display all of the complexity and variety of approaches to the problem of evil is not possible in a diagram. While having clear limitations Table 5 below attempts to provide a visual representation that maps out some of the main approaches.

Table 5: Theodicies and the Problem of Evil[210]

DETERMINISM	FREE WILL DEFENSE		ATHEISM
	FULL GREATER GOOD THEODICY (No Gratuitous evil)	**LIMITED GREATER GOOD DEFENSE** (Gratuitous evil)	
	G W Leibniz *(Best of all Possible Worlds)*		
Divine Glory Defense	Alvin Plantinga *(Felix Culpa)*	Michael Peterson	David Ray Griffin *(Process Theology)*	Mackie *(Logical POE)*
	Augustine *(Early Augustine)*		
Augustine *(Late Augustine)*	John Hick *(Soul-Making)*	Bruce Reichenbach *(Natural Law)*	Mormon Theology	Rowe *(Evidential POE)*
	Richard Swinburne *(Natural Order)*		
	FULL THEISM	FINITE THEISM	ATHEISM
Sceptical Theism Defense *(Stephen Wykstra, William Alston)*		**ANTI-THEODICY**	
		PRACTICAL *(Kenneth Surin)*	PROTEST *(John Roth)*	PURE *(Atheists)*

CONCLUSION: COMMON STRATEGIES AMONG THEODICIES

After this survey of the problem of evil, particularly in its evidential form, a common strategy among theodicies can be observed. This observation can be stated in the following way: In responding to the problem of evil *theodicies tend to add a missing premise (usually one or more justificatory patterns) while readjusting either the theological premise (doctrine of God / model of providence) or the factual premise (deny gratuitous evil)*.[211] This will

---

210. Michael Peterson's theodicy appears Open Theist. Gregory Boyd's is open theist (Boyd will be examined in the following chapter) as is William Hasker; see *Providence*. Hasker is also in the Natural Law category. Also in the Natural Law (but not Open theist) category is Bruce Little in his *A Creation-Order Theodicy*.

211. Feinberg outlines a generic four-stage strategy common for theodicy or defense-making, see, Feinberg, *The Many Faces of Evil*, 489–90.

help in analyzing cosmic warfare theodicies. This wider discussion highlights the following areas and questions to be asked when formulating a Great Controversy theodicy. What justificatory patterns are utilized? What approach is taken to the question of a greater good? Is there such a thing as gratuitous evil? Does God have limitations, chosen or imposed? What is the doctrine of God (including the question of divine suffering)? How are divine attributes understood? What is the doctrine of providence? What role is given to atonement? And does the Great Controversy significantly depart from well-established approaches? What is similar and what is different?

Chapter 2

Gregory Boyd's Trinitarian Warfare Theodicy

The previous examination of theodicy in chapter 1 has shown that the problem of evil has evoked a wide range of theological and philosophical responses. However, that survey deliberately omitted cosmic warfare theodicies (of which the Great Controversy theodicy is one) to which this study will now turn. One of the most thorough applications of a cosmic warfare worldview to the problem of evil is that of Gregory Boyd.[1] Boyd's warfare perspective appears in many of his works but it is spelled out in detail in his two volumes *God at War* and *Satan and the Problem of Evil*.[2] This study will now examine Boyd's work.[3] It will center on these two works but will also weave in insights and perspectives from his other works.[4] In *God at War*, Boyd introduces the problem of evil[5] and presents the biblical case

---

1. C. Peter Wagner argues that from within the spiritual warfare perspective Boyd's works are "unrivaled in the literature of theodicy." In Bielby and Rhodes, *Understanding Spiritual Warfare*, 169.

2. These two books are part of a series. A follow-up volume is tentatively entitled *Myth of the Blueprint*. *Is God to Blame? Moving Beyond Pat Answers to the Problem of Evil* is a popular explanation of his theodicy. Warfare theodicy also appears in Boyd, *Letters from a Skeptic* and Boyd, *God of the Possible*.

3. This chapter will not critique Boyd's views. Critique will take place in chapters 4 and 5.

4. These include other books, articles, papers and blog entries.

5. William Rowe used paradigmatic stories ("Bambi" the suffering fawn and Sue

for a warfare worldview which provides a necessary foundation and biblical justification for his theodicy.[6] Boyd constructs a specifically Christian version which he terms a Trinitarian Warfare Theodicy.[7] In his follow-up work, *Satan and the Problem of Evil,* Boyd works out in detail the philosophical-theological-historical argument of his theodicy and deals with challenges and objections.

BOYD'S FOIL: THE BLUEPRINT WORLDVIEW

The main foil[8] to Boyd's warfare theodicy is the traditional and predominant approach to theodicy, which he calls the "classical-philosophical" approach[9] or alternatively the "blueprint worldview."[10] This approach "assumes that everything somehow fits into 'God's secret plan'" or "a divine blueprint."[11] For Boyd this view covers different theologies. Some versions state "that God *ordains* all things, others that he simply *allows* tragic events to occur," but what is common to all of them is that they share the assumption that "there is a *specific divine reason* for every occurrence in history."[12] This blueprint worldview is another way of speaking of "greater good" theodicies in which there is a divine reason behind all evils, and it is this element which Boyd is at pains to challenge and reject.[13] According to Boyd's definition this blueprint worldview takes in the majority of classical Christian thought after Augustine (including Augustinian,[14] Thomist, Calvinistic,[15] Molinist, and

---

the raped and murdered five-year-old girl) to make concrete the Evidential argument; likewise, Boyd uses paradigmatic stories. In *God at War* Boyd refers to Zosia, a young Jewish girl in Warsaw who had her eyes cut out by German soldiers in front of her mother and was later killed. Boyd, *God at War,* 33–34. See also Boyd, *Is God to Blame?* 11–15. These stories highlight how difficult extreme evil is for all theodicies.

6. Warfare theodicies focus on a conflict between spiritual good (e.g., God) and evil (e.g., demons, etc.). Boyd, *God at War,* 13. Boyd argues that this is the worldview of the Bible and the church pre-Augustine. See Boyd, "Trouble with Angels," 1–32.

7. Boyd, *Satan,* 18.

8. Boyd does contrast the biblical warfare worldview with spiritualistic or animistic warfare perspectives, but they are not the main foil. See Boyd, *God at War,* 9–17.

9. Boyd, *God at War,* 20.

10. Boyd, *Satan,* 13.

11. Boyd, *Satan,* 13

12. Boyd, *Satan,* 13. In keeping with Boyd I will also use the phrase's "classical" view or "classical theism" or the "blueprint" view.

13. Boyd, Satan, 19, 179, 290. Boyd, *God at War,* 48, 56.

14. Boyd, *God at War,* 35.

15. Boyd, *God at War,* 35. The classical blueprint view is "expressed with the most logical consistency by Calvin and the Reformed tradition."

even some Arminian theology). This classical viewpoint finds its roots in the encounter between Christian and Hellenistic thought[16] and produces a theology that seeks to work out the doctrines of God, providence, and theodicy, from a commitment to such constructs as impassibility, immutability and timelessness.[17]

The Issue of Divine Power and Meticulous Providence

The problem of evil concerns the tension between God's power and goodness and evil's existence. Boyd argues that the classical view of divine power is the real problem. This is because the classical view defines omnipotence as omnicontrol, "an equation that forces the problem of evil to be seen as a problem of God's sovereignty."[18] This understanding of power gives rise to a doctrine of meticulous providence (i.e., God meticulously controls and wills every event) which has the effect of absorbing and domesticating the warfare worldview.[19] Cosmic or spiritual war is turned into a "sham war."[20] After all, a war that is played out exactly as one side has determined is hardly a real war.

This leads to a search for a divine reason behind each and every evil. The difficulty suggests "that perhaps the understanding of providence which lies behind this formulation of the problem [of evil] is mistaken."[21] Boyd argues that the classical approach has generally framed "evil as a problem of God's providence and thus of God's character."[22] What kind of God (i.e., moral character), who controls all things (i.e., has power and providence), would ordain such evil? Like Peterson, Boyd rejects the common assumption that theism necessarily entails a belief in "meticulous providence" because this reframes the problem as one of "locating a loving and good purpose behind evil events," and this view of divine providence makes theodicy an impossible and unsolvable task.[23] Because a mysterious divine plan

---

16. Christian thought "shows the unmistakable imprint of a biblical-classical synthesis in which the ontological categories of Greco-Roman philosophy have been untied with the personal-dramatic categories of biblical faith." Bloesch, *God the Almighty*, 205.

17. Boyd, *God at War*, 35, 49, 67; Kärkkäinen, *The Doctrine of God*, 54–55.

18. Boyd, *God at War*, 44.

19. Boyd, *God at War*, 67.

20. Boyd, *God at War*, 67.

21. Boyd, *God at War*, 33.

22. Boyd, *God at War*, 20. "If God is the sort of God who is capable of ordaining such evils, then you can't trust God's character." Boyd, *God of the Possible*, 155.

23. Boyd, *God at War*, 20. Boyd footnotes Surin and reveals an affinity with practical anti-theodicy. See also the following, "It is *this* conclusion [a specific divine purpose

or greater good purpose is assumed to be behind evil events, the problem of evil becomes "an intellectual problem to be solved rather than a spiritual opponent to be overcome."[24] This is a crucial point for Boyd. Classical theism intensifies and to a significant degree creates the problem of evil while rendering it unsolvable.[25]

Undermining the Free Will Defense

All this has implications for theodicies' use of free will. Some forms of classical theism appeal to free will as a partial explanation for evil.[26] However, Boyd argues that under the influence of Platonic/Aristotelian thought, climaxing in Augustine's neo-platonic/Christian synthesis, freedom was subsumed within the sovereign will of God; this meant that there was a transcendent divine purpose behind the freely chosen evil making it contribute to some higher good.[27] This undermines the free will defense because whatever freely chosen evil that happens is also what God deliberately willed or ordained to happen. The point of the free will defense is to deny this connection and instead affirm that the freely chosen evil was contrary to God's will.[28]

The Issue of the Minimal Recognition of a Personal Satan

Boyd's wider objection to classical theodicy is its failure to appreciate the central role of angelic freedom and particularly that of Satan in understanding evil.[29] This understanding, while not entirely absent from classical the-

---

behind every specific evil] more than anything else that creates the problem of evil." Boyd, *God of the Possible*, 99.

24. Boyd, *God at War*, 21, 67.

25. Boyd, *God at War*, 43–44.

26. Such theodicies assume libertarian understanding of free will in contrast to deterministic theologies which assume a compatibilist form of freedom. Libertarian free will refers to the ability to choose between alternatives (it is not compatible with the determinism of only one alternative), whereas compatibilist freedom refers to the ability to choose to freely *do* what you desire to do, but you cannot choose what your desires will be (they are determined by other factors).

27. Boyd, *God at War*, 47–48, 67.

28. Boyd argues that classical theists who are Arminian and affirm free will still maintain a qualified "blueprint" version of providence and are still left with the unsolvable question of what loving reason God had for allowing Zosia's suffering. Boyd, *God at War*, 49. Boyd outlines four reasons why this is so; see Boyd, *God at War*, 49.

29. Boyd, *God at War*, 53, 54.

ism, exists more as an echo, and especially since the time of Augustine few thinkers have "conceived of Satan as a being in any way relevant to, let alone central to, the solution of the problem of evil."[30] Instead of Satan and the corresponding warfare explanation for evil, the ultimate explanation for evil has been God's meticulous providence. "By contrast, the New Testament and early postapostolic church always thought of the problem of evil in the context of spiritual warfare. The world is caught up in a cosmic battle and thus is saturated with horrifying suffering and diabolical evil. *That is the final explanation of evil*."[31] For Boyd, the combination of undermining the ultimate role of angelic freedom, and thus the ultimate explanatory power of cosmic war, for the sake of preserving the view of meticulous providence, generates the unsolvable nature of the problem of evil.[32] Bringing together these ideas, Boyd states that "the main difference between the warfare worldview and the blueprint worldview is that the former does not assume that there is a specific divine reason for what Satan and other evil agents do. To the contrary, God fights these opponents precisely because *their* purposes are working *against his* purposes. The reason why they do what they do is found in them, not God."[33]

REFRAMING THE PROBLEM

Against this blueprint worldview Boyd offers the cosmic warfare worldview, which will now be explored. The essence of the warfare worldview is that "divine goodness does not completely control or in any sense will evil; rather, good and evil are at war with one another."[34] The world has become a place of competing wills with no secret purpose behind every evil. One of the most important implications of this view is that evil, especially gratuitous evil, is to be expected in a condition of war. *Gratuitous evil is normative*.[35] Boyd's acceptance of the factual premise of the evidential problem of evil (i.e., gratuitous evil exists) and the denial of the theological premise (meticulous providence) marks a significant departure from the majority

30. Boyd, *God at War*, 55.
31. Boyd, *God at War*, 56.
32. Boyd, *God at War*, 56.
33. Boyd, *Satan*, 15.
34. Boyd, *God at War*, 20. "This assumption obviously entails that God is not now exercising exhaustive, meticulous control over the world. In this worldview, God must work with, and battle against, other created beings. While none of these can ever match God's own power, each has some degree of genuine influence within the cosmos."
35. Boyd, *God at War*, 20.

of theodicies. Positing a cosmic war with gratuitous evil and locating all evil in the will of creaturely rebels and not in the will of God allows Boyd to distinctly separate evil from God. God does not will evil; he fights it. If this is true then much of the force of the problem of evil (in its evidential form) is overcome. Does this move by itself completely resolve the problem of evil? Boyd cautiously avoids such a claim. He argues that because God is the sole creator of all things, the metaphysical question still remains of why God would create a world capable of cosmic war in the first place. Boyd concedes that due to this, *"the problem of theodicy remains, even within a warfare worldview,"* but immediately contends that "unlike the futile quest for the elusive good divine motive for any particular evil within the world, this metaphysical question is *answerable*."[36]

This optimism is based, in part, in Boyd's belief that solving the problem of evil is linked to a correct framing of the issue. "It is all a matter of where one starts: do we start with a view of God as being at war with evil or with a view of God as controlling evil?"[37] This reframing radically alters the entire response.[38] The problem changes from unanswerable to answerable. Instead of an intellectual conundrum to solve, it is transformed into the practical problem of a spiritual opponent to be overcome.[39] Freed from fruitless speculations as to why God might will or ordain evil, we can rise up and combat evil. Another way of saying this is that a warfare theodicy leads to a theology of revolt against evil rather than a theology of resignation. Theologies of resignation theologize about evil (and personal sin) rather than fight it.[40]

Despite this sanguine note, Boyd still has to face a continued challenge to warfare theodicy: even if God doesn't ordain evil, he still has the power

---

36. Boyd, *God at War*, 21 (emphasis mine). Boyd wants to demonstrate that the warfare worldview produces a theodicy philosophically superior to all alternatives. Boyd, *God at War*, 23.

37. Boyd, *God at War*, 291.

38. Boyd, *God at War*, 291. "The centrality of this warfare motif is the single most important observation to be made as one approaches 'the problem of evil.' How one tries to resolve this problem depends entirely upon how one frames the problem. And how one frames the problem is decisively colored by the kind of world, the kind of God and the kind of evil that one thinks needs explaining."

39. Boyd, *God at War*, 21, 291. "When we accept the warfare worldview of Scripture, the intellectual problem of evil is transformed into the practical problem of evil, just as it was in the New Testament." Boyd, *God at War*, 291.

40. Boyd, *God at War*, 22. "Jesus spent his entire ministry revolting against the evil he confronted" (and thus so should we). Boyd, *God of the Possible*, 102. Boyd also links this resisting evil to the belief that the future is settled and not open, 93, 94. See also Boyd, *God at War*, 21–22, 201, 214, 217.

to prevent it. The dilemma is thus: "It seems we must either believe that God does not prevent certain events because he *chooses* not to or because he is *unable* to." It appears that the "warfare worldview must accept that at least sometimes God is *unable* to prevent them. But how can we continue to affirm that God is all-powerful?"[41] The goal of Boyd's volume *Satan and the Problem of Evil* is to answer that very question and thus render the warfare view philosophically coherent.[42] Boyd's answer is summed up in one word: love. God is love. He designed creation for love. But "the possibility of love among contingent creatures such as angels and humans entails the possibility of its antithesis, namely, war. If God wanted the former, he had to risk the latter."[43] Love is risky.

This summary might appear to be merely a restatement of the free will defense, but Boyd has a very important caveat. The warfare theodicy is epitomized by Satan and cosmic war. The fallout arising from the dark possibility inherent in contingent love is first and foremost a struggle between God and Satan.[44] Because Satan is more powerful than any other creature opposing God, and because he is the leader of this opposition, to account for him is to account for lesser rebels. Cosmic war and evil is epitomized in Satan.[45] Boyd appears to wager the success of his warfare theodicy on its account of Satan. This will be of particular interest in this study. While some might conclude that Satan will function as Boyd's ultimate explanation for moral evil and not natural evil, he pre-emptively states that "there is a class of evils in the world that cannot be explained adequately except

---

41. Boyd, *Satan*, 16.

42. Boyd, *Satan*, 16.

43. Boyd, *Satan*, 16–17. "To create a cosmos populated with free agents (angels and humans) who are capable of choosing love requires that God create a cosmos in which beings can choose to oppose his will, hurt other people, and damn themselves. If love is the goal, this is the price. *The solution to the problem of evil, I believe, is found in this insight.*" *God of the Possible*, 135. Emphasis mine.

44. Cosmic war "is first and foremost a struggle between Satan and God. Thus, insofar as our goal is to render this cosmic struggle intelligible and understand evil in our lives in the light of it, it made sense to express it as centred on Satan and the problem of evil." Boyd, *Satan*, 17.

45. Boyd, *Satan*, 17. Because "Scripture depicts Satan as being far more powerful than any of the demonic or human beings that are under him, *he represents the ultimate challenge for our theodicy. The challenge of explaining how God could create beings who can resist his will and genuinely war against him is epitomized by Satan. If we can account for his existence, we shall have thereby accounted for the existence of all lesser evil agents.*" Boyd, *Satan*, 17. (emphasis mine).

by appealing to Satan."[46] By this Boyd means natural evils and animal suffering.[47] Traditionally, explaining natural evil has been considered a major weakness of free will theodicies.[48] But here Boyd turns everything on its head and argues that natural evil constitutes evidence for a cosmic warfare explanation rather than against it.[49]

SIX THESES OF BOYD'S TRINITARIAN WARFARE THEODICY

This study will now turn from an overview of Boyd's approach and its comparison to the blueprint viewpoint to a closer examination of Boyd's central theses. Boyd's argument can be summarised in six tightly argued interlocking theses. For these theses Boyd uses the abbreviation "TWT" which stands for *Trinitarian Warfare Theodicy*. This study will follow Boyd in this and maintain his nomenclature. The six theses are:

1. TWT1: Love must be freely chosen.
2. TWT2: Love entails risk.
3. TWT3: Love and freedom entails that we are to some extent morally responsible for one another.
4. TWT4: The power to influence one another for the worse must be roughly proportionate to our power to influence for the better.
5. TWT5: Love entails a freedom that is within limits irrevocable.
6. TWT6: Our capacity to freely choose love is not endless.[50]

Formal similarities with the free will defense can now be noted. Theses 1, 3, 5, and 6 explicitly mention the notion of freedom. Chapter 2 of *Satan*

---

46. "While appealing to Satan is not sufficient to explain 'natural' evil, I shall argue that no explanation that ignores his activity is adequate." Boyd, *Satan*, 17–18.

47. Boyd, *Satan*, 17–18.

48. The traditional theodicy of free will theism "provides no answer to the question of what is usually called 'natural evil,' meaning the forms of evil that are not due to human volition." Griffin, "Creation out of Nothing, Creation out of Chaos, and the Problem of Evil," 117.

49. Boyd, *Satan*, 17–18.

50. The theses are outlined on pages 23–24 and detailed in chapters 2–6 of *Satan and the Problem of Evil*. A different wording of the theses appears in the article "Six Theses of the Warfare Worldview." This version is: 1. Love Requires Freedom; 2. Freedom Implies Risk; 3. Risk Entails Moral Responsibility; 4. Moral Responsibility is Proportionate to the Potential to Influence; 5. Power to Influence is Irrevocable; 6. Power to Influence is Finite.

and the Problem of Evil is entitled "The Free Fall: Free Will and the Origin of Evil." The cosmic warfare theodicy clearly uses the free will defense as a justificatory pattern and is thus a version of a free will theodicy. But Boyd is not simply trying to present a free will theodicy. Instead, and this constitutes part of his uniqueness and importance, he is trying to place freedom within the larger issue of cosmic warfare and situate freedom as a dimension of a more foundational characteristic of love. Boyd is moving free will beyond a mere defense against the problem of evil to a viable theodicy by means of cosmic warfare based in the metaphysical requirements for love.

TWT1: Love must be Freely Chosen

Why does Boyd start here? Why position freedom within love, and why place love first? Boyd argues that because the Trinitarian God is a God of love his desire for his creation is that it loves also. God's goal for creation is a "bride" who would receive, embody and reflect his love back to him.[51] He then asks, "If love is the goal, what are its conditions?" More specifically, what are the kinds of creatures that must be created in order to participate in this goal?[52] Creatures who love can only do so if they love freely. Creatures who love must have the capacity not to love.[53] Many things can be forced or compelled but, as everyone knows by experience, love cannot be coerced or forced.[54] "The possibility of saying no to God must be metaphysically entailed by the possibility of saying yes to him."[55]

---

51. Boyd, *Satan*, 51.

52. Boyd, *Satan*, 52.

53. The same is not true of God. God is not a contingent creature but a necessary being whose essence could not be other than it is. Boyd, *Satan*, 53.

54. Boyd illustrates this with his "perfect wife" analogy, in which a computer chip is placed into his wife's head which would make her behave in a deterministic fashion (and yet she would experience it as her own freely chosen decisions). Although exhibiting loving behaviours, would she be genuinely loving her husband? Would Boyd find this love unfulfilling knowing that she is not feeling or deciding this of her own accord but only in accordance with the computer chip. She is in effect a puppet. Boyd would really be interacting with himself in the form of the computer chips. See Boyd, 55. This illustration appears in a simpler, briefer form in *God of the Possible*, 134–35.

55. Boyd, *Satan*, 53. The very fact that people can and do say "no" to God is itself evidence that God created people with this ability.

Libertarian Freedom vs. Compatibilistic Freedom

Boyd's view requires a libertarian view of freedom as opposed to a compatibilist view of freedom. Libertarian freedom as a view recognizes the power of various influences and the constraints of particular circumstances upon a person's decision but believes that the final decision is nevertheless determined by the individual. The final and ultimate explanation for an agent's decision is the agent herself/himself. People possess a *self-determining freedom* rather than one truly determined by someone or something else.[56] A person could have chosen otherwise.[57] Pre-existent conditions influence but do not coerce the decision. This contrasts with compatibilist freedom in which all that is required for someone to do something freely is for them to do what they want to do. But they are not free to determine what they want (this is determined by other causes whether circumstances, history, biology, or divine activity through secondary agents or direct primary causation). Hasker explains compatibilism as "the claim that everything we do is causally determined, either by the "strongest motive" (psychological determinism) or by physical causes . . . [or] with the theological view according to which everything we do is determined by immutable divine degrees."[58] In this view, predestination (as absolute divine sovereignty) and freedom are not seen as contradictions because "we 'freely' choose to do exactly what God has predestined us to do."[59] Boyd offers two main reasons why he rejects compatibilism. First, it does not adequately explain moral responsibility. Second, its "failure to consistently affirm agents as the ultimate producers and ultimate explanations of their own actions intensifies the

---

56. "The nature of the freedom TWT1 postulates is self-determining freedom." Boyd, *Satan*, 56.

57. See Boyd's discussion in *Satan* 56–57. Roger Olson explains libertarian freedom this way, "When an agent (a human or God) acts freely in the libertarian sense, nothing outside of the self (including realities within the body) is causing it; the intellect or character alone rules over the will and turns it one way or another. Deliberation and then choice are the only determining factors, although factors such as nature and nurture, and divine influence come into play. Arminians do not believe in absolute free will; the will is always influenced and situated in a context. Even God is guided by his nature and character when making decisions. But Arminians deny that creaturely decisions and actions are controlled by God or any force outside the self." Olson, *Arminian Theology*, 150.

58. Hasker, *The Triumph of God over Evil*, 150.

59. Hasker, *The Triumph of God over Evil*, 150. "In compatibilist free will, persons are free so long as they do what they want to do—even if God is determining their desires . . . people sin voluntarily and are therefore responsible for their sins even though they could not do otherwise." Olson, *Arminian Theology*, 75.

problem of evil."[60] From Boyd's perspective "compatibilism and the problem of evil are inextricably connected."[61] The significance of this for Boyd's view is his claim that the ultimate explanation for moral evil is to be found in the agents themselves.[62] This means that there is no need to look outside of the person's choice for the ultimate explanation for evil to some higher greater good which God wishes to achieve and in which he requires certain evils in order to achieve it.

TWT2: Love entails risk

Boyd's first thesis is crucial, and everything else follows from accepting this account of love and freedom. Given the nature of love as freely chosen, it follows that a free individual may choose not to love. This is the "metaphysical price" God pays for love. "The possibility of evil is not a second decision God makes; it is implied in the single decision to have a world in which love is possible."[63] There is a *risk* in making creatures who can love, hence the second thesis—*love entails risk* (TWT2). This means that it is logically impossible for God to both create creatures who can freely choose to love and yet creatures who can never freely choose not to love. God cannot both give and withhold freedom. The positive side of this realization is that God is not expected to do the logically impossible; therefore, it is no slight on God if he cannot guarantee that love will always be chosen. This "inability" needs to be understood as a *voluntary self-limitation*[64] that God has freely willed and chosen once he decided to make this kind of creature. This limit is not imposed on God by nature or reality or another power. In this way Boyd steers clear of finite theism.[65] This also means that a risky creation conflicts with the idea of divine sovereignty as divine control of all events

---

60. Olson, *Arminian Theology*, 60–61. "For the same reason it is also difficult to render intelligible the warfare motif of Scripture within this view." Olson, *Arminian Theology*, 60–61. The warfare motif is rendered inauthentic. It is only a mock war.

61. Olson, *Arminian Theology*, 61.

62. That the "Creator is all-holy and thus does not himself will evil, leads inexorably to the conclusion that these cosmic forces have *made themselves* evil . . . Only this view can provide an adequate foundation for theodicy within a creational-monotheistic framework." Boyd, *God at War*, 99; Boyd, *Satan*, 56–57.

63. Boyd, *Satan*, 55.

64. Boyd, *Satan*, 183.

65. Two significant versions of finite theism are Process theology and Mormon Theology. For Mormon theodicies see Mosser, "Evil, Mormonism," 56; Mosser, "Exaltation and Gods," 46; Potter, "Finitism and the Problem of Evil." For a Process theodicy see Griffin, *God, Power and Evil*.

(i.e., Augustinian and Calvinist determinism). The nexus of freedom and love involves a risk that divine power cannot eliminate without also eliminating those very things. But interestingly, Boyd chooses not to make this point in the chapter which outlines this second thesis, even though earlier he has stated that traditional understandings of divine power are the problem. Instead, Boyd chooses to highlight what he sees as the incompatibility of risk with divine foreknowledge. Classical theism believes God possesses *exhaustive definitive foreknowledge* (EDF) of the future. This means the future is not an unsettled field of possibilities but a fixed and known fact to God. Therefore, "attributing risk to God seems to contradict the classical understanding of God's foreknowledge."[66] This is where Boyd introduces his open theism into his theodicy.[67] He proceeds to contrast simple foreknowledge with open theism.[68] Simple foreknowledge believes that God simply "looks" and sees the future. God does not determine the future by divine decree, as in Calvinism, or by selecting a potential world to actualize, as in Molinism. The problem for Boyd with simple foreknowledge is that while it affirms genuine risk for God, it is a risk that God is unable to change. The future is fixed. God's foreknowledge is more like hindsight and offers God no providential advantage in response to what will happen.[69] In contrast to this, Boyd argues that the "open view of God (or of the future, as I prefer) avoids the difficulties associated with the EDF [exhaustive definitive foreknowledge] doctrine and allows us to consistently attribute risk to God."[70]

Having highlighted problems with exhaustive definitive foreknowledge, especially in the form of simple foreknowledge, Boyd then pulls back from his presentation of open theism.[71] His point "is not that believers

---

66. Boyd, *Satan*, 86.

67. Boyd's discussion of open theism is extensive and takes up the greater part of chapters 3 and 4. These chapters rehearse Boyd's views which are detailed in a number of other works, see Boyd, *God of the Possible*; Boyd, "The Open-Theism View," 11–47; Boyd, *Four Views on Divine Providence*, 183–208; Boyd, "Neo-Molinism," 187–204. For how neo-molinism helps improve standard open theism understandings of God and the future (in this case Clark Pinnock's) see, Boyd, "Unbounded Love and the Openness of the Future."

68. Boyd only focuses on simple foreknowledge as representative of exhaustive definitive foreknowledge (EDF) even though Calvinism and Molinism also affirm EDF. For Boyd's critique of Calvinistic determinism and Molinism see his contributions in Boyd, *Four Views on Divine Providence*.

69. Boyd, *Satan*, 88–90.

70. Boyd, *Satan*, 90.

71. The appearance of open theism in the second thesis may imply that the remaining theses are essentially constructed on an open theism platform, but this is not so. This is for two reasons. Firstly, Boyd makes clear that it is possible to understand this thesis from non-openness perspectives. Secondly, none of the remaining theses are

cannot embrace the Trinitarian warfare worldview without also embracing the open view of the future, that is, without denying that God possesses EDF."[72] Rather he wishes other Arminians to see that their current views are inconsistent and that there are advantages in approaching the warfare view from an open theological perspective. Boyd finishes by saying "it is not my intention to wager the entire credibility of the Trinitarian warfare theodicy on my defense of the open view of the future. At its heart, the Trinitarian warfare theodicy is simply an expansion and fleshing out of the free will theodicy that Arminians have always appealed to."[73] Boyd positions his view within Arminian theology as a theology that is compatible with a warfare view but in such a way to show the advantages of his own position. The rest of Boyd's presentation of the warfare view will reflect this stance. The warfare view unfolds in a way that does not necessitate open theism but it will often appear as the preferable providential model for the warfare perspective.

Risk and Divine Sovereignty

The first two theses (TWT1 and TWT2) aimed to show how evil is an unavoidable *risk* that is entailed in the creation of beings who love. This is a standard free will defense. In many respects what Boyd has done is offer a variation of the free will defense, only this time articulated through the lens of love. A free will defense may explain evil *per se*, but can it explain the magnitude and extremity of evil? Boyd's theodicy develops beyond a free will defense by looking further at the implications of love in the context of cosmic war. Now that risk has been introduced it is hard not to be struck by the scale and dimensions of the risk involved in a cosmic warfare perspective. Risk is a disturbing idea if even God is subject to it. It should be noted that for Boyd's cosmic warfare theodicy the issue of risk has been severely heightened by the inclusion of open theism, especially in comparison with traditional "no-risk" doctrines of providence.[74] Boyd is aware of this and the issue of risk will preoccupy the rest of Boyd's six theses. After all, the God of open theism may be

---

specific or peculiar to open theism. Boyd, *Satan*, 86–87. In fact this is the only thesis that specifically lends itself to (but does not necessitate) open theism, and so it makes sense that this is where Boyd chooses to flag his providential commitments.

72. Boyd, *Satan*, 86.

73. Boyd, *Satan*, 87.

74. Tiessen, *Providence and Prayer*, 31–336, lists open theism among the "risk" theories of providence. No-risk theories are the Thomist, Barthian, Calvinist, Fatalist, and Tiessen's own middle-knowledge Calvinism.

viewed as an irresponsible gambler uncertain of the future yet risking both our and his future. Boyd wants to show why this is not the case.

Leaving aside open theism for issues more central to our concerns, there are a number of questions following from the element of risk that arise as a result of these initial two theses and must be dealt with by any warfare approach (open theist or non-open theist). How can God be guaranteed to win a cosmic war if he can never be guaranteed of winning each or any particular battle? It appears theoretically possible that God could fail and that no one will choose God's way. Why will this not happen? How can we *trust* a God who is not in meticulous control of the world? He may be God but why trust him? An additional question asks why creatures that reject love are allowed to then significantly hurt others? Why doesn't God prevent angels and humans from harming each other?[75] Abusing your own freedom is one thing; abusing someone else's is another. The risk seems to be the creature's as much as the Creator's. These questions are particularly important because they represent the objections that the blueprint worldview, with its meticulous providence and no-risk stance, levels against free will theologies.[76]

Because the remaining theses (TWT3–TWT6) deal with risk, Boyd considers the development and understanding of these as the heart of the Trinitarian warfare theodicy.[77] These theses aim to explain and mitigate the nature of that risk. They reveal that the evils resulting from cosmic war operate within limits. Therefore, God's risk is a rational and knowable (even if not exhaustively known in the classical sense) risk, and because God perfectly understands the parameters of this risk, he is able to deal with it.[78] In showing how the warfare theses dealing with love can answer the blueprint objections, Boyd also shows how his alternative understanding of divine providence and sovereignty (general as opposed to meticulous) is also not subject to these objections. The problem of evil always concerns the tight connection between the *God-World* relationship. Boyd's *six theses* explain the nature of the *World* God has made, while *doctrines* of divine sovereignty and providence explain the *God* involved. One cannot work without the other. Thus, Boyd's discussion of his theses on the nature of love constantly

---

75. Boyd, *Satan*, 145–46.

76. Boyd's example is R. C. Sproul, who argues that if chance exists then God cannot be sovereign. Even one lone molecule not under God's control could prevent Christ from returning! Boyd, 146–147. See, Sproul, *Chosen by God*, 26; Sproul, *Not a Chance*, 3.

77. Boyd, *Satan*, 145.

78. Boyd uses his divine chess master analogy here (Boyd, *Satan*, 112–4). While the precise details of the future are not exhaustively known, the limits on the possibilities of the future are clearly knowable to God. For more references to the divine chess master see also Boyd, "The Open-Theism View," 44.

requires clarifying and arguing for the complementary theological framework in which they work. Meticulous providence, divine determinism, divine power as omni-control, all nullify or falsify a free-will-and-cosmic-warfare theodicy. The cosmic warfare worldview only emerges from the interaction between a particular understanding of God and a particular understanding of the world (the same is true for blueprint worldviews). Therefore, before Boyd moves to his remaining theses (about the world-reality) he makes way for them by outlining how his doctrines of providence (God-reality) mitigate risk.

Consequently, Boyd presents four arguments against the idea that risk threatens divine sovereignty. All address divine determinism in some way. The first two concern God and the last two concern the world. First, Boyd wants to affirm a sovereignty that is *adventurous* rather than unilaterally controlling. His sovereignty is adventurous because it allows for God the experience of risk and novelty rather than simply control.[79] Second, Boyd argues that a God who must unilaterally control all things, else he would not be God, is an inferior God. This view *undermines real divine sovereignty*. Such a God is a weaker God who is threatened if he is not controlling everything. In reality this is a denial of real sovereignty. An analogy is apparent in human leadership. Leaders who must control others to get their own way are viewed as insecure, manipulative, and weak in comparison to leaders who lead by character.[80] Third, *general determinism* and *specific indeterminism* are not opposites but complementary.[81] What this means is that God can know the general and ultimate outcome of history even if he cannot know or control every specific event. Boyd is thinking here of current scientific theories which map the interaction of order and chaos in nature and even society. The indeterminism of the quantum world yields surprisingly predictable and determinable outcomes. A world filled with indeterminism does not mean a world that is unpredictable. Risk, on a general level, is not complete or unknowable risk. The spiritual world is analogous to the quantum world.[82] Advocates of no-risk providence fail to understand that it is a question of

79. Boyd, *Satan*, 147–48.
80. Boyd, *Satan*, 148–51.

81. Boyd, *Satan*, 151–53. The terms "general" and "specific" are mine. I use them to distinguish general-term determinism from the theological idea of divine determinism. This helps clarify Boyd's use. Boyd simply uses in his subheading determinism and indeterminism.

82. "The *laws* that keep the world relatively predictable do not need to be meticulously coercive on a quantum level to be binding on a phenomenological level. *In the same way*, God's providence does not need to be meticulously controlling on the level of free agents to ensure that his sovereign plan for the world will be accomplished." Boyd, *Satan*, 153. Italics mine.

balancing control and freedom;[83] not a question of either/or. Fourthly, the complementary nature of determinism and indeterminism is *universal*. Whether it be the behavior of subatomic particles, the economy, the flight pattern of bees, prevalence of crime or disease, the rate of suicides in a particular area, all of these are predictable. While it is not easy to predict what any individual will do, the behavior of groups or systems is quite predictable.[84]

Even with these four arguments, people may continue to ask if God might still fail. Boyd adds two important additional arguments. First, in giving humans freedom *God actively sets the parameters of that freedom.* God knows what humans, created in a certain way, are capable of. He also knows the percentages of how creatures will act. This capacity and percentage is one he can deal with.[85] A somewhat similar point entailed in Boyd's metaphysics of love in TWT6 can be seen. But whereas TWT6 concerns the metaphysical limitations of a creation capable of love, Boyd's point here is theological and providential. God knows and thus actively sets limits to human action. These ideas will later develop into Boyd's important ideas on "probation." Second and logically related, *God knows his own character and ability*. He knows he can cope with the situation. Elsewhere Boyd makes this point through two related theological affirmations: *Infinite intelligence*[86] and *Omni-resourcefulness*.[87] Infinite intelligence is the idea that God's intelligence is never taxed or divided up. God is able to devote complete and total attention to each and every challenge as if it was the only challenge he faces. No number of situations to attend to could ever lessen God's capacity devoted to them. God's intellect can never be "spread thin" as ours is. We can handle only one focus at a time whereas God can handle an infinite number of focuses as if each of them were the only focus he had.

In this outline and defense of Boyd's providential model, risk is reduced but uncertainty still remains high especially in the areas of specifics.[88] For example, Boyd suggests that God reasoned about the future in terms of

83. Critics fail to appreciate that the "game" is "all about *balancing control and freedom*. God is in control precisely because he can and does limit creaturely freedom, and agents have freedom precisely because God does not exercise exhaustive and unilateral control." Boyd, *Satan*, 153. Italics mine.

84. "The behaviour of groups is far more predictable than the behaviour of individuals." Boyd, *Satan*, 154.

85. Boyd, *Satan*, 156.

86. Boyd, *Satan*, 103.

87. Boyd, *Satan*, 109.

88. In classical Arminianism God exercises general providence but has specific and definitive foreknowledge of the risk and the actual outcome, whereas in Boyd's open theism God only has partial or general knowledge of the future outcome of the specific risks.

percentages (i.e., before creating God knew that a fall into sin was a high possibility or even inevitable. God also knew that a certain percentage of people would reject an offer of salvation and a certain percentage of people would accept).[89] The uncertainty in regards to who and how many will be saved parallels uncertainty about *when* God's goal of the acquisition of a "bride" will be achieved. This means the end of the cosmic war which frustrates God's goal is uncertain. In response, Boyd declares that God's love "refuses to give up" and will do whatever it takes "for however long it might take" to see his plan fulfilled.[90]

TWT3 and TWT4: Moral responsibility and Proportionality and Risk

Clarifying God's providence has shown that risk is not a total threat to God's plan, yet it still leaves a great many questions about risk. Boyd then moves to questions about the range, effects, and value of God's risk. God might be able to handle the risk and ensure he achieves his goal of a "bride," but is it worth it? Or has God wagered too much in his "gamble"? These questions shift the discussion from querying God's power and ability to handle risk to his wisdom and goodness in allowing such a risk. Specific questions include: Why does God allow free agents so much influence and power over other free agents (specifically to harm and even to kill)? Why can angelic decisions influence human agents to such a vast degree? Has God overplayed his hand and wagered too much on angelic and human freedom? Is Satan's freedom worth it? Considering the degree of suffering in cosmic war, is freedom itself worth it?[91] These questions all address the issue of the balance between control and freedom in Boyd's theodicy. They ask if God has got the balance wrong. Wasn't a different balance possible?

Boyd relies heavily on ideas of necessary proportionality and responsibility to illustrate the unavoidable conjoined value and cost of the risk. It is within an understanding of a relational creation that Boyd articulates further his metaphysics of love with his 3rd and 4th theses in answer to these questions. Boyd argues that Creation (both in its sentient and inanimate forms, and "above"/heavenly and "below"/earthly dimensions) is an interconnected whole which operates on the same moral principles, and as a result there necessarily exists within it an interlocking moral tapestry

---

89. Boyd, *Satan*, 156.
90. Boyd, *Satan*, 157.
91. These questions appear in Boyd, *Satan*, 163–77.

which includes both the human and the angelic.[92] To love is to be able to relate, influence, and affect others deeply. Unfortunately, this capacity to bless others, when freedom goes wrong, turns into the capacity to curse others. Because freedom involves the ability to bless or harm others, by granting it God has made us "morally responsible for each other."[93] This is "the dark side of the potential to love."[94] This articulates the third thesis that *love and risk means we are morally responsible to and for each other*.[95] Boyd recaps the sequential logic by stating that just as *"love requires freedom* (TWT1) and *freedom requires risk* (TWT2), *risk entails moral responsibility* (TWT3)."[96] Moral responsibility means that God could not have created us with the capacity to influence each other and yet that influence have no moral dimension. Influence is unavoidably moral (i.e., good or evil). Because angels and humans are part of the same creation they participate in this shared moral influence and responsibility. Boyd is quick to caution that other free agents may influence us, but they cannot determine our choices or behavior. There can be no blaming of other free agents for our own decisions.[97] Thus Boyd is able to defend God's wisdom because he shows God could not have made creatures with the capacity to love while withholding from them the unavoidable moral responsibility that comes with love. The unifying idea is that of influence. To give or receive love is to influence or be influenced. To influence is to be responsible for what you do. Here is where Boyd also brings out the *social* aspect of love. Love requires others. With this element risk is no longer simply the created agent's risk to God (rejecting his love) but, importantly, free agents' risk to each other. This helps address some of the questions which ask about the cost of risk to beings other than God. Freedom for an individual to love is predicated on the interlocking shared freedom of others to love. Freedom to love cannot be isolated to an individual or cordoned off from society. Therefore, freedom for part is entailed in freedom for the whole. Freedom to love requires the existence of others, power to influence them, and responsibility to others. The *social* and the *moral* are inseparable.

Having answered why it is that free agents (including angels) can potentially cause harm to other free agents Boyd tackles the follow-up question.

92. The Bible depicts "the world 'above' as very much like the world 'below' and as inextricably interconnected with it" Boyd, *Satan*, 166. "Angels are part of the moral tapestry that weaves all creation together." Boyd, *Satan*, 167.

93. Boyd, *Satan*, 165.

94. Title of subheading on Boyd, *Satan*, 163

95. This point appears in Boyd and Boyd, *Letters from a Skeptic*, 23.

96. Boyd, *Satan*, 165.

97. Boyd, *Satan*, 167–69.

Is freedom itself worth it? This is the abstract form of the question. In a cosmic warfare context it has a special concrete epitomizing counterpart. Is the freedom of the one being Satan worth it?[98] After all, Satan seems to be the free agent who is the genesis for evil and suffering. Surely it would have been possible and permissible to have compromised his freedom to prevent the resulting evil? Has God gambled too much on freedom?[99] In a special way Satan is the paradigm case for cosmic warfare theodicies. To account for Satan and God's treatment of him is to be able to explain lesser and resultant evil as well as the wider foundational problem of evil. To answer this element of the problem of risk Boyd introduces his fourth thesis—the principle of proportionality. "As the fourth structural thesis of the trinitarian warfare theodicy, therefore, I submit that *moral responsibility is proportionate to the potential to influence others* (TWT4)."[100] Moral responsibility establishes the *fact* of influence and risk, proportionality establishes the *scope* and *scale* of that influence and risk. Boyd's theory suggests that God undertook a God-sized goal with a God-sized risk. Boyd points out that if TWT2 (freedom entails risk) says "Nothing ventured, nothing gained," then TWT4 goes further and says, "The more that is ventured, the more that can be gained—or lost."[101] We should expect that the proportional potentiality of good, and hence of evil, inherent in creation to be truly immense. "Why does it seem that God risks so much—sometimes, seemingly, too much—on freedom? According to TWT4, *it is because he is aiming too high*."[102]

Not all creatures or free agents have the same level of influence or potential. Proportionality varies. Some free agents are capable of great good or evil while others possess more modest limits. The question of Satan then is partially answered by acknowledging that he is a creation who possessed the highest potential. The "extremity of Satan's evil is itself an indication of how much potential for love was thrown away by his fateful decision."[103] Boyd illustrates this by making the point that a world capable of a Mother Theresa must allow for the possibility of a Adolf Hitler. In like manner if God wanted a glorious Lucifer, he had to accept the possibility of a diabolical

---

98. Boyd illustrates this question using Hitler as a comparable example. "Wagering the potential destruction of six million people on how one person will use his freedom seems to be a very poor wager. *Wagering the welfare of the entire creation throughout history on the will of one agent (Lucifer) seems even worse*." Boyd, *Satan*, 173. Italics mine.

99. "We must yet question why God would wager *so much* on both human and angelic freedom." Boyd, *Satan*, 169.

100. Boyd, *Satan*, 170.

101. Boyd, *Satan*, 170.

102. Boyd, *Satan*, 172.

103. Boyd, *Satan*, 173.

Satan.[104] Satan is an example of *degree* not kind. Eliminating him would not eliminate the dark side of love, but simply a creature of high potential for love or harm. The principles of love, freedom, risk, influence, and moral responsibility remain. He is not a special case in a metaphysical sense. He is a special case in an individual, historical sense. He, and not someone else, sinned first, but this is not because he was of a different metaphysical make-up or nature. His sinning is so significant because his original potential was so significant.

Nevertheless, Boyd has another important point to make. Proportionality applies to groups and not simply individuals. Moral responsibility is both individual and collective. Satan's degree of power could not happen without the cooperation of others. The scale of evil is the result of many free agents, angelic and human, using their influence and potential in a way that aligns with Satan. "Evil on a grand scale, like goodness on a grand scale, always involves cooperation on a grand scale."[105] Moral potentiality is shared potentiality. Proportionality and its collective application mean that elimination of evil is not as simple as it seems. There is a catch. God can only eliminate creation's potential for evil by also eliminating its potential for goodness. This seems to exist in an inverse relationship. Some might say that God shouldn't have allowed as much evil as has happened. But Boyd makes the argument that whatever point God decides to cap our capacity to love or harm, it would invariably seem too much to us.[106] Boyd's argument has been to show that while risk was an inevitable part of God's decision to make a creation capable of love, it was a good and wise risk. This is especially so because God knew he would succeed and acquire a bride (he knew some would choose his way even if he didn't know initially who would). The overall claim then is that *love is worth the risk*. This may sound like the standard greater good approach, but it is not. It says God has good reasons for creating a world with the possibility of evil. It does not say that God wills or ordains every evil for a specific good. This is a soft or partial greater good claim, not the traditional greater good approach.

TWT5 and TWT6: The Irrevocability and Finitude of Freedom

Boyd then moves to his last two theses, which round out the Trinitarian warfare theodicy. Worded in such a way to highlight the continued development of the nature of love TWT5 states that "love entails a freedom that is

104. Boyd, *Satan*, 172.
105. Boyd, *Satan*, 174.
106. Boyd, *Satan*, 175.

within limits irrevocable,"[107] and TWT6 states that "our capacity to freely choose love is not endless." Put more succinctly, *freedom is irrevocable* and *freedom is finite*. These theses build on and complete the previous four theses, extending the cosmic warfare theodicy's ability to answer questions put to it. The questions Boyd has in mind are three in particular:

1. Why does God tolerate the on-going activity of evil agents?
2. Why is God arbitrary in his intervention? Why does he sometimes allow evil and sometimes intervene to stop it?
3. Will heaven be eternally risky?

TWT5 and TWT6 form their own complementary tension. One proposition (TWT5) argues that there is something about freedom which places a (self-created and self-accepted) limit on God, while the other proposition (TWT6) clarifies that there is a limit to creaturely freedom. TWT5 will help explain why God can allow evil but not himself be culpable for doing so. TWT6 will help explain why evil will not be indefinite and eternal and assure us of God's triumph without resorting to arbitrary divine action or meticulous divine control. God's ending of evil is in accordance with the nature of freedom and love. While Boyd has shown how evil appears as a slim but tangible dark potential in contingent love, he hasn't explained why God has allowed evil to go on so long. This is particularly important because, unlike process theology, Boyd affirms divine omnipotence. God has the power, so why doesn't he exercise it and destroy the rebels and end pain?[108] Boyd's answer is that freedom is irrevocable. The claim is essentially an argument about the vital, unavoidable importance of *temporality* to love, freedom, and relationships. Creatures "must have the power to exercise their influence over time, for better or for worse."[109] Creation exists in time or it doesn't exist at all. No time means no love and no influence. "Hence, in my view, once God gives the gift of self-determination, he *has to*, within limits, endure its misuse. This constitutes the fifth structural thesis of the warfare theodicy: *the power to influence is irrevocable* (TWT5)."[110]

Irrevocable influence applies to the ongoing distinct decisions and actions of agents. This means that if God allows a free agent to exist he cannot then unilaterally or coercively pick and choose what decisions and actions he will allow the free agent to make. "If God were to retract our

---

107. This point appears in Boyd and Boyd, *Letters from a Skeptic*, 23.
108. Boyd, *Satan*, 179.
109. Boyd, *Satan*, 181.
110. Boyd, *Satan*, 181; Boyd, *Is God to Blame?*, 115.

freedom every time we were about to choose something against his will, then it cannot be said that he really gave us freedom or that we are in fact genuinely *self*-determining."[111] God either creates real "others" or he does not. We are presented with mutually exclusive options—either ongoing existence with freedom or not. "In short, the *genuineness* of the gift of self-determination hinges on its *irrevocability*."[112] This genuineness is measured in allowing free agents time and the absence of coercive micro-control during that time. The two points go together. For this last point Boyd argues for an implicit, divinely-chosen covenant. "God's design to have creatures who are capable of *moral* decision-making requires a sort of '*covenant of non-coercion*' with each of them."[113] Without this covenant of non-coercion, the gift of temporal existence would be meaningless and agents would be incapable of real freedom and love or even mental deliberation.[114] Without non-coercion, agents could not live and develop as moral beings. Any moral decision would ultimately be, at best, a choice about continuing to have power over our own thoughts or have God assume control over certain of our thoughts, or at worst, a choice to continue to exist or be eliminated by God in view of a wrong choice. As Boyd puts it, the "choice to follow God would be a matter of *survival*, not of *morality*."[115] God cannot have a creation with the potential to love unless he opts for a creation whose basic freedom is irrevocable. Eliminating the potential for evil could be forestalled only by "creating a risk-free robotic creation" without the possibility of genuine love.[116] The covenant of non-coercion highlights freedom's riskiness and irrevocability.[117] God can't undo the risk of evil without also undoing the goal of good.[118]

---

111. Boyd, *Satan*, 182.

112. Boyd, *Satan*, 182.

113. Boyd, *Satan*, 183.

114. An agent "must be able to conceive of herself as enduring through time" to make decisions. Boyd, *Satan*, 182–83.

115. If disobeying God entailed immediate destruction, then "the choice to love God or not (as well as every other choice between godly and ungodly alternatives) would have the same moral character as the 'choice' to breathe or not." Boyd, *Satan*, 183.

116. This non-robotic potential for rebellion that God must genuinely struggle against "is simply the dark side of a beautiful potential." Boyd, *Satan*, 184.

117. The fifth thesis of freedom's irrevocability "answers the most compelling criticism raised against the notion of a self-limiting, omnipotent God," which is that a God who self-limits can un-self-limit. Boyd, *Satan*, 184.

118. Boyd illustrates this by noting that God cannot create a mountain without at the same time creating a valley. He cannot create a triangle and at the same time have it be a circle. Boyd, *Satan*, 184.

TWT5 seems to place God in a very limited position largely at the behest of creation. On the one hand it seems creation has too much power, so how can God end evil without ending freedom? On the other hand, it also seems to contradict what we see in Scripture, where God does seem to revoke freedom by ending life in judgment and punishment. Why does God seem to violate his own covenant of non-coercion? And why are these violations arbitrarily applied, with God sometimes abiding by this covenant of non-coercion and sometimes not? In response, Boyd's delicate balancing act continues and is rounded out in his final thesis, TWT6. Freedom's irrevocability and temporality is open-ended, but not eternal; it is genuine but not unconditional.[119] Freedom has limits. "This constitutes the sixth and final structural thesis of the Trinitarian warfare theodicy: *the power to influence is finite* (TWT6)."[120] Temporality is given with purpose. Freedom is not an unconditioned absolute. It is given within the wider context of God's plans and purposes. TWT5 is an important part of the story but it is not the whole story. With this last thesis Boyd aims to finally tame the risk that has haunted his model. This last thesis explains in principle three crucial issues: 1) Why God can intervene in the world sometimes but not always; 2) Why God can eventually win the cosmic war but not immediately; and 3) Why we can never know the extent of an agent's freedom and thus why God's interaction with agents can appear arbitrary to us.[121]

How is freedom finite and how is it relevant to Boyd's argument? To answer this Boyd references a complex interaction of a diverse range of factors. Experience teaches us that freedom is constrained by elements of creation such as by our genetic make-up, our environment, and the free will of other agents. It is also wisely limited by the Creator who, like a wise shareholder, would never give away so many shares that he lost power.[122] However, the most important arguments, which lie at the heart of TWT6, concern the interaction between divine providence and creaturely probation in relation to the development of character. Boyd argues that God has given us a probationary period in which to develop character. This is an inherently finite process. In this probationary period "we make the choices,

---

119. "TWT5 thus does not entail that God can *never* exercise coercive power in his interactions with free creatures. Nor does it entail that creatures have the power *eternally* to exercise an evil influence on the creation." God would lose only if freedom was "unconditional in nature and *unlimited* in scope or duration." Boyd, *Satan*, 185.

120. Boyd, *Satan*, 186.

121. Boyd, *Satan*, 186.

122. Boyd, *Satan*, 186–89. Boyd also argues from the nature of contingent creatures. Creatures are finite in every other way. Nothing about them is infinite. A finite, conditioned, contingent being with infinite freedom would be a contradiction.

though in time our choices make us."[123] Our moral choices over time form our moral character.[124] Eventually we take on a particular moral character. "Self-determining freedom is about what morally responsible contingent beings choose to *do* on their way to deciding what they are going to permanently *be*." Eventually the shape of our character becomes morally settled and fixed. "For better or worse, *we irreversibly become the decisions we make.*"[125] Boyd terms this "character solidification."

How does solidification of character relate to cosmic war, providence, risk, and the problem of evil? The question of character provides answers to the question of time. Character needs time to develop, but a thoroughly evil character is no longer owed time. Boyd links the length of the probationary period attached to character to several factors. The first factor is the relative state of an agent's *character*. When an agent's character is settled, their probation is up, this leaves God free to intervene and thus curtail evil. Once an agent has spent their freedom, God is under no obligation to refrain from intervening on the agent's freedom.[126] The mechanism and logic behind Boyd's conclusion is important to understand for reasons that will become apparent later on. Boyd describes probation as a process in which our freedom is changed from libertarian freedom to compatibilistic freedom.[127] This is equivalent to saying the libertarian "power to do otherwise" diminishes over time. Eventually we can no longer change.[128] Freedom has the divinely intended goal of becoming "a person who eternally receives and reflects God's love" and "self-determining freedom is not an end in itself—it gives way either to higher freedom (love) or lower bondage."[129] The second factor affecting probation is the original state of an agent's moral *potential or capacity* to influence for good or evil. This capacity or potential is distinguishable from character. God's toleration of an agent "depends on the potential he originally gave to the agent . . . The more that is risked, I have argued, the more that can be gained and lost (TWT4). What I am now arguing is that this dual potentiality must have a temporal element to it. If Satan has the capacity to corrupt the cosmos for billions of years, it is only because

123. Boyd, *Satan*, 189.

124. "Our choices become our habits, and our habits eventually become our characters." Boyd, *Satan*, 188.

125. Boyd, *Satan*, 189.

126. Boyd, *Satan*, 191.

127. Boyd, *Satan*, 189. "Our *libertarian freedom is the probationary means by which we acquire compatibilistic freedom* either for or against God." Italics mine.

128. The most that can be said then is that we *could have been* (past tense) otherwise. Boyd, *Satan*, 189.

129. Boyd, *Satan*, 190.

he originally had the capacity to bless the cosmos for this same length of time. He could not have the former without having the latter."[130] The third factor is the relative state of an agent's salvation decision about God. God is waiting to see if free agents will choose him or not. This is obvious for human beings who are invited to choose God in the invitation of the gospel. But curiously for Boyd it also applies to a certain class of angels. "True, there seems to be a certain class of angels whose destiny is not yet resolved for or against God. God thus corrects them, warns them and encourages them to follow his ways, lest they perish (e.g., Ps 82)."[131] In summary, probationary time is delimited by character, capacity, and choice.

TWT6 is especially important in completing the explanatory power of Boyd's cosmic warfare worldview. TWT6 allows Boyd to affirm that the cosmic war is not an eternal war.[132] Boyd can therefore avoid classical theodicy's ("blueprint") problem of finding higher reasons (greater goods) for particular evils on the one hand and also avoid process dualism where evil is never finally overcome on the other hand.[133] One cannot make sense of the genuineness of the war and its length without TWT5 (freedom's irrevocability), but one cannot make sense of the certainty of God's victory without TWT6 (freedom's finitude). TWT6 shows that love entails risk but not eternal risk. Once an agent has spent their freedom God is under no obligation (no longer bound by the covenant of non-coercion) to refrain from intervening on the agent's freedom.

Arbitrariness, Divine Intervention, and the Quality of Freedom

While TWT5 (freedom's irrevocability) and TWT6 (freedom's finitude) explain in principle why God can sometimes intervene and why he sometimes cannot, it does not answer the charge of God's arbitrariness. Sometimes God intervenes and sometimes he doesn't. Why does God intervene when he does (e.g., the killing of Ananias)? And why does he not intervene more often and in cases which seem warranted (e.g., when a person is about to kill an innocent baby)? Boyd answers this charge, in part, with his discussion of the *quality* of freedom. Any particular event (involving intervention

---

130. Boyd, *Satan*, 182.

131. Boyd, *Satan*, 180. Boyd appears to distinguish this group of angels from Satan and his angels who are eternally doomed.

132. Boyd, *Satan*, 190. "TWT6 also provides a plausible explanation of how it is that the possibility of love entails risk without holding that heaven will be eternally risky." Boyd, *Satan*, 191.

133. Boyd, *Satan*, 190–91.

or non-intervention) can only be understood in relation to all the variables affecting someone's freedom. These variables condition, but do not determine, the quality of our freedom and its irrevocability.[134] Boyd lists five variables. First, *quality of freedom is conditioned by the ongoing influence of God.* Creation is not left to itself. God is the providential ruler of the world. God controls factors external to our will, such as the environment, but our actual 'will' he influences but does not attempt to control. This is in order to maintain us and our personhood as this "freedom is, I believe, the core of what it means to be made in the image of God."[135] Second, *quality of freedom is conditioned by our original constitution.* We are all created different but we "do not know the scope of any agent's original potential or the extent to which this agent has solidified his or her character through expenditure of this potential."[136] Third, *quality of freedom is conditioned by previous decisions.* Because character is a work in process, an agent's quality of freedom is dynamic. "The current of the life gains momentum the further it flows."[137] Each decision an agent makes conditions his or her freedom in terms of both moral direction but also remaining probationary existence. However, we cannot know exactly how morally fixed someone's character is or what remains of someone's probationary potential.[138] Fourth, *quality of freedom is conditioned by other agents.* No one lives in isolation. Other agents, their influence, power and decisions all act to condition and limit another's freedom. For better or for worse "freedom is a dynamic reality largely defined by its relationship to everything else."[139] It is important for Boyd to recognize that the quality of our freedom is conditioned by both angels and humans. Social responsibility applies to angelic influence on humans individually and collectively.[140] Boyd is arguing that we must see TWT5 in light of TWT3 "More specifically, we cannot understand God's covenant of noncoercion with any individual agent without understanding God's covenant of noncoercion with every *other* agent. The choices any particular agent makes have consequences

---

134. Boyd, *Satan*, 192.
135. Boyd, *Satan*, 193.
136. Boyd, *Satan*, 197.
137. Boyd, *Satan*, 198.
138. "The particular decisions that a free agent makes condition the direction as well as the parameters of his or her future freedom." Boyd, *Satan*, 198.
139. Boyd, *Satan*, 201.
140. The principle of social responsibility applies to angels who are "given charge over us" and can "carry out this duty well or poorly." Their actions, including interactions with each other (e.g., warfare), affect "our lives individually and corporately—including our quality of freedom." Boyd, *Satan*, 201.

for the quality of irrevocable freedom for all the others."[141] Consequently, to understand God's interaction with someone we would need to understand his interaction with everyone else. The dizzying array of interactions between such a vast number of beings is something utterly impossible for human beings to fully trace. Boyd terms this the *sociological nature of the cosmos* and it means moral and social responsibility is always shared.[142] Every event has been influenced (but not determined) by an entire history of choices by a vast society of people. Fifth, *quality of freedom is conditioned by prayer*. Prayer plays a very important part in Boyd's overall theology and he devotes an entire chapter of *Satan and the Problem of Evil* to the issue of prayer. This fifth condition is a profound extension of variables one (the on-going influence of God) and four (the influence of other agents).[143] But here God and people are not separate influences. Instead the divine and human combine. "God has significantly bound himself to the power of prayer, so much so that there are things he would like to do that will not be done unless people of faith pray."[144] Together these five variables relieve God of the charge of arbitrariness and also clarify why we, in our limited knowledge and understanding, can misjudge God as arbitrary.

Mystery of Creation

These five variables contribute to another wider overarching explanation Boyd has for not only the apparent arbitrariness of God but also for the impenetrable arbitrariness and mystery of evil itself. Boyd appeals to the sheer complexity of creation. But importantly in a warfare theodicy "the impenetrable mystery is *not about God's character or plan*, as in blueprint worldview. It is rather a mystery about *the complexity of creation*. Relocating the mystery of evil is, I believe, one of the most distinct features of the trinitarian warfare

---

141. Boyd, *Satan*, 202.

142. "In a sense we must conclude that *every single event* in the cosmos is to some extent a universally influenced, sociologically determined event. Every event within the whole is to some extent influenced by the whole and in turn influences the whole." Boyd, *Satan*, 213.

143. Boyd actually sees nine variables as necessary to understanding prayer; see *Is God to Blame?* These variables affecting the outcome of prayer are: 1) God's will; 2) The faith of the person being prayed for; 3) The faith of people praying for others; 4) Persistence of prayer; 5) The number of people praying; 6) Human free will; 7) Angelic free will; 8) The number and strength of spiritual agents; 9) The presence of sin. Boyd, *Is God to Blame?*, 135–47.

144. Boyd, *Satan*, 203.

theodicy."¹⁴⁵ This complexity means we can attain a general understanding of why evil happens, but there are so many variables at work that it is impossible for us to trace exactly why God does or doesn't act in respect to any particular situation. Life's arbitrariness is only apparent not real. "God seems arbitrary, not because he is arbitrary, but because the world he interacts with is unfathomably complex."¹⁴⁶ This perception of arbitrariness is due to our epistemological limitations not God's unwillingness to act. "If we saw what God sees, we would understand why God did what he did and we would see that he is always concerned with maximizing goodness and minimizing evil."¹⁴⁷

Conclusion to Six Theses

With this Boyd rounds out his six theses. For Boyd at least, he has tamed the profound risk which lies at the heart of his theodicy. If these theses are accepted, he contends that "we can make sense out of the fact that a world created by an all-good and all-powerful God could become a nightmarish war zone."¹⁴⁸ He also believes these theses can account for the epitome of the problem of evil—Satan. "In short, these theses take us a long way in explaining Satan and the problem of evil, for Satan represents the paradigmatic case of a free agent turned bad."¹⁴⁹ Boyd then narrates Satan's story through the lens of each thesis. It is worth quoting in full:

> God created Lucifer free, for he created him with the potential to love (TWT1). This meant there was a risk involved in creating Lucifer (TWT2), as there is with every free agent, for Satan's potential to become evil and to harm others had to be proportionate to his potential to become loving and to bless others (TWT3–4). Unfortunately, Lucifer chose an evil course that God must tolerate (TWT5) until the power of Satan's influence is spent (TWT6). The incredible amount of destruction Satan has brought about in God's creation is a testimony to the vast amount of love and benefit he could have brought had he chosen

---

145. Boyd, *Satan*, 215–216. "The inscrutable mystery of the problem of evil is the mystery of a largely *unknowable creation*, not the mystery of an *unknowable God*." Boyd, *Satan*, 197; Boyd, *Is God to Blame?*, 79–106.
146. Boyd, *Satan*, 204.
147. Boyd, *Satan*, 204.
148. Boyd, *Satan*, 205.
149. Boyd, *Satan*, 205.

a different path. God could not have hoped for the former, however, unless he was willing to risk the latter.[150]

COSMIC WARFARE AND NATURAL EVIL

Boyd's six theses offer a significant extension of the free will defense within a cosmic warfare theodicy and explicitly deal with the problem of moral evil. That extension does not yet answer the formidable question of natural evil.[151] (This is often seen as the "Achilles's heel" of the free will defense[152]). How can moral evil explain "evidential" evils unrelated to human choice (e.g., suffering due to earthquakes, genetic diseases, etc.)? At this very point there is an apparent problem. One of the delimitations of this study involves restricting the discussion to *moral* evil rather than natural evil. How can we ignore the Achilles's heel? Interestingly, it is Boyd's approach to natural evil (which shares some similarities to the Great Controversy) that justifies this delimitation. Boyd denies that natural evil is "natural."[153] Instead, he affirms the radical unnatural influence and input of non-divine moral agents, specifically Satan and demons, on nature.[154] Rather than natural evil being the weak link, in his adapted free will theodicy Boyd claims that failing to utilize Satan makes natural evil unsolvable.[155] Creation is not as God intended, just as humanity is not as God intended.[156] God is not the only one at work in nature. Nature exhibits diabolical features because diabolical

---

150. Boyd, *Satan*, 205.

151. The problem of "natural" evil is "arguably the most formidable objection that can be raised against the belief in an all-powerful, all good God." Gregory A. Boyd, "Satan and the Corruption of Nature," 2019.

152. Warburton, *Philosophy: The Basics*, 25. Griffin, "Process Theology and the Christian Good News," 16–17.

153. Augustine also denied the existence of "natural evil," but his meaning is different to Boyd's. Augustine's privation theory means evil has no "substance," therefore anything natural is "good." Evil is a privation of the good. No "thing" is intrinsically evil. See Griffin, *God, Power and Evil*, 70–71.

154. Boyd advances seven arguments in favour of Satan's corruption of nature being the necessary explanation of natural evil in an essay on his website. For the arguments see Boyd, "Satan and the Corruption of Nature," 2019.

155. "I'm going to argue that we cannot adequately explain 'natural' evil unless we accept that Satan and other rebellious cosmic forces have had a corrupting influence on creation. This is not to deny that there aren't other important things to consider in explaining 'natural' evil. But my contention is that if we leave Satan and other nefarious spirit-agents out of the picture, no explanation of 'natural' evil can be adequate." Boyd, "Satan and the Corruption of Nature," 2019.

156. Boyd, *Satan*, 247.

agents are either directly or indirectly behind the "unnatural" features of nature.¹⁵⁷ "Arguably, nowhere is the distinctiveness of the Trinitarian warfare theodicy more apparent than on this point."¹⁵⁸ With this move Boyd places the problem of natural evil as a subcategory within moral evil. The problem of natural evil ultimately flows out of the problem of moral evil. Therefore, when a cosmic warfare theodicy deals with moral evil it is also dealing with natural evil. This study's concern is not to critique this view (or to chart all of Boyd's argument) but understand and recognize this. It is to find how the Great Controversy as a (cosmic warfare) theodicy resolves the problem of evil. As will be shown the Great Controversy shares a similar, although not identical, approach to Boyd. It too ultimately sees natural evil as arising due to moral evil. Explain moral evil and you have the key element needed to account for natural evil.

In his discussion of "natural evil" Boyd explores over seven different approaches to natural evil¹⁵⁹ (some of which he agrees with and others he does not) before offering his own cosmic warfare account.¹⁶⁰ The main difference between Boyd's approach and the others is that Boyd places the other explanations in a cosmic warfare perspective that recognizes the neglected agency and activity of Satan and the demonic.¹⁶¹ This crucial satanic/demonic dimension transforms the previous explanations and their ability to account for natural evil. Boyd argues that a neutral medium of relationally (the natural order) which is necessary if free moral agents are to communicate and affect one another, is subject to either good or evil

---

157. Plantinga, drawing from Augustine, mentions Satan as a possible explanation for natural evil in his free will defense. See Plantinga, *God, Freedom and Evil*, 58,59. Plantinga presents this merely as logically compatible with his free will defense. What is distinct with Boyd is his use of moral evil (via Satan) in constructing a theodicy, not simply a defense, his rejection of natural evil as a separate category, and his assertive claim that only by recognising the centrality of Satan is an adequate explanation of natural evil possible.

158. Boyd, *Satan*, 247.

159. The seven approaches are 1) Augustine's "Natural evil" fulfils a "higher" purpose. 2) "Natural evil" is due to human sin. 3) Hick's Soul-making theodicy. 4) Nature as kenotic process (Boyd has in mind Murphy and Ellis, *On the Moral Nature of the Universe*). 5) "Natural" evil exists because God is inherently limited (Process theology). 6) "Natural" evil exists because there are inherent limitations in creation—dual potentiality and randomness (drawing from Peterson, *Evil and the Christian God*, 111). 7) Natural evil as Barth's Nothingness (drawing from Karl Barth *Church Dogmatics*, 3.3: 289–368). Boyd, *Satan*, 248–85.

160. Boyd's own account of natural evil combines features of all seven approaches. For his position see Boyd, *Satan*, 290–91.

161. Boyd, *Satan*, 291, 293–318.

influence from the same agents.[162] Thus in a warfare context, it is appropriate to speak of nature's potential use as a tool or weapon.[163] Boyd summarises what he believes is pivotal: "The problem of evil is not a problem of occasional bad things happening on the otherwise pristine stage of God's creation, as is frequently portrayed. Rather, evil permeates *the structure of the stage itself*, for the one given authority over the structure (Satan) has become corrupt."[164] This view leans heavily on the assumption that Satan had an initial God-given authority over matter or creation which was not revoked following rebellion. It is this authority which allowed spiritual agents to effect *structural* change to creation. He emphasizes that this "insight lies at the heart of the Trinitarian warfare worldview."[165]

One more element of Boyd's view will prove significant to later discussions. This is the issue of when Satan was able to effect structural change in the cosmos. In more recent discussions Boyd has developed the idea that evolution itself is a "sort of warfare between the life-affirming creativity of an all-good God, on the one hand, and the on-going corrupting influence of malevolent cosmic forces, on the other."[166] Boyd even speculates when Satan and his cosmic forces may have initially rebelled against God and started corrupting nature. He suggests that the appearance of predatorial life forms during the Cambrian explosion half a billion years ago might be the point

162. Boyd, *Satan*, 297. A stable shared common medium is where "(1) all parties can *influence* others by influencing their environment, and (2) no party can exhaustively *control* others or their environment." This "shared medium must be pliable enough for us to influence it but resistant enough that no one can exhaustively control it." Boyd, *Is God to Blame?*, 113–4. While God can still intervene in this world, too much overriding of the order could compromise its stability. In "creating a stable, non-chaotic world, God ruled out a world in which he could intervene any time, place or manner he desires." Boyd, *Is God to Blame?*, 115.

163. Boyd finds precedent for this in the early church fathers and modern theologians/ philosophers who believe Satan can use nature in such a way: Boyd, *Satan*, 294–301. This early attributing of natural evil to Satan was eclipsed in the early church by the later Augustinian turn to a deterministic view of divine sovereignty. Later still enlightenment rationalism and naturalism made belief in evil spirits even more problematic. Boyd, *Satan*, 295.

164. Boyd, *Satan*, 301.

165. Boyd, *Satan*, 301. What is this structural change? It appears to be the introduction of death and disorder into the natural realm and its manipulation by the demonic so that nature manifests a pain-ridden, bloodthirsty, hostile character.

166. Boyd, "Evolution as Cosmic Warfare," 127. This is a shift of views for Boyd. Earlier he advocated a "restorationist" or "gap" reading of Genesis 1:1, 2. See Boyd, *God at War*, 103–13. In this view verse 1 describes an initial ancient creation billions of years ago which ended with a war between God and Satan, while verse 2 transitions to a recent creation. Boyd, *Satan*, 313–17. Now Boyd advocates a warfare reading of evolution.

in time.[167] This is reinforced by other statements which speak of the "battle God has been waging for millions upon millions of years."[168] This ongoing divine battle which had creation as the first stage, Jesus as the culmination, and is now being carried on by the church, has been raging "for millions of years and, for all we know, it may go on for a million more" but "*cannot*—go on forever."[169] Overall, one can see the pivotal cosmic importance of Satan for subsuming natural evil into moral evil. Satan first rebels then uses his original capacity, power, and authority to introduce deep-level structural evil to the natural order (as well as ongoing specific evils). Denying Satan would mean eliminating an adequate explanation for natural evil. But Boyd does affirm Satan as the cause of natural evil, and so God is not to blame. In this view, human evil is secondary to Satan's. Satan is on the level of a demonic demiurge. Boyd has clearly pushed Satan's theodic explanatory power to the maximum. One wonders if he has pushed it too far.

A THEOLOGY OF REVOLT AS THE PRACTICAL SIDE OF THEODICY

Having outlined the way the Trinitarian Warfare Theodicy theoretically handles the problems of moral and natural evil, it is time to look at the practical side of warfare theodicy. One of the truly distinctive and appealing elements of Boyd's warfare theodicy is the natural way his theodicy becomes a practical response to evil rather than an intellectual one. Traditional theodicies are marked by a philosophical and theoretical approach to evil often with minimal practical relevance. Anti-theodicy opponents have even accused theoretical theodicies as being a part of the problem of evil. In contrast, Boyd's theology of revolt helps him avoid this major criticism. It could be argued that Boyd's warfare approach is both a theodicy and an anti-theodicy at the same time. The warfare worldview naturally and seamlessly integrates theodicy, atonement theory, practical action, mission, spiritual warfare and ecclesiology. As God fights against evil, so does the church. The practical is not an add-on to the theory; it is the theory in action. But before spelling out the practical ongoing ecclesiastical-based revolt against evil there is need to look at the event which begins, enables, models, empowers, and grounds all revolt against evil—the saving work of Christ.

---

167. Boyd, "Evolution as Cosmic Warfare" 143, fn 38.
168. Boyd, "Evolution as Cosmic Warfare," 145.
169. Boyd, "Evolution as Cosmic Warfare," 145.

Christus Victor—Atonement as Warfare and Revolt

It is no surprise that for Boyd salvation is viewed through the warfare lens. A number of different models of atonement have been developed in Christian theology.[170] Boyd believes that that the foundational atonement model is the Christus Victor view.[171] Due to it being more fundamental, the other models should be seen in the context of the Christus Victor theory not vice versa.[172] In the Christus Victor model Satan has profound power and authority over the fallen world, and salvation consists in deliverance from the devil by Christ. The plight of humanity is primarily defined as bondage to evil forces (rather than guilt, shame, weakness, ignorance, disease) and thus the solution is freedom from evil powers. This freedom is achieved by union, incorporation, or participation in Christ's victory.[173] In this model, in contrast to other views, the cosmic significance of Christ's work is ontologically more fundamental than its soteriological (individual) significance.[174] Salvation is "a cosmic reality before it is anthropological reality, and it is the

---

170. There are many theories or models of atonement and ways of grouping them. John McIntyre, for example, lists no less than 13 models: (1) ransom; 2) redemption; 3) salvation; 4) sacrifice: 5) propitiation: 6) expiation; 7) atonement; 8) reconciliation; 9) victory; 10) punishment; 11) satisfaction; 12) example; 13) liberation; see McIntyre, *The Shape of Soteriology*. However, these are synthesized into more complex models, the most prominent of which are the Ransom or Christus Victor theories (Ireneaus, Gustav Aulen), Satisfaction theory (Anselm), Moral Influence theory (Peter Abelard) and the Penal Substitution theory (Calvin; see Green and Baker, *Recovering the Scandal of the Cross*, 142–91. To these could be added the Governmental (Hugo Grotius), Healing (Reichenbach), and modern non-violent theories (Rene Girard).

171. Boyd rejects the patristic idea that God offered Jesus as payment to the devil in exchange for humanity or that God used Jesus as bait (knowing that Satan would be unable to resist seizing Christ but nor could he contain him); Boyd, "Christus Victor View," 36. Boyd also differs from ancient models by declining to explain in detail exactly how Jesus' life and resurrection defeated the powers, only that he did so. Ancient advocates became incredulous because they pressed details too far. Boyd, "Christus Victor View," 37 fn 23. Lastly, Boyd sees Jesus' victorious death as an extension of his loving life and ministry, and that both Christ's life and death are acts of divine warfare against evil. Atonement is not limited to Christ's death. Boyd, "Christus Victor View," 38–42.

172. Boyd, "Christus Victor View," 24. Boyd argues that the cosmic view is able to encompass within its single framework all the other elements of truth expressed in other models of atonement. In these he includes penal substitutionary views, recapitulation, healing model, moral governmental model, exemplar models. Boyd, "Christus Victor View," 42–45.

173. "All who trust in Christ are incorporated into him and therefore share in this cosmic victory. This is the essential meaning of 'salvation' in the New Testament" Boyd, "Christus Victor View," 33. The "concept of salvation is centered on our participation in Christ's cosmic victory over the powers." Boyd, "Christus Victor View," 35.

174. Boyd, "Christus Victor View," 33.

latter because it is the former."175 For Boyd, the superiority of the Christus Victor view is evident in its ability to incorporate the whole of Jesus' life, his ministry, as part of salvation, and not just Christ's death and resurrection. The "other models tend to isolate the meaning of Jesus' death from other aspects of life," whereas in Christus Victor every aspect of his life is "most fundamentally *about one thing*: victoriously manifesting the loving kingdom of God over and against the destructive, oppressive kingdom of Satan."176 And all of this is a manifestation of cross-like love.

The Christian life as Spiritual Warfare and Practical Revolt

What does a theology of revolt (practical ecclesiastical theodicy) look like in the life of the church? It looks like Jesus' kingdom. What does that look like? "The kingdom looks like Jesus. It looks like Jesus' self-sacrificial love. It looks like Jesus being crucified for the very people who crucified him."177 Boyd describes it as "anti-political social activism."178 It is modeled on Jesus. For Boyd, Jesus engaged in political revolt.179 By this Boyd means that Jesus rejected in his life the socio-political order of the world which demeaned women, foreigners, outcasts, achieves and maintains power by violence, exalts nationalism, abuses the poor, etc. Jesus also engaged in spiritual revolt.180 Here Boyd refers to Jesus' revolt against the spiritual principalities and powers by his exorcisms, healings, and self-sacrificing death on the cross. This was a revolt against the cosmic powers which empower world evil. The two (socio-political revolt and spiritual revolt) are intimately linked. To revolt against one was to revolt against the other.181

    175. Boyd, "Christus Victor View," 35.

    176. Boyd, "Christus Victor View," 40.

    177. Boyd, "Advancing the Cruciform Revolution," 415. "Jesus' life, his ministry and teachings, and especially his death and resurrection manifest the kingdom of God. The kingdom always has a cruciform character, a self-sacrificial character, a loving character. The kingdom always looks like Jesus." Boyd, "Advancing the Cruciform Revolution," 408.

    178. Boyd, "The Kingdom as a Political-Spiritual Revolution," 23. Boyd also calls it being a "anti-political political activist," 25.

    179. Boyd, "The Kingdom as a Political-Spiritual Revolution," 23–25.

    180. Boyd, "The Kingdom as a Political-Spiritual Revolution," 25–27.

    181. "Every act of revolt against oppressive, unjust, and dehumanizing socio-political and religious systems was *at the same time* an act of revolt against the Powers that fuel these systems. Jesus' solidarity with the poor, for example, was itself a revolt against the Powers that fuel greed and poverty. In this sense, Jesus was a political and spiritual revolutionary, and he was the one because he was the other. He was, in short, a political-spiritual revolutionary." Boyd, "The Kingdom as a Political-Spiritual Revolution," 27.

The church is called to participate in this political-spiritual revolution. This means a revolt against idolatry, judgment, religion, individualism, violence, social oppression, racism, poverty and greed, abuse of creation, abuse of sex, and secularism, by means of non-violent love.[182] This is "displaying the reign of God in love.'"[183] This is spiritual warfare and is the ground level practical expression of cosmic warfare.[184] "Jesus' radically counter-cultural ministry wasn't first and foremost a form of social and political protest, though it certainly was that. It was, rather, most fundamentally a form of spiritual warfare."[185] Boyd believes the church is simply called to live out this radical social-spiritual revolution. That is participation in cosmic warfare and part of God's response to evil. This is part of theodicy. This approach avoids the path of the Christian Left with its political activism or the paths of the Christian Right's conservative attempts to taking society back for God or social retreat which only focuses on saving souls.[186] This Jesus revolution is both political and anti-political. It is political in the sense that everything it does has political implications. It is anti-political in that Jesus never showed any interest in the power politics of the world or setting up a kingdom now amid the world's political order.[187] This is divine love fighting on its own terms.

ESCHATOLOGY—FINAL VICTORY OVER EVIL

In Boyd's Trinitarian Warfare Theodicy eschatology is not an addition to soteriology but an extension of it. The Christus Victor model is an expression of 'inaugurated eschatology' which follows the widely held 'already-but-not-yet' dynamism of the New Testament eschatology.[188] Jesus in his life, ministry, death, and resurrection achieves victory over Satan and evil. This means the eschaton has already been achieved in principle in Jesus but

---

182. See Boyd, *The Myth of a Christian Religion*.

183. Boyd, "Advancing the Cruciform Revolution," 411.

184. Boyd, "The Ground-Level Deliverance Model," 129–57.

185. "In Jesus, and in the movement he came to establish, the long expected apocalyptic battle between God and the Powers was—and still is—being waged." And Boyd clarifies that "when Jesus refused to live in accordance with his culture's assumptions, laws, and social taboos regarding nationalism, race, gender, class, wealth, he wasn't just waging a social protest; he was engaging in warfare against the Powers that oppress people by empowering these things." Boyd, *The Myth of a Christian Religion*, 31.

186. Boyd, "The Kingdom as a Political-Spiritual Revolution," 23. Boyd, *The Myth of a Christian Nation*.

187. Boyd, "The Kingdom as a Political-Spiritual Revolution," 29–30.

188. Boyd, *God at War*, 213.

is not yet fully manifested. Christ has set in motion forces which will eventually eliminate Satan and evil and restore creation. Until the finalization of Christ's victory the cosmic war continues and the church in its spiritual warfare is called to continue the same ministry of Jesus and its revolt against evil. But in this section the questions is: What does the consummated side of eschatology look like in Boyd's theodicy?

Boyd has relatively little to say about the Second Coming of Jesus apart from affirming that it will happen. Boyd sees most detailed eschatological discussions about the order of events leading up to or surrounding Christ's return as a waste of time.[189] His discussions are more concerned with heaven, hell, and the afterlife. Boyd's thinking is not always clear in this area.[190] He has held a number of different positions indicating that his thinking has undergone significant change and may continue to undergo further change. In *Satan and the Problem of Evil* Boyd tended toward a more traditional understanding of hell as eternal punishment although significantly modified by Barth's idea of nothingness.[191] At the time he displayed some sympathy with annihilationist positions but without accepting them. Since then, Boyd has continued to shift in his thinking and now leans toward the annihilationist position.[192] What can account for this change? Boyd indicates that the burden of theodicy and his understanding of God's love are motivators for these changes. Boyd cannot reconcile the God who eternally inflicts suffering due to an insatiable vengeance and the God of Calvary's self-sacrificing love.[193] Boyd appears to be bringing his eschatology in line with his doctrine of God inspired by the concerns of theodicy.

Like most annihilationists Boyd now seems to affirm conditional immortality[194] and yet he also appears to affirm an ongoing intermediate state

---

189. See Boyd, "What's Your View of the Tribulation Period and the Rapture?," 2007. Boyd leans toward preterism but is not completely convinced.

190. Boyd confesses that "it's admittedly hard to put together into a coherent scheme the various things Scripture says about the afterlife." Boyd, "What about the Thief on the Cross?," 2009. We should note that most of this information about eschatology comes from Boyd's blog and may indicate the secondary status it holds in his overall thinking.

191. Boyd, *Satan*, 319–57.

192. Boyd's statements are slightly unclear; for example, he states, "While I am not completely convinced of this position, I think it is worthy of serious consideration." Boyd, "The Case for Annihilationism," 2008. Yet he also says "I'm strongly inclined toward the annihilationist position. The reason is that it strikes me as the view that has the best biblical support." Boyd, "Are You an Annihilationist, and if So Why?," 2008.

193. Boyd, "Are You an Annihilationist, and If So, Why?," 2008.

194. Boyd, "Are You an Annihilationist, and If So, Why?," 2008.

for the (believing) dead between death and eternity.[195] Into this state Boyd entertains the idea of some form of "purgatory." This is not a medieval-style purgatory (with indulgences, etc.) but rather a post-mortem place of refinement. What Boyd seems to have in mind is that after death the sanctification process continues for believers as they enter a place called "paradise" where, paradoxically, they undergo a purifying (which involves pain and punishment) of their character in the presence of the fire of God's love. This is a place and state that precedes the coming of the Kingdom and resurrection of bodies. Elsewhere, he refers to this refinement as happening at the "judgment seat of Christ" (which is different to the Great White Throne judgment). Whether this is the equivalent to paradise or at the end of paradise is not clear.[196] On top of this, Boyd has developed the idea of a post-mortem opportunity of salvation for babies who die without having the chance to decide for or against Christ.[197] Boyd reasons that as love must be freely chosen, babies will be allowed to mature in the afterlife and then decide whether or not they want to submit to Christ. Processes not completed in this life are completed in the next life. This view later becomes a generalized post-mortem salvation as Boyd opens this possibility up to all (not just babies) who have not solidified a decision for or against Christ.[198] In all of these changes to his eschatology we can see Boyd trying to work out in his theology his commitments to his understandings of freedom, love, and theodicy.

CONCLUSION

Boyd's cosmic warfare theodicy resolves the problem of evil by an appeal to the *metaphysics of love*. On one hand there is the contingent conditional love of the creature and on the other hand the unconditional love of the creator. The possibility of contingent creaturely love (reflecting the triune God of love) entails the necessity of a libertarian freedom and with that the

---

195. Boyd's scattered thoughts on eschatology leave open many questions. His affirmations of an intermediate state (implying anthropological dualism) appear to be in conflict with his conditional immortality (implying anthropological monism/holism). Boyd is even open to the possibility of near death experiences (although he is very cautious); see Boyd, "Review of Proof of Heaven," 2012. This ambiguity and lack of clarity characterises his eschatology in general and suggests a work in need of more progress. Boyd admits that it's "hard to put together into a coherent scheme the various things Scripture says about the afterlife." Boyd, "What about the Thief on the Cross?," 2009.

196. See, Boyd, "Purgatory and the Judgment Seat of Christ," 2009.

197. Boyd, "What Happens to Babies That Die," 2007.

198. Boyd, "What Happens to Babies That Die," 2007.

risk of its abuse leading to a cosmic war in which creation resists its creator. Cosmic war and evil are not willed by God; instead God fights against it but without revoking freedom itself. Unfortunately, in war gratuitous evil becomes normative. Just such a war eventuated through the rebellion of a high-ranking angel, Satan, and those who followed him. Satan is the originator of rebellion, its leader, and therefore functions as the paradigm of creaturely evil. To account for Satan is to account for all lesser rebels. Satan's profound original power, authority, and potential help account for the pervasive presence of suffering and corruption that exists in the natural world ("natural evil"). Nevertheless, divine love is the answer to the metaphysical risk inherent in creaturely contingent love. Creaturely love needs freedom and freedom introduces risk. But divine love redeems freedom and ends the risk. Thus the nature of love is the resolution to the problem of evil in a dual and complementary sense. Firstly, contingent creaturely love resolves the theoretical and metaphysical problem of how evil or war against God can arise and yet God not be blameable for it. Secondly, love resolves the practical issue of evil because (divine) love is the force and power which can and will redeem fallen creation from evil and end the cosmic war. Boyd's cosmic warfare theodicy is also a theodicy of practical response and not simply theoretical explanation. Love in both its creaturely and divine forms accounts for evil's origins and its end. Love forms an explanatory circle around the problem of evil allowing for, without absolutizing, its occurrence, and tempering without trivializing its challenge.

Chapter 3

Initial Construction of a Great Controversy Theodicy

This study now turns its focus to the cosmic warfare theodicy which is our focus, Seventh-day Adventism's idea of a "Great Controversy" between Christ and Satan.[1] This theodicy has a number of similarities to Boyd's, as well as salient differences to Boyd and all other theodicies. Until now it has charted its own course by not living within traditional discussions that are so often closely tied to philosophy and metaphysics. The previous analysis of Boyd revealed his warfare theodicy flows from a *metaphysics of love;* this exploration of the Great Controversy will demonstrate that it is a theodicy grounded in a *metanarrative of love* which offers some unique responses to the questions surrounding the problem of evil. First, the origin of evil within the Great Controversy theodicy through the person of Lucifer/Satan, how he initiates a cosmic controversy with God, and how such a controversy is even possible will be examined. This will require an exploration of the Great Controversy understanding of love, law, and the "mystery of evil." This chapter concludes by detailing the divine response of atonement. The conclusion outlines the analytical and constructive findings.

---

1. The construction of the Great Controversy Theodicy will be mainly but not exclusively drawn from Ellen White. For a purely biblically-based theodicy with some complementary similarities to White's, see John Peckham's *Theodicy of Love.*

FOUNDATIONAL IDEAS

The Great Controversy is built on one primal assumption—God is love. Ellen White begins her *Conflict of the Ages* series,[2] in which is most fully developed her thinking, with the sentence: "'God is love' (1 John 4:16). His nature, his law, is love. It ever has been; it ever will be."[3] She ends the same series with the phrase "God is love," thus forming a conceptual envelope within which all cosmic conflict is to be understood. The opening chapter is entitled "Why was Sin Permitted?," indicating from the outset a concern with theodicy. Here she subsumes divine sovereignty and power within the idea of divine love. "Every manifestation of creative power is an expression of infinite love. The sovereignty of God involves fullness of blessing to all created beings."[4] She then immediately places the primal truth about God (divine love) within a cosmic conflict setting. "The history of the great conflict between good and evil, from the time it first began in heaven to the final overthrow of rebellion and the total eradication of sin, is also a demonstration of God's unchanging love."[5] Her next move is to introduce Christ, his divinity and oneness with the Father, and his work in creating and ruling all things.[6] This is important because the cosmic conflict has a specific personal element that focuses on Christ versus Satan. Finally, in this important opening which sets the scene for everything else to follow, the importance of God's law of love and the idea of freedom of the will is introduced.[7] The main ideas which will prove foundational to the Great Controversy theodicy are present: God is love, creation and sovereignty defined by divine love, an ensuing great conflict between good and evil, Christ's supremacy, God's law, and freedom of the will.

CREATION AND CONDITIONS

To understand cosmic warfare as Great Controversy, it is necessary to understand God's original purpose in creating the universe and the conditions

---

2. This series is Ellen White's narrative commentary on all of history and Scripture. It consists of the books: White, *Patriarchs and Prophets*; White, *Prophets and Kings*; White, *The Desire of Ages*; White, *The Acts of the Apostles*; White, *The Great Controversy*.

3. White, *Patriarchs and Prophets*, 33.

4. White, *Patriarchs and Prophets*, 33.

5. White, *Patriarchs and Prophets*, 33.

6. White, *Patriarchs and Prophets*, 34. Special mention is made of angels as God's servants in contrast to the Son who is equal to the Father and co-rules with him.

7. "He takes no pleasure in a forced obedience; and to all He grants freedom of will, that they may render Him voluntary service." White, *Patriarchs and Prophets*, 34.

of that fulfillment. God wanted a universe populated with creatures who were like him in character and capable of entering into communion with him. In such a universe, creaturely existence would be a ceaseless education or "school" in which intelligent beings would constantly learn of, know, and grow in a moral knowledge of God, by a collective exploration of God and his works.[8] Communion with God and each other was both the goal and means to the goal.[9] The vastness and near infinity of the universe is an indication of the eternal scope of the divine plan and purpose for creation.[10] In continually uncovering new depths to God's wisdom, power, love, and goodness, creatures would more fully reflect God's glory and in this process experience their own holistic development.[11] The cosmos was constructed infinitely deep with a mutually beneficent character reflective of its creator.

Achieving such a goal required a particular universe populated with specific kinds of beings. To become "like God" in character required the possession of "God-like" faculties. "Every human being, created in the image of God, is endowed with a power akin to that of the Creator—individuality, power to think and to do."[12] Yet this individuality was not autonomous individualism. Adam and Eve were to "have no interest independent of each other; and yet each had an individuality in thinking and acting."[13] Individuality was in service to wider, higher, deeper realities. Individual powers were given in order to enjoy communion with God and others, explore the universe, and "comprehend moral responsibilities and obligations" (i.e., God's law).[14] These powers enable and express free will. Humans were created as free moral agents[15] rather than mere "machines" or "automatons."[16] God would not force the will or accept service unless willingly and intelligently given, as "forced submission would prevent all real development of mind or character; it would make man a mere automaton."[17] Yet freedom

---

8. White, *Education*, 18.

9. "In this communion is found the highest education. It is God's own method of development." White, *Education*, 14.

10. White, *The Ministry of Healing*, 100.

11. White, *Education*, 15.

12. White, *Education* 17.

13. White, *Testimonies*, 3:484.

14. White, *Education*, 20.

15. "God made them free moral agents, capable of appreciating the wisdom and benevolence of His character and the justice of His requirements, and with full liberty to yield or to withhold obedience." White, *Patriarchs and Prophets*, 48.

16. White, *Patriarchs and Prophets*, 49. See also, White, *Steps to Christ*, 43–4. White, in "Ellen White Comments," 1:1084.

17. White, *Steps to Christ*, 43–44.

was subservient to the higher moral and social principles of God's law and government.[18] We were made to love God and each other. Contingent creaturely freedom and love is conditioned by moral responsibility or law.[19] That is, God's love gives and also places conditions upon freedom. God's love is a law. The Great Controversy theodicy mirrors the basic free will defense but with its own emphasis on love and law.

LUCIFER'S STRUGGLE AND FALL

This original created order is described as producing a universal harmony "so as long as created beings acknowledged the allegiance of love."[20] The note of conditionality and contingency which attends this unity is sounded again in the description of the social dimensions of the allegiance of love (deliberately evocative of the two great commandments) and by the use of the word "while." "And *while* love to God was supreme, love for one another was confiding and unselfish."[21] This is a picture of a tightly integrated and perfectly balanced social unity, built on a supreme love for God which secures every other resultant love. Creation is morally and relationally centered and secured in an unselfish God whose love-nature is reflected in his subjects. Creation possesses a moral fine-tuning necessary for social life analogous to the physical fine-tuning of the universe that is essential to biological life. Into this picture radical change took place. Discord first arose in the heart of an exalted angel called Lucifer and later spread to other hearts. Utilizing a free will-styled defense White states that there "was one who *perverted the freedom* that God had granted to His creatures. Sin originated with him who, next to Christ, had been most honored of God and was highest in power and glory among the inhabitants of heaven."[22]

The Great Controversy follows the early church tradition of seeing Satan's fall in Isaiah 14 and Ezekiel 28 but develops it in its own way.[23] Satan

---

18. "God placed man under law, as an indispensable condition of his very existence. He was a subject of the divine government, and there can be no government without law." White, *Patriarchs and Prophets*, 49.

19. This means, following Adventist theologian John Peckham's model of divine love, that God's love is "fore-conditional." Peckham, "The Concept of Divine Love."

20. White, *Patriarchs and Prophets*, 35.

21. White, *Patriarchs and Prophets*, 35.

22. White, *Patriarchs and Prophets*, 35. Italics mine.

23. See, Bertoluci, "The Son of the Morning."; Davidson, "The Chiastic Literary Structure of the Book of Ezekiel," 71–94; Tonstad, *Saving God's Reputation*. For the alternative and predominant contemporary position which denies Isaiah 14 and Ezekiel 28 refer to Satan, see, Oswalt, *The Book of Isaiah*, 320, and Block, *The Book of Ezekiel*, 119.

was once a perfect angel, a covering or anointed cherub[24] who was created sinless, good and holy.[25] Perfection means faultlessness, not impeccability (being incapable of sinning) or infallibility (since God alone is infallible). He was the highest in glory, power, intellect, and wisdom among all the angels and created beings.[26] In terms of heaven's government he was next after God and Christ in position and honor.[27] He was given the greatest talents and gifts a created being could possess.[28] In terms of goodness and beauty he was as near as possible to being like God himself.[29] Accordingly, he was greatly loved by the angelic host and had considerable influence over them.[30] He was foremost among created beings in revealing God's purposes to the universe.[31]

The fall of Lucifer and his transformation into Satan is described in remarkable detail by Ellen White in a number of places in her writings.[32] The fall was a process that need not have happened and could have been averted at a number of points if Lucifer had been willing to listen to God. Lucifer's fall is not a sudden event. It runs through two main stages. There is an initial, private, inner struggle which continues to grow and becomes concurrent with a second outward public revolt.

---

24. Ezek 28:14; White, "Ellen White Comments," 4:1143,1163; White, vol. 7: 969, 972; White, *Desire of Ages*, 21, 116, 758; White, *The Great Controversy*, 496–7, 669; White, *Selected Messages*, 1, 222; White, *The Story of Redemption*, 427.

25. Ezek 28:12,15; White, *The Great Controversy*, 493–4, 513; White, *Patriarchs and Prophets*, 35.

26. Ezek 28:12; White, *The Desire of Ages*, 758; White, *The Great Controversy*, 493, 495; White, *Patriarchs and Prophets*, 35, 37; Whtie, *Selected Messages*, 1958, 1:341.

27. White, *Fundamentals of Christian Education*, 175; White, *Christ Triumphant*, 27; White, *Patriarchs and Prophets*, 35–36.

28. "The greatest talents and the highest gifts that could be bestowed on a created being were given to Lucifer, the covering cherub. Before his fall he was a glorious being, occupying a position next to Christ, but he sought to be equal with God, and brought upon himself irretrievable ruin." White, *This Day with God*, 287.

29. White, "Without Excuse." Angels, while a different order to humans, also possess a likeness to God.

30. White, *The Great Controversy*, 494–95; White, *Patriarchs and Prophets*, 37, 41.

31. White, *The Desire of Ages*, 758.

32. The most significant are the parallel chapters "Why was Sin Permitted" in White, *Patriarchs and Prophets*, 33–43; and "The Origin of Evil" in White, *The Great Controversy*, 492–504.

First Stage: Mysterious Origins, Covert Emergence & Private Struggle

The Great Controversy begins with a perfect and happy being, Lucifer. It then turns to a strange, unaccountable, and subtle psychological, spiritual, mental, emotional shift within him. Mysteriously, deep within the psyche of Lucifer, his thoughts began to turn toward himself in such a way that his attitude toward God changed. The exact genesis of these thoughts is impossible to fully trace. The process is briefly outlined as, "Little by little Lucifer came to indulge a desire for self-exaltation."[33] This internal drift was known only to Lucifer and God. At some point Lucifer began to accept these self-exalting thoughts. New unprecedented and questionable feelings toward God were toyed with and eventually embraced as valid. This genuinely new and unprecedented thinking can be summarised as a turn to the self as center, or a turn to selfishness. It is characterized by an interrelated mix of two attitudes: pride and envy. In White's narration, the feelings of pride arose from an inordinate estimation of his own glory, perfection, and importance, and this was symbiotically related with feelings of envy and jealousy which centered around a comparison to Christ's position. Pride was the burgeoning attitude to himself and envy was the emerging attitude toward Christ. Both are expressions of selfishness. Lucifer became self-referential. Selfishness is the summary category and root attitude, while pride and envy are the specific species and manifesting fruit of it.

Descriptions of Lucifer's selfishness occur in a number of ways. His thoughts turned toward himself in self-seeking,[34] self-indulgence,[35] and self-exaltation.[36] He desired to live for self. He developed a disposition to serve self instead of Creator.[37] He wanted to "make himself a center of influence"[38] in opposition to the only ultimate center—God. The essence of Lucifer's rebellion was a turn to self or selfishness. The most explicit statement of selfishness as sin's origin is this: "Sin originated in self-seeking."[39]

Lucifer's pride is associated with his beauty and brilliance. Lucifer gloried in his brightness and exaltation.[40] Being highly honored and admired

---

33. White, *Patriarchs and Prophets*, 35. White, *The Great Controversy*, 494.
34. White, *Christ Triumphant* 32; White, *Desire of Ages* 21–22.
35. White, *Patriarchs and Prophets* 48.
36. White, *Desire of Ages* 22; 435–36; White, *Great Controversy* 494, 503–4; White, *Patriarchs* 35,37; White, *Testimonies* 2:440; White, *Testimonies for the Church*, 6:237.
37. White, *Patriarchs and Prophets*, 55.
38. White, *Testimonies*, 5:236.
39. White, *Desire of Ages*, 21.
40. White, *The Great Controversy*, 495.

by others, Lucifer thought of himself as the favorite among angels.[41] He was taken in by his own glory.[42] Pride in his own glory could only happen as Lucifer started to think "selfishly" or without reference to God. How? In a crucial statement, Ellen White relates how Satan had enjoyed serving God "until he began to think that his wisdom was not derived from God, but was inherent in himself and that he was as worthy as was God to receive honor and power."[43]

An inflated sense of self explains pride but not envy. Comparisons with lesser beings would reinforce pride but not generate envy. Envy requires a comparison with someone perceived as greater in brilliance and position. In Lucifer's case, it was Christ. Pride is internally focused, envy is externally focused. Pride indulges. Envy covets. By observing the place and position of Christ Lucifer developed "dissatisfaction with his position."[44] He desired Christ's power, position, authority, and honor. Lucifer coveted the glory invested in Christ and the homage that was due to him.[45] He wanted the honor which the Father bestowed upon the Son.[46] Thus, he developed and nurtured an intense envy and jealousy toward Christ.[47] To desire Christ's unique position requires displacing him.[48] This would place himself above the entire created realm. He eventually wanted to "gain control of heavenly beings, to draw them away from their Creator, and to win their homage to himself."[49] Pride and envy combined to create an unholy ambition.[50]

Identifying pride and envy as the main descriptions of Lucifer's fall has a long history within theology. The majority view within the early Christian tradition saw Lucifer's sin as *pride* (Origen, Chrysostom, Jerome, and Ambrose), usually working from Isaiah 14 and Ezekiel 28, while the

41. White, *The Story of Redemption*, 14.

42. White, *Patriarchs and Prophets*, 37.

43. White, "The Weapon against Satan's Delusion." See also, "though all his glory was from God, this mighty angel came to regard it as pertaining to himself." White, *Patriarchs and Prophets*, 35.

44. White, 3 *Spiritual Gifts*, 36.

45. White, *The Great Controversy*, 502; White, *Patriarchs*, 35; White, *Testimonies*, 5:702.

46. White, The *Great Controversy*, 494.

47. White, "Ellen White Comments," 5:1149–1150; White, *Early Writings*, 145; White, *The Great Controversy*, 495, 669; White, *Patriarchs and Prophets*, 36–37; White, *Spiritual Gifts*, 3:36–38; White, *The Story of Redemption*, 38.

48 He desired to exalt himself and be above Christ. White, *Desire of Ages* 129; White, 3 *Spiritual Gifts* 38.

49. White, *The Great Controversy* 494–95; White, *Patriarchs* and *Prophets* 35.

50. For comments on ambition see White, *Patriarchs and Prophets*, 403; White, *Early Writings*, 145; White, *Testimonies*, 5:242, 702; White, *Spiritual Gifts*, 3:37.

minority opinion emphasized *envy* (Irenaeus, Tertullian, Justin Martyr, and Cyprian).[51] Within the envy position, it was commonly held that Lucifer was envious of humanity whom God had created in his image.[52] The Great Controversy follows the majority view in seeing pride as central but also accepts the importance of envy (pride providing a foundation for envy). It rejects, however, the minority view that Lucifer was envious of humanity. In contrast, Lucifer is pictured as specifically envious of Christ as supreme ruler and creator of humanity. In the Great Controversy account, the context for Lucifer's fall is christological not anthropological. Lucifer's envy is particularly aroused by certain exclusive divine councils between the Father and Son. He is described as desiring to enter divine councils and purposes[53] and was curious to know what God had not designed he should know.[54] He developed a dissatisfaction at not knowing all of God's secrets.[55] His exclusion was taken as a personal slight and mistreatment. In his mind, he had closed the infinite gap between himself and Christ. All of this subjective envy is unjustified, arbitrary, and without cause. Thus, Lucifer's rebellion is linked to an inordinate curiosity, a sense of entitlement to know divine mysteries, a refusal to accept on trust that some things belong to God alone, a confidence that he was capable of understanding and worthy to do so, and a resentment that God had not considered this so. While pride was the internal incubator of his sin, it is envy of Christ that proves the catalyst for outwardly questioning God. This perceived mistreatment by God becomes delusional justifications for his envy and "evidence" for others that his feelings are legitimate. Personal selfishness, pride, and envy will now manifest as public disaffection.

Second Stage: Initial dissemination, Covert Dissatisfaction to Overt Questioning

With pride established and envy of Christ developed, Lucifer started to act on his ambitious desire for supremacy. He is described as slowly and

51. See Russell, *Satan*.

52. King, "Augustine and Anselm on Angelic Sin," 262.

53. Satan "*desired to enter into the divine counsels and purposes, from which he was excluded by his own inability, as a created being, to comprehend the wisdom of the Infinite One. It was this ambitious pride that led* to his rebellion." White, *Testimonies*, 5:702. Italics mine.

54. White, *The Great Controversy*, 523; White, *Testimonies*, 5:503.

55. White, *The Great Controversy*, 523. He had wanted to be consulted regarding the plan to create humanity. Exclusion from this exclusive divine council especially ignited Lucifer's envy. White, *Spiritual Gifts*, 3:36; White, *The Story of Redemption*, 13–14.

selectively voicing his thoughts to others (initially to those directly under his command) in such a way that it was not immediately clear what his purposes were.[56] Lucifer was so highly exalted and considered perfect that he had the natural trust of these angels and was able to illicit their sympathies. These angels in turn began disseminating to others the thoughts that he had implanted within them. This gave the appearance of a wider movement questioning the order of things when in fact it was all traceable to Lucifer.[57] He initially presented himself as a victim of injustice and unfairness.[58] This was all in relation to Christ. The request for equality with Christ masked a desire for pre-eminence. While subtly engendering sympathy for himself, Lucifer was challenging the order of heaven.

White indicates that God responded to Lucifer's accusations with ways and means that only divinity could develop to help all fully understand what was happening, its dangers, and how to turn back.[59] White indicates that this had an initial calming effect on all, including Lucifer.[60] But this did not last. As "again he [Lucifer] was filled with pride in his own glory. His desire for supremacy returned, and envy of Christ was once more indulged."[61] At this point Lucifer deserted his place as covering cherub in the immediate presence of God.[62] Renewing his work amid the angels, Lucifer began to repeat his basic arguments but now with new additions while

---

56. "He began his work of rebellion with the angels under his command, seeking to diffuse among them the spirit of discontent. And he worked in so deceptive a way that many of the angels were won to his allegiance before his purposes were fully known. Even the loyal angels could not fully discern his character, nor see to what his work was leading." White, *Selected Messages*, 1:222.

57. "When Satan had succeeded in winning many angels to his side, he took his cause to God, representing that it was the desire of the angels that he occupy the position that Christ held." White, *Selected Messages*, 1:222.

58. "When Satan became disaffected in heaven, he did not lay his complaint before God and Christ; but he went among the angels who thought him perfect and represented that God had done him injustice in preferring Christ to himself." White, *Testimonies*, 5:291.

59. "The spirit of discontent. . . . was a new element, strange, mysterious, unaccountable. Lucifer himself had not at first been acquainted with the real nature of his feelings; for a time he had feared to express the workings and imaginings of his mind; yet he did not dismiss them. He did not see whither he was drifting. But such efforts as infinite love and wisdom only could devise, were made to convince him of his error. His disaffection was proved to be without cause, and he was made to see what would be the result of persisting in revolt." White, *Patriarchs and Prophets*, 39.

60. White, *Patriarchs and Prophets*, 37.

61. White, *Patriarchs and Prophets*, 37.

62. "*Leaving his place in the immediate presence of the Father*, Lucifer went forth to diffuse the spirit of discontent among the angels." White, *Patriarchs and Prophets*, 37.

maintaining great care to disguise his deeper designs. His accusation that Christ's exaltation above him was an injustice was now presented as part of a wider injustice facing all the angels. Here is a crucial turning point in his argument, although in reality it brings out what has been happening in clearer terms. Lucifer claims the essential problem is with the order and law of God.[63] In the Great Controversy, this questioning of divine law and the lawgiver's character will become his essential argument. God's laws are, like Christ's exaltation over Lucifer, advanced as an arbitrary imposition reflecting an unjust order. Lucifer argues that the angels are like God in nature and not capable of erring (impeccable). Therefore, such law is unnecessary and onerous.[64] Arbitrary divine law like Christ's unfair exaltation threatens everyone's liberty and freedom. Lucifer offers a new approach as a solution to this "problem." The solution consists in a change to the law and order of God.[65] Through this argument Lucifer was able to position himself as a loyalist and reformer only aiming to improve the situation while still leaving the implication that the error is with God and especially Christ. Strategically speaking, Lucifer's rivalry with Christ was personal and had limited appeal to other angels, but the new emphasis on dissatisfaction with divine law, which the angels were also under, had wider appeal. "Satan could establish pronounced enmity toward God only by bringing into contempt the laws of his government."[66]

Having rejected all divine outreach, Lucifer finally and fully hardened himself and publicly completed his rejection of Christ.[67] Discarding the pretence of loyalty to God he openly and boldly asserted an alternative form of government.[68] He now denounced loyal angels as deluded slaves.[69] Lucifer had now irreversibly become Satan. To strengthen and secure his following

---

63. "He worked with mysterious secrecy, and for a time concealed his real purpose under an appearance of reverence for God. He began to insinuate doubts concerning the laws that governed heavenly beings . . ." White, *Patriarchs and Prophets*, 37.

64. "He began . . . intimating that though laws might be necessary for the inhabitants of the worlds, angels, being more exalted, needed no such restraint, for their own wisdom was a sufficient guide. They were not beings that could bring dishonor to God; all their thoughts were holy; it was no more possible for them than for God Himself to err." White, *Patriarchs and Prophets*, 37.

65. White, *The Great Controversy*, 499; White, *Patriarchs and Prophets*, 37.

66. White, "The Cross Incontrovertible Evidence."

67. White, *Patriarchs and Prophets*, 39.

68. "He promised those who would enter his ranks a new and better government, under which all would enjoy freedom. Great numbers of the angels followed . . . he hoped to win all the angels to his side, to become equal with God Himself, and to be obeyed by the entire host of heaven." White, *Patriarchs and Prophets*, 40.

69. White, *Patriarchs and Prophets*, 40.

and prevent any of his sympathizers from going back to God, Satan added a new argument and deception. He now declared that they all had gone too far, God would not show mercy nor would he forgive.[70]

As a result of this process all angels made their decisions and took sides. Divisions were complete and solidified. An attempt was made by Satan and his allies to assert their new liberty by use of force. God permitted Satan to develop his work until its rebellious aggressive nature revealed itself. The final stage in the primordial rebellion was expulsion. Christ and his angels cast Satan out from heaven. From here, however, he managed to take his rebellion to earth. This raises the important question of why God expelled but did not destroy Satan (either as soon as he sinned or after his opposition became open). Having seen the origin of sin which triggers cosmic war, the reasons why sin, suffering, and cosmic war have been allowed to continue will be explored.

SATAN'S CHARGES/ACCUSATIONS: THE BASIS FOR THE GREAT CONTROVERSY

The Great Controversy understands the problem of evil to arise out of something subtler than even the description "cosmic war" would warrant. Behind war is its catalyst. This catalyst is a moral-spiritual-political-philosophical controversy. Controversy, not simply sin, precipitates cosmic war. What in turn drives and sustains this "Great Controversy" and thus explains why the cosmic war continues for a long time are the questions, accusations, lies, or charges raised by Satan against God.[71] Hence, it is moral controversy and not a metaphysical explanation which ultimately accounts for the origin and continuation of evil (as well as its end). These audacious satanic charges, along with God's necessary response, together constitute the core elements of the "controversy" which lies beneath the cosmic war. The core of the charges is that God, his character, his law, and government, are the problem and Satan's rebellion is justified. An actual detailing of the charges reveals the breadth, daring, scope, and inner logic of the ideology driving the controversy which fuels the cosmic war. First, an overview of the charges will be given, and then an examination of how they work together.

---

70. "Many wanted to return . . . yet Lucifer had another deception ready. The mighty revolter now declared that the angels who had united with him had gone too far to return; that he was acquainted with the divine law, and knew that God would not forgive . . . they needed to assert their liberty." White, *Patriarchs and Prophets*, 40.

71. Most of these accusations are present at the very beginning but some originate later on.

The Claim that God Himself is the Problem

In the Great Controversy theodicy, Lucifer misrepresents God's character. He maintains that God desires his own self-exaltation,[72] is severe and tyrannical,[73] selfish, and oppressive, claiming all and giving nothing.[74] God exacts self-denial from others but practices no self-denial or self-sacrifice himself.[75] Satan questioned whether the Father or Son had sufficient love for man to exercise self-denial and sacrifice.[76] He declared that God knows nothing of self-denial, mercy, love but is stern, exacting, and unforgiving[77] Therefore, Satan claims God is the ultimate author of sin, death, and suffering. In effect, Satan attributes to God his own satanic character. This is a very bold assertion and the complete reversal of reality.

The Claim that God's Law is the Problem[78]

Much of Satan's accusations are "justified" by attacks on God's law. God is not just in imposing law.[79] This law is faulty,[80] tyrannical,[81] and cannot be obeyed.[82] Adam's sin (and human sin) is proof that God's law is unjust and

---

72. Satan "misrepresented God, attributing to Him the desire for self-exaltation. With his own evil characteristics he sought to invest the loving Creator." White, *Desire of Ages*, 21–22.

73. White, *The Great Controversy*, 500.

74. White, *The Desire of Ages*, 57; White, *The Great Controversy*, 502.

75. Satan "had declared that, while the Creator exacted self-denial from all others, He Himself practiced no self-denial and made no sacrifice." White, *The Great Controversy*, 502.

76. White, *Patriarchs and Prophets*, 69.

77. "Satan had declared that God knew nothing of self-denial, of mercy and love, but that He was stern, exacting, and unforgiving. Satan never tested the forgiving love of God; for he never exercised genuine repentance . . . his representations of God were incorrect." Ellen G. White, "Christ Represents the Beneficence of the Law," *The Advent Review and Sabbath Herald*, March 9, 1897.

78. "From the first the great controversy had been upon the law of God." White, *Patriarchs and Prophets*, 69.

79. White, *Patriarchs and Prophets*, 44.

80. White, *Desire of Ages*, 763.

81. White, "Manuscript 1, 1902" *Manuscript Releases*, vol 21.

82. "He [Satan] declares that it is impossible for us to obey its precepts." White, *Desire of Ages*, 24, 761.

cannot be obeyed.[83] God's unjust restrictions are the real cause of the fall.[84] God's law is a law of selfishness.[85] Law is a restriction on liberty,[86] a yoke of bondage,[87] and needs to be changed.[88] God's law is not perfect or immutable, but defective and subject to change.[89] If God's law is changeless then the penalty cannot be remitted,[90] pardon for sin is impossible and must be punished.[91]

The Claim that God's Government is the Problem

Satan charges that God's government is based on blind submission and unreasoning control.[92] Satan argues that God treated him unjustly in the beginning.[93] God's order is unstable and Satan only wanted to improve the divine order and bring stability and harmony.[94] If God hadn't reproved Satan, then, he asserts, he would not have rebelled.[95] God, who knew the consequences of sin, is unjust in having permitted man to transgress the law.[96]

---

83. White, 117. Concerning the fall of Adam and Eve, "Satan declared that he would prove to the worlds which God had created, and to the heavenly intelligences, that it was an impossibility to keep the law of God." White, "Obedience the Fruit of Union with Christ."

84. "[He] declared that God's unjust restrictions had led to man's fall, as they had led to his own rebellion." White, *The Great Controversy*, 500.

85. "Satan represents God's law of love as a law of selfishness." White, *Desire of Ages*, 24.

86. White, *The Great Controversy*, 499.

87. White, *Patriarchs and Prophets*, 504.

88. White, *Patriarchs and Prophets*, 69.

89. "Satan [said] . . . that His law was faulty, and that the good of the universe required it to be changed . . . In the controversy it was to be shown whether the divine statutes were defective and subject to change, or perfect and immutable." White, *Patriarchs and Prophets*, 69.

90. White, *The Great Controversy*, 502.

91. White, *Desire of Ages*, 761.

92. White, *Steps to Christ*, 43–44.

93. In dialogue with other angels in pre-fall heaven Satan "represented that God had done him injustice in preferring Christ to himself." White, *Testimonies*, 5:291.

94. "While claiming for himself perfect loyalty to God, he urged that changes in the order and laws of heaven were necessary for the stability of the divine government . . . [he Incited rebellion and discontent ubt claimed his sole purpose was to] . . . promote loyalty and to preserve harmony and peace." White, *Patriarchs and Prophets*, 38.

95. White, *The Great Controversy*, 499–500.

96. White, *Patriarchs and Prophets*, 331. This is a post-expulsion argument.

Satan claims that due to the rebellion of humanity, the world now rightly belongs to him (his government is legitimate).[97] He asserts that God's justice is severe and unforgiving.[98] Ultimately, Satan claims that God is responsible for the fall and is therefore the author of sin, death, and suffering.[99]

The Claim that the Principles of God are Inconsistent and Contradictory

Working from these assertions, Satan maintains that the principles God claims to operate on are inconsistent and contradictory opposites. God's principles make forgiveness impossible.[100] Sin must be punished and it cannot or will not be forgiven or pardoned.[101] God's justice is inconsistent with mercy, and as a result, God cannot be just and show mercy at the same time.[102] To this must be added the last but very crucial post-cross accusations. So far, all of the accusations were originated before the coming of Christ and his redemptive work. As will be shown, Christ's redemptive work answers these accusations. However, in response to Christ's redemptive work, Satan comes up with another accusation (while strategically maintaining all previous ones). The last accusation is that mercy destroys justice. If Christ's sacrifice brings mercy, then his death has abrogated the law.[103] Satan does not care if abrogation is perceived as applying to all or only part of the law.[104]

97. White, *Desire of Ages*, 114, 115; White, *Confrontation*,16.

98. White, *Desire of Ages*, 22.

99. "The fall of our first parents, with all the woe that has resulted, he charges upon the Creator, leading men to look upon God as the author of sin, and suffering, and death." White, *Patriarchs and Prophets*, 24.

100. "He had declared that the principles of God's government make forgiveness impossible. Had the world been destroyed, he would have claimed that his accusations were proved true. He was ready to cast blame upon God, and to spread his rebellion to the worlds above." White, *Patriarchs and Prophets*, 37.

101. "When he tempted and overcame Adam and Eve . . . He claimed that it was impossible that forgiveness should be granted to the sinner, and therefore the fallen race were his rightful subjects, and the world was his." White, *Patriarchs and Prophets*, 69.

102. White, *Desire of Ages*, 761.

103. "Another deception was now to be brought forward. Satan declared that mercy destroyed justice, that the death of Christ abrogated the Father's law . . . the very means by which Christ established the law Satan represented as destroying it. Here will come the last conflict of the great controversy between Christ and Satan." White, *Desire of Ages*, 762.

104. That the law of God is faulty and parts of it have been set aside is "the claim which Satan now puts forward. It is the last great deception that he will bring upon the

The "Logic" of the Accusations

These accusations should not be thought of as a random collection of charges. While sometimes situational and opportunistic, they also form a cumulative argument. The case they develop has its own progression. Each charge is meant to complicate any possible defense or vindication of God and give the impression of being unanswerable. The charges suggest a hopeless "Catch-22" dilemma from which God cannot escape unless he concedes Satan's points. That would give Satan victory and legitimacy. John Woods summarises the structure of Satan's accusations as revolving around three clusters of ideas: 1) God is a harsh, unjust, unfair tyrant. The basis for this is that God has arbitrarily imposed an absolute law which he had no intrinsic right to do. 2) God cannot (or will not) forgive. Justice destroys mercy. God is in a dilemma about what he will do with rebels. Justice and mercy are incompatible opposites. 3) With the first two arguments having collapsed at the cross Satan now argues that mercy destroys justice and abrogates law.[105] Norman Young presents the various accusations in a basic sequence of five charges. Charge 1) God is a harsh dictator; Charge 2) Holy creatures need no external restraint (Law); Charge 3) It is impossible to obey God's law; Charge 4) Justice excludes mercy; Charge 5) Mercy excludes justice (post-cross claim).[106] Below a fuller summation is offered in order to show the interrelated progression of charges. Each charge is self-contained, yet together they form part of a progressive argument. A more detailed outline of the logic of Satan's arguments is as follows:

1. Generic Accusation: God is the Problem.

   God himself is arbitrary, harsh, and unjust in his character, government, and law.
   Therefore, there is a justification for the alternative Satan advocates.

2. Controlling Accusation: God's Law is the Essence of God's Problem.

   God's Law is prime evidence of the generic accusation.
   God's unjust law is an arbitrary, unnecessary restriction on creatures.
   God's law is for God's own self-exaltation and control of others. It is selfish
   Therefore, God's law needs to be changed.

---

world. He needs not to assail the whole law; if he can lead men to disregard one precept, his purpose is gained." White, *Desire of Ages*, 763.

105. The three ideas are summarised in Wood, "'All Must Appear,'" 641. Wood also deals with the first two ideas in more detail in "The Mighty Opposites, Part 1" 694–709, and the third is dealt with in "The Mighty Opposites, Part 2," 710–30.

106. Young, "Five Charges Against God," 11–12.

Satan only wants to improve things and bring liberty by a change in God's law.

3. Subordinate Accusation A: It is impossible to obey God's unjust law.

    Humanity's fall (and continued sin) is evidence of this, Angelic rebellion is evidence of this.
    It is unfair to ask obedience to an unjust law.
    Therefore, disobedience was/is justified and unavoidable (this is evidence for the second accusation that the law needs to be changed).

4. Subordinate Accusation B: God's justice/law cancels out mercy and the possibility of forgiveness.

    God will not forgive (he is cruel and unmerciful) because,
    God cannot forgive and must punish (God's unjust law requires it).
    If/when God shows mercy/pardon he is unjust, inconsistent, and untrue.
    Therefore, the law can neither be obeyed yet nor can humanity be forgiven. An impossible, unworkable, unjust situation (this confirms the first three accusations).

5. Counter Accusation (Post-Cross): Mercy cancels out justice and abrogates law.

    God can't have it both ways—it is either justice or mercy.
    God has compromised his justice by mercy.
    Therefore, mercy abrogates law and shows that it should have been changed originally as Satan said.

This is how Satan presents himself as a liberator and reformer instead of a rebel. His broad claim is against God's character, that he is an unjust selfish tyrant, but when examined closely everything hinges on Satan's attack on God's law. Law is the *prima facie* evidence for the claim that God is unjust. Most steps in some way work back to a challenge to God's law. Satan tries to place the divine administration on the horns of a dilemma. If God upholds his law he is cruel, if he shows mercy he is inconsistent. Either way, Satan claims self-justification and noble motives for his rebellion.

WHY SATAN, SUFFERING, AND EVIL CONTINUE

It is now possible to return to the important question of why God expelled Satan from heaven but did not destroy him and thus why God has allowed evil and suffering to continue for so long.

God's Realm: Angels, Humans, Unfallen Worlds

The Great Controversy asserts that God's government is not restricted to angels (unfallen and fallen) and humanity (believing and non-believing). To this it adds the idea of *unfallen worlds*. These are planets and societies of other intelligent, free beings comparable in some sense to angels and humans. It is implied that there are many of these.[107] They function as observers of the conflict between God and Satan.[108] They are intellectual participants capable of persuasion either way. Satan hoped to win them to his position and has made his accusations against God before them.[109] God and Satan act in reference to this group and not just in reference to humanity. God acts in such a way to keep the hearts and minds of this group (unfallen worlds, unfallen angels) on his side as well as win back the hearts and minds of hostile, fallen humanity.[110]

This means that God in his wisdom did not immediately destroy Satan but allowed his activity to continue for a number of very important reasons. First, as will be discussed later, evil is a mystery, especially its first appearance. Only God could fully understand evil. Even the loyal angels could not discern the true nature of evil or see through Satan's advocacy of it.[111] To undo evil, and the satanic deceptions, in such a way that it never can arise again requires a particular, complex, and exceedingly difficult course of action. Evil must be unmasked. Satan must be given enough time and opportunity to reveal himself. "His own work must condemn him."[112] Second,

---

107. "Unnumbered worlds." White, *Christ Triumphant*, 66; White, *Christ's Object Lessons*, 190.

108. White, *Patriarchs and Prophets*, 78; White, *The Desire of Ages*, 759.

109. White, *The Great Controversy*, 497.

110. In his saving work God has "carried the worlds unfallen and the heavenly universe with Him, but at a terrible cost." White, *Manuscript Releases*, 18:362.

111. "Until fully developed, it could not be made to appear the evil thing it was; his disaffection would not be seen to be rebellion. *Even the loyal angels could not fully discern his character or see to what his work was leading.*" White, *Patriarchs and Prophets*, 41. "The inhabitants of heaven and of the worlds, *being unprepared to comprehend the nature or consequences of sin*, could not then have seen the justice of God in the destruction of Satan." White, *Patriarchs and Prophets*, 42. Italics mine.

112. "Satan had made it appear that he himself was seeking to promote the good of the universe. *The true character of the usurper and his real object must be understood by all. He must have time to manifest himself by his wicked works* . . . [Satan declared all evil] to be the result of the divine administration . . . *therefore God permitted him to demonstrate the nature of his claims, to show the working out of his proposed changes in the divine law* . . . Satan had claimed from the first that he was not in rebellion. The whole universe must see the deceiver unmasked." White, *Patriarchs and Prophets*, 42. Italics mine.

questions asked cannot be unasked. Even loyal creatures cannot pretend otherwise. For the sake of both the faithful and the hostile, God needs to provide answers. Furthermore, from the divine perspective, these answers must comprehensively answer every dimension and facet of the challenge of evil and Satan. God, his law, his character, and government must "be forever placed beyond question."[113] Thirdly, destroying Satan immediately would have appeared to confirm Satan's charges. Satan would have won a victory even in defeat. Creatures would no longer serve God due to love but fear.[114] The spirit of doubting and distrusting God would have remained alive amid intelligent free beings and become the seedbed for repressed disaffection and potential future rebellion(s).[115]

Creaturely Limitation

All of these reasons relate to a brute fact. If God wants to win the hearts and minds of his finite creatures then he must act according to creaturely limitations. Created beings face *epistemological limitations* that God must work within.[116] Their knowledge, understanding, and reasoning ability is finite and fallible (though not originally perverse). All creaturely understanding is interpretative; however, the controverted points that God wishes to make plain must be placed beyond a conflict of interpretations. God must enable answers to the Great Controversy to emerge from a level of evidence so compelling that even Satan will freely acknowledge the truth (even if he is no longer willing or able to embrace its implications). Another part of this epistemological problem is an *experience limitation*. Many truths cannot be known by abstraction or theorization. Morality and spirituality cannot be learned in the same manner as maths. Many things can only be known by experience.[117] This experience limitation does not necessitate evil

---

113. "For the good of the entire universe through ceaseless ages, he must more fully develop his principles, that his charges against the divine government might be seen in their true light by all created beings, and that the justice and mercy of God and the immutability of His law might be forever placed beyond all question." White, *Patriarchs and Prophets*, 42.

114. "Had he [Satan] been immediately blotted out of existence, some would have served God from fear rather than from love." White, *Patriarchs and Prophets*, 42.

115. Had Satan been immediately eliminated "the influence of the deceiver would not have been fully destroyed, nor would the spirit of rebellion have been utterly eradicated." White, *Patriarchs and Prophets*, 42.

116. "The entrance of sin into the world, the incarnation of Christ, regeneration, the resurrection, and many other subjects presented in the Bible, are mysteries too deep for the human mind to explain or even to fully comprehend." White, *Testimonies*, 5:698–99.

117. "The plan of redemption is so far-reaching that philosophy cannot explain it

for any individual creature, as shown by the unfallen angels who avoided evil by trusting God and experiencing his trustworthiness.[118] But if any part of creation does embrace evil then creation can only know the answers to the Great Controversy by experiencing (either by direct experience or observing the experience of others) the fruit of evil or the fruit of grace. Related to this is the *historical-temporal limitation*. Heavenly and earthly events take time.[119] The development of ideas, the minds or cultures that process them, the resulting historical impact, and the persons or societies which perform them, take time. Time is needed for individual and collective decisions and actions to manifest and work out as well as be evaluated. God cannot simply cut short history if history is the domain of demonstration required to answer the issues in the Great Controversy.[120] Humans (and angels and unfallen beings) are complex, socially-located beings. It is not possible to separate ideas, their development, and their demonstration from all these complexities or the particularities of history itself. There is no creaturely context-free, neutral, timeless view from nowhere. Creatures can only know anything from within history. There is no way to rush history and no demonstrable answers (as opposed to claims whether divine or satanic) without it. Sin can only be seen for what it really is if it can properly express its horrible nature. If evil is gratuitous then this requires allowing evil to be seen for what it is. Otherwise, God's claims about sin could be controverted as exaggerations, or, without historically-observed cause and effect, be blamed on God.

Complicated by Deception

All of these limitations are further complicated by the deceptive strategy of Satan. "God could employ only such means as were consistent with truth and righteousness. Satan could use what God could not—flattery and deceit."[121] Multiplying and changing deceptions is a very effective tactic continually

---

"It will ever remain a mystery that the most profound reasoning cannot fathom. The science of salvation cannot be explained; but it can be known by experience." White, *Desire of Ages*, 494–95.

118. For evil not to arise, unfallen beings must trust God in the face of any test, whether benign/benevolent testing like the Tree of Good and Evil or sinister temptations like those of the serpent.

119. The Great Controversy theodicy affirms that the foundational nature of reality is temporal not timeless; see Canale, *A Criticism of Theological Reason*.

120. For an example of this see Ellen White's discussion of God sparing Cain: White, *Patriarchs and Prophets*, 78.

121. White, *Patriarchs and Prophets*, 42.

complicating any divine defense. Until God's demonstration of truth and error is fully complete, any divine action can be misused and thrown back at him via deceptive means. God can be accused of being too slow too quick, too harsh, too lenient, too absent, too present, and so on. Only the full story independently clarifies the truth. Thus, the history of the Great Controversy between God and Satan is itself the answer to Satan's charges and the problem of evil. This history functions as a "lesson," a "perpetual testimony," a "history of this terrible experiment"[122] (the experiment is Satan's and ours, not God's. God does not experiment with his creation) for all creation and all time which not only answers every question raised about God's rule but, due to its comprehensive nature, functions as a perpetual safeguard which ensures that evil will never arise again.[123] At the end of the Great Controversy, God can eliminate sin with universal acknowledgment of his justice whereas he couldn't at the start. The intervening process means that creation has been tested, proved, educated, and, in humanity's case, redeemed. This creation will never and can never now turn from or doubt a God whose fathomless love and infinite wisdom have been so fully revealed.[124] The universe is eternally safe and secure from evil. God's foreknowledge allows him to know not only how to do this but that this undertaking will succeed and one day all (loyal and disloyal) will freely understand and assent to God's righteousness and goodness.

PAIN, SUFFERING AND NATURAL EVIL

The Great Controversy is clear that God is not the author of moral or natural evil (evil not resulting from moral choices, i.e., earthquakes).[125] Sin broke the original created order and introduced the antagonistic principle of death into creation so that it now produces suffering.[126] Natural evil is not the inevitable by-product of having a lawful universe. Natural evil results from *disobedience* to the laws of nature, not the laws themselves.[127] Natural evil arises due to moral evil. All natural evil is either directly or remotely

122. White, *Patriarchs and Prophets*, 42.
123. White, *Patriarchs and Prophets*, 42.
124. White, *The Great Controversy*, 504.
125. "God did not create evil, He only made the good, which was like Himself... Evil, sin, and death were not created by God; they are the result of disobedience, which originated in Satan." White, *Testimonies*, 5:503.
126. "God is the life-giver. From the beginning all His laws were ordained to life. But sin broke in upon the order that God had established, and discord followed. So long as sin exists, suffering and death are inevitable." White, *Patriarchs and Prophets*, 522.
127. Duah, "A Study of Warfare Theodicy," 225–26.

due to disobedience to God's laws.[128] Through Adam's and Eve's fall, Satan implanted the seeds of death within nature which has corrupted and distorted it.[129] Continued disobedience to moral and physical laws produces ever-increasing levels of suffering.[130] The more evil escalates the more suffering multiplies. Adams and Eve's fall also gave Satan access to creation and allows him to exercise a usurped and contested but real dominion on earth.[131] This provides him with opportunities to manipulate creation in a malevolent way as far as he can.[132] God does not cause pain and suffering.[133] Instead, God seeks to work amid pain and suffering and overrule it for good.[134] God permits pain and suffering to awake people to righteousness and compassion.[135] At other times God permits pain, suffering, and evil to come upon people as judgment. But this is often not the case. Much suffering indiscriminately affects the just and the unjust. Such is the confused, disordered, fallen condition of the world.[136] Amid all this God is constantly restraining Satan and the full effects of sin and evil in the world. If God did not do this then natural evil would be far greater.[137]

---

128. Duah, "A Study of Warfare Theodicy," 341.

129. White claims that the seeds of death and even noxious, poisonous plants are in some way Satan's doing. See White, *Selected Messages*, 2:288.

130. White, *Patriarchs and Prophets*, 461; White, *Counsels on Health*, 19.

131. Creation is a finished work. Satan does not have authority over creation in terms of its origins or formation. Sin is a foreign, anti-life, anti-god principle implanted in a completed and good creation. This implantation of the death principle is by inducing the fall of Adam and Eve. It is not due to any inherent power of Satan to change the fundamental laws of the universe, contra Boyd.

132. White suggests Satan has studied and experimented with nature and whenever it is advantageous and possible seeks to bring about natural evil. White, *The Great Controversy*, 589–590. The exact way and degree to which this is possible is unclear.

133. "It is not God who causes pain and suffering, but that man through his own ignorance and sin has brought this condition upon himself." White, *Testimonies*, 6:280.

134. "The history of Job had shown that suffering is inflicted by Satan, and is overruled by God for purposes of mercy." White, *Desire of Ages*, 471.

135. "The Lord permits suffering and calamity to come upon men and women to call us out of our selfishness, to awaken in us the attributes of His character—compassion, tenderness, and love." White, *Counsels on Stewardship*, 23.

136. White is against viewing all great calamities as an index of crimes or sins. This is sometimes true and sometimes false. White, "MS 56, 1894" in "Ellen White Comments," 3:1140.

137. White, *The Great Controversy*, 36.

THE INTERCONNECTIONS BETWEEN EVIL, LOVE, AND LAW

In order to truly understand the inner logic of the Great Controversy as theodicy, there is a need to look at some of the distinctive ideas about love, law, and evil. This requires returning to and understanding the idea of the "mystery of iniquity." It also requires understanding love more deeply, especially the relationship between love and law (love's immutable minimum). And "understanding the unlimited depths of divine love revealed in God's saving mystery of godliness" (love's supererogatory maximum). Appreciating these mysteries will help understand the idea that the Great Controversy resolves the theodicy through a metanarrative of *love*. Love is the counterpoise to evil.

The Mystery of Iniquity (Mystery of Evil)

To understand the problem of evil properly within Adventism's Great Controversy metanarrative requires understanding the essential nature of evil. Now it is time to examine the central Great Controversy idea of the logic-defying irrationality of evil. Ellen White notes that the "great perplexity" caused by evil and the inability to explain it leads many to the wrong responses of skepticism, rejecting God via anti-theistic arguments from the problem of evil, or traditionalism, which offers theological solutions that do not properly represent God.[138] White then makes the most important and defining statement on evil's origin for the Great Controversy theodicy. It is necessary to quote it in full:

> It is impossible to explain the origin of sin so as to give a reason for its existence. Yet enough may be understood concerning both the origin and the final disposition of sin to make fully manifest the justice and benevolence of God in all His dealings with evil. Nothing is more plainly taught in Scripture than that God was in no wise responsible for the entrance of sin; that there was no arbitrary withdrawal of divine grace, no deficiency in the divine government, that gave occasion for the uprising of rebellion. Sin is an intruder, for whose presence no reason can be given. It is mysterious, unaccountable; to excuse it is to defend it. Could excuse for it be found, or cause be shown for its existence, it would cease to be sin. Our only definition of sin is that given in the word of God; it is "the transgression of the law";

---

138. White, *The Great Controversy*, 492. Unfortunately, these are not here specified.

it is the outworking of a principle at war with the great law of love which is the foundation of the divine government.[139]

This statement suggests the possibility of a narrative account of evil's origin and a defense of God, but not an explanation of the first evil. In fact, explanation is unambiguously rejected. Evil is inexplicable. This is the "*Mystery of Evil.*" Everything in the Great Controversy theodicy hinges on it. No reason can be given because evil is in essence irrational, absurd, and unfounded. It is a "species of insanity."[140] Reason can be mounted to justify God and his ways ("no arbitrary withdrawal of divine grace, no deficiency in the divine government") but not for evil itself. Evil is incomprehensible. In terms of its origin, it is metaphysically, philosophically, ontologically, and rationally without the possibility of elucidation.[141]

Evil's mystery is not like paradoxical theological truths (e.g., the Trinity or Incarnation) which are rational even while going beyond reason. Neither is it a mystery so as to avoid the problem of evil. It is not that this is a mystery beyond current human reason but, nevertheless, still lies within the greater realm of reason (explainable perhaps in the hereafter or known to God). It is rather that evil is inherently inexplicable. It doesn't transcend reason, it both lacks and overthrows reason. The mystery is that this self-destructive, irrational, unjustifiable, maddening insanity called "evil" was ever chosen. Evil is a mystery in its own unique category. Evil defeats reasoning. It is its own black hole from which nothing coherent escapes. And reason itself becomes perverted if this realization is not understood. Reason can be fooled (or fool itself) into imagining that there is some point to evil. But reason cannot solve evil or save us from it. Reason needs something deeper and more profound to protect it from evil (i.e., divine wisdom). Reason is vulnerable. Therefore, the problem of evil cannot be resolved by an appeal to autonomous human reason (what antitheists demand in the logical or evidential versions) or theological reason (as certain theodicies attempt). Any answers to evil, practical or theoretical, can only come from God. But that does not involve God giving a rationale for evil.

This understanding has important practical implications. What the Great Controversy theodicy claims is this: understanding evil as an

---

139. White, *The Great Controversy*, 492–93.

140. "All sin is selfishness. Satan's first sin was selfishness. He sought to grasp power, to exalt self. A species of *insanity* led him to seek to supersede God." White, *The Ellen G. White 1888 Materials*, 1763.

141. Adam's sin is also called unexplainable, inexcusable, and irrational. White, Letter 191, 1899, in "Ellen White Comments," 1:1083. While both are equally unjustifiable, it is also true that Satan sinned with full knowledge of God while Adam was deceived. Satan's fall was incurable, but Adam's was not. See White, *Desire of Ages*, 761–62.

inherently mysterious insanity incapable of rational explanation is the only correct and proper logical stance that enables an account of evil which itself does not try and rationalize the irrational or justify the unjustifiable. To do so would itself be an evil (as per anti-theodicy). To "understand" evil properly is to realize it cannot be understood and to refuse to be seduced into attempting to do so.[142] Evil must be opposed, exposed, and overcome, but not rationalized. However, doesn't this essential insight appear, at least on the surface, to be evasive, even absurd? Such would be true if we were dealing with rationally-explicable phenomena. To designate something rational as irrational is to misrepresent it. But it is equally wrong to provide a logical justification for an absurdity, to arbitrarily turn nonsense into sense. The Great Controversy claims that evil is inherently *confounding*.[143] The only logical statement to make about evil's origin is to affirm its illogic.[144]

This is, of course, "circular reasoning" or "begging the question." How can one assume *a-priori* evil's absurdity when this is the point to be proven? This apparently intractable objection actually helps get to the heart of the Great Controversy as theodicy. There is no theoretical proof (independent of God's declaration) that this characterization of evil's mystery is correct. God's law declares evil unjustified (with eternal death as evidence) but the key point is that Satan has disputed this very divine declaration. The Great Controversy doesn't avoid this objection of circular reasoning but embraces it. It is precisely because God cannot appeal to something beyond himself (beyond the divine character or law) to justify himself (there is nothing more basic than God) that necessitates God reveal the truth about evil by demonstration. In the Great Controversy theodicy demonstration, not explanation, lies at the heart of the divine response to evil and Satan's justification of evil. Demonstration is long, slow, painful, and complex, especially when it must exhaust the multiple lies of a deceptive adversary. This means creation must learn by painful experience the truth of what God has said.

This point is too easy to miss as one point among many. But it is the lynchpin of any correct response to the problem of evil. This is the starting point. Any view which fails to build on this will go wrong. The Great

---

142. The phenomenon of evil and its effects, however, can be studied. We can learn about evil, discern patterns, and construct models. While evil is not rational, it does exist within rational beings and a rational world. We can learn how evil corrupts the created order but no explanatory theory or model can be made of evils origin or justification.

143. This aligns with the anti-theodicy views of Surin, *Theology and the Problem of Evil*, 52–53.

144. On top of that inherent ontological confounding, Satan adds another mystifying layer of confounding lies.

Controversy claim may best be understood by saying *even God cannot explain or give a reason for evil*, precisely because there is no reason to explain.[145] This is precisely why God opposes it. It can be explained why evil is a possibility, why it is wrong and dangerous, why God allowed evil to occur, what God does in response, but evil itself can never be explained.[146] Once evil's absurd nature is accepted and understood, then and only then can helpful insight be gained into evil's origin without mistaking for explanation. The Great Controversy theodicy can then attempt to throw light on the mystery of how a perfect being could fall into sin, all the while adamant that such elucidation never functions as a justification of the sin. The Great Controversy theodicy does this by history/narrative. Evil's insanity is "understood" by observing the actions and thinking of the originator of evil. Lost in the inner workings of Lucifer is the irrationality of the first sin. But in his actions and words (and all who cooperate with him) it is possible to document, describe, and delineate evil, but not explain it. Another key conclusion to draw from evil's mystery and absurdity is to grasp that on this understanding sin is inherently gratuitous. Gratuitous evil exists. The originating sin was completely pointless and gratuitous. It had no justification. The Great Controversy theodicy avoids the traditional Greater Good (and meticulous providence) response which denies the reality of gratuitous evil.

Centrality of Love

The opposite of sin and evil is the law of love. The nature of love is central to the Great Controversy. A denial of divine love set off the cosmic controversy.[147] The vindication of divine love will end it. This vindication is revealed by a metanarrative of love. The word "love" has a notoriously wide range of meanings. Its basic, generic meaning is the attraction to, attachment to, affection toward someone or something. While acknowledging this, the Great

---

145. "Does this position imply, then, that God doesn't have an explanation for all evil? Yes. If something is, by definition, inexplicable, then it can't be explained, period." Clifford Goldstein, "The Inexplicable Unexplained," 10. Coming from the different perspective of Thomist natural theology, Neil Ormerod makes a strikingly similar claim: "Not even God understands evil, because in a real sense there is nothing there to be understood. The stance refuses to put good and evil on the same ontological basis. They are not equiprimordial; rather, evil is parasitic on the good." Ormerod, *A Public God*, 165.

146. "Theodicy means the justification *of God*, not the justification *of evil*, a crucial distinction. Sin and evil won't be justified; God will, and central to that understanding is the Cross." Goldstein, "The Inexplicable Unexplained," 10.

147. "The great apostasy originally began as a denial of the love of God, as is plainly revealed in the Word." White, *The Upward look*, 149.

Controversy asserts that more must be said. Not all love is worthy. Love itself may be good or evil. Ultimately, love can only be fully understood theologically, that is, in relation to God. The link is intimate. "'God is love' (1 John 4:16). His nature, His law, is love. Ever has been; ever will be."[148] God's character or nature is unselfish. "It is His nature to give. His very life is the outflow of unselfish love."[149] This theologically or God-derived conception of love centers on divine "unselfishness"[150] and "self-sacrificing love," which is revealed in divine actions and especially Jesus. God's "law of self-renouncing love is the law of life."[151] This is a non-generic biblical and Christian "definition" of love. It is based in a Trinitarian conception of love which assumes relationality as native to divine nature.[152] The Triune God is the source of love itself. Creation is an expression of divine love. The Great Controversy pictures the (pre-fall) creation as a "circuit of beneficence" built on the principle of self-giving love which is the "law of life for the universe." Love and life flow out from the Father, the "great Giver," to all through Christ (to whom the Father has given all things), and through Christ love and life from all things freely "returns in praise, joyous service, and a tide of love" back to God.[153] The work of redemption stands above even this, for redemption is an act of love to those who have rejected the very cycle of love itself. Ultimately, Jesus in his saving work is the most perfect demonstration and revelation of love. Calvary is its highest expression.[154] Salvation reveals God's supererogatory love.

Love and Law

While divine salvation reveals the heights of true love, the concrete principles of God's law express love's irreducible minimum. For the Great Controversy this tight connection between God, love and law is absolute and crucial. Everything hinges on this. This study will term the Great Controversy understanding of law as "deep law." "Deep" refers to the deepest level of the divine moral essence or character. "The law of God is as sacred as

---

148. White, *Patriarchs and Prophets*, 33.
149. White, *Thoughts from the Mount of Blessing*, 77.
150. White, *Education*, 154.
151. White, *Desire of Ages*, 19.
152. Whidden, "God Is Love—Trinitarian Love!," 98–124.
153. White, *The Desire of Ages*, 21.
154. "In the light from Calvary it will be seen that the law of self-renouncing love is the law of life for earth and heaven; that the love which "seeketh not her own" has its source in the heart of God." White, *The Desire of Ages*, 19.

God Himself. It is a revelation of His will, a transcript of His character, the expression of divine love and wisdom."[155] God's law, like God himself, is immutable[156] and "holy, just and good" (Rom 7:12). Moral law (especially the Decalogue) must be understood as God's essential essence communicated propositionally in commandments (or consciously as cognitive moral intuitions written on the heart/conscience[157]). Understanding moral law as an expression of 'deep law' clarifies that there is nothing arbitrary or voluntaristic about moral law. Morality and moral epistemology emerge from divine ontology. Deep law gives rise to moral law. The latter is an enunciation of the former and the former is the source and essence of the latter. They are not two different laws. Moral law is an expression of deep law's *minimum nonnegotiable immutable principles*. Whatever love is, it can never be less than these. God, of course, is constantly expressing his love beyond the minimum. Nowhere more so than in the maximum expressions of the life of Jesus[158] and especially the cross.[159] Understanding this minimal-maximal spectrum of love is important for the Great Controversy theodicy.[160]

---

155. White, *Patriarchs and Prophets*, 52.

156. "It [God's Law] is eternal, immutable as God Himself." Manuscript 163, 1897 in "Ellen White Comments," 7:47.

157. Romans 2:14–15

158. "The law, revealed in the character of Christ, was a perfect manifestation of the Father." White, "The Cost of Salvation." The law reveals God's character as principles, but Jesus reveals God's law as a living person.

159. "This gift was given to man to convince him that God had left nothing undone that he could do, that there is nothing held in reserve, but that all heaven has been poured out in one vast gift . . . Calvary represents his crowning work." White, "Humanity the Lost Pearl."

160. Depth is further illustrated in the Great Controversy narrative in other ways. First example, "When Satan rebelled against the law of Jehovah, the thought that there was a law came to the angels almost as an awakening to something unthought of. In their ministry the angels are not as servants, but as sons." White, *Thoughts from the Mount of Blessing*, 109. Law was a deep internalized disposition, the idea of external propositions seemed strange. Law existed in created beings in a way analogous to how it is God's very nature. The second example, "deep law," helps explain how moral law can exist in different expressions while still being the same law. God's law has been adapted and contextualized for angels and fallen humans. White, *Selected Messages*, 1:220; White, *Spiritual Gifts*, 3:295. It can be expressed as the two great commandments (Love God/love your neighbour), the Decalogue, or in further more specific and detailed commandments. White, *Patriarchs and Prophets*, 305.

God's 'Deep Law' is the Basis of Resolving the Problem of Evil

The real problem of evil for the Great Controversy is that it seems to provoke God to act simultaneously in opposite, contradictory ways. God needs to destroy sin yet save sinners, to punish and not punish, to save and not save. This tension is what Satan uses against God.[161] His charges suggest a hopeless contradiction within God's government. The seeming irreconcilable tension between justice and mercy in the face of sin confirms this. All this, Satan claims, points to the need for his alternative. The Great Controversy maintains that this confusion is not due to any contradiction within God. Evil and sin, not God, introduced an unjustified conflict into *existence* and only God can remove it. If God's government was helplessly contradictory then he would have immediately destroyed all sinners (a harsh justice but without mercy and the complete failure of the creation project) or offered mercy arbitrarily and forgone his moral law (a capricious rather than gracious mercy from a God who has denied his own character). The former option would have produced external obedience due to suspicion and fear[162] while the latter option would have only immortalized and embodied sin.[163] But the atoning sacrifice of the cross reveals that God resolves the problem of evil *not by repudiating himself but by more fully expressing himself—his deep self*. Not by denying his law but by upholding his law. God upheld the law and executed judgment most fully on humanity but this humanity was Jesus — our representative and substitute. Motivated by deep love the Father gave his Son and the Son gave himself for sinners. The moral law is not sidestepped or ignored. It is upheld. Love is not withheld from sinners and enemies but lavished on them. God resolves the self-destructive "mystery of iniquity" by an even greater life-giving "*mystery of godliness.*"[164]

---

161. "The opposites, justice and mercy, are both moral qualities that exist in and proceed from the infinite, intrinsic righteousness of God, but they seem irreconcilable. Ellen White presents these two Satanic arguments [first is that God is an arbitrary tyrant with an arbitrary law, the second is that this arbitrary law means that when justice and mercy are in tension and God will not forgive but will opt for a harsh justice] as virtually unanswerable and a deep dilemma for the inexperienced, finite creatures of the universe." Wood, "The Mighty Opposites, Part 1," 698.

162. "Had he [Satan] been immediately blotted from existence, they would have served God from fear, rather than from love." White, *The Great Controversy*, 499.

163. "There could have been no pardon for sin had this atonement not been made. Had God pardoned Adam's sin without an atonement, sin would have been immortalized, and would have been perpetuated with a boldness that would have been without restraint." White, "The Great Standard of Righteousness."

164. The mystery of godliness is the humiliation, condescension of God to give his Son to die for a rebellious race, White, *The Upward Look*, 90. White, *The Sanctified Life*, 75. White, "Ellen White Comments," 5:1133. It is God's love in giving Christ to be

Evil's gratuity is overcome by a more wonderful divine gratuity. This divine gratuity, made possible by the mystery of godliness, is summed up in the Great Controversy theodicy concept of atonement as the practical answer to the problem of evil.

THE ATONEMENT

When evil is understood from the perspective of cosmic controversy and not simply as the classic philosophical trilemma then the practical atoning or redemptive work of Christ becomes the solution and not theoretical theodicy. The Great Controversy view involves a very broad understanding of atonement.[165] Most theologies view atonement as how God deals with the human sin problem. The Great Controversy affirms this but also sees atonement as how God resolves the problem of evil as cosmic controversy.[166] Atonement is understood as a process and not as a particular model or even a collection of models.[167] The various models of atonement are placed within a larger category of atonement as process.[168] There are several ways to approach atonement. It is sometimes limited to a singular model, or, more commonly, a particular model is seen as having priority and given a controlling foundational role over other models.[169] The mosaic or kaleidoscopic

---

propitiation for men's sins: White, *Christ's Object Lessons*, 128–29. Christ's incarnation is mystery of mysteries: White, "Ellen White Comments," 6:1082. It includes his birth, his life, sufferings and death. Jesus as God in flesh is a mystery which increases when contemplated: White, *Testimonies to Ministers and Gospel Workers*, 371.

165. George Knight treats the atonement as "a process that began at the time sin entered the universe and will continue until the close of the millennium." Knight, *The Cross of Christ*, 10.

166. "The real issue in the great struggle between good and evil is not the justification of humanity, but the justification of God. Human justification is a by-product of God's." Knight, *The Cross of Christ*, 10. Norman Gulley contrasts the more limited Salvation Worldview with a broader Cosmic Controversy Worldview. Gulley, *Systematic Theology: Prolegomena*, 392, 416.

167. Norman Gulley states that "one theory of the atonement is inadequate to describe fully the atonement." See Gulley, *Systematic Theology: Creation, Christ, Salvation*, 599. "In Scripture atonement is looked at from a variety of perspectives that are complementary." Gulley, *Systematic Theology: Creation, Christ, Salvation*, 602.

168. "The biblical view of atonement includes the incarnation, life, and death of Christ, and His present ministry in heaven's sanctuary, which embraces the final judgment and the eradication of sin and sinners." Gulley, *Systematic Theology: Creation, Christ, Salvation*, 605.

169. Gregory Boyd (Christus Victor model), Thomas Schreiner (penal substitution model), and Bruce Reichenbach (healing model), while acknowledging some value in other models and a variety of metaphors, all give one model priority; see Beilby and

approach has more recently acknowledged the need for multiple models but without any particular model being granted priority or grounding status for the others.[170] The Great Controversy understanding of atonement shares some similarity to a mosaic approach but differs in that the multiple models of atonement are seen as existing within a specific atonement process. This atonement process is structured around the sanctuary system which is seen as typologically revealing a comprehensive program of atonement.[171] The context for the atonement process is the Great Controversy metanarrative. This narratively-situated and sanctuary-structured atonement process unifies the various models so that they don't simply exist independent of each other (as in a mosaic/kaleidoscopic approach). One model does not ground the others; instead, all models are grounded in a higher-level explanation contained in the cosmically contextualized atoning process. Christ the mediator (sanctuary) and protagonist (Great Controversy narrative) is the unifying center to atonement and theodicy.[172]

What does this process look like? It is a 3-staged atonement process[173] preceded by a preparatory, pre-emptive stage. This first stage will be called stage "0" (zero) to distinguish it from stages 1–3 in which the atonement is

---

Eddy, *The Nature of the Atonement*.

170. See Beilby and Eddy, *The Nature of Atonement*, 157–85.

171. "The intercession of Christ in man's behalf in the sanctuary above is as essential to the plan of salvation as was His death upon the cross. By His death He began that work which after His resurrection He ascended to complete in heaven . . . there the light from the cross of Calvary is reflected. There we may gain a clearer insight into the mysteries of redemption." White, *The Great Controversy*, 489. See also Wallenkampf and Lesher, *The Sanctuary and the Atonement*; Adams, *The Sanctuary*; and especially Davidson, "Sanctuary Typology."

172. Richard Davidson suggests the Great Controversy as the orientation point for Biblical theology and the Sanctuary as the organising principle for systematic theology; see Davidson, "Cosmic Metanarrative," 105.

173. These basic three stages correspond to other three-fold patterns that are not uniquely Adventist; there is the older ubiquitous pattern of salvation as justification-sanctification-glorification (although this tends to be individualistic). More recently is the "now, not yet" understanding of God's kingdom (the period between the "now/not yet" makes for three stages) as an inaugurated kingdom awaiting its future consummation; see Ladd, *The Presence of the Future*. Adventist theology affirms this pattern but they are given special unity as a process by the structure and content found in a typological reading of the three-phased/-zoned pattern in the sanctuary (Courtyard or sacrifice/ Holy Place or priestly intercession/ Most Holy Place or judgment). Holbrook describes these as atonement by sacrifice, mediation, and judgment. Holbrook, *The Atoning Priesthood of Jesus Christ*, 50–52. Richard Davidson argues that biblical typology parallels this threefold pattern. He terms the first stage "Christological," the second is the "Ecclesiological," and the third is the "Eschatological." See Davidson, "Sanctuary Typology," 129–130. Christ's atoning ministry fulfils the specific work associated with the three phases of the sanctuary and happen in their order.

enacted and accomplished. Stage "0" reaches right back to the eternal nature and life of God as well as including all his activity before the incarnation. The Great Controversy works with a high view of divine foreknowledge, particularly God's knowledge of himself.[174] God has always known of the fall and he has always given himself for the redemption of creation. From all eternity God has had an "eternal covenant" for the salvation of humanity. God has always been God for us.[175] Because of this, the prospect of evil did not prevent creation's possibility; instead, the prospect of salvation ensured creation's actuality. God has always known and willingly embraced the inherent risk involved in creating creatures with the freedom necessary for them to possess the capacity to express God-like love.

The risk of contingent creatures requires that they be under probation and a period of testing. This applies to all intelligent creatures.[176] This testing is not to fail anyone; rather it is to authenticate their fitness and substantiate and confirm them in righteousness. When Adam and Eve failed their first probation, Jesus immediately pledged himself as the basis for a second probation.[177] "As soon as there was sin there was a savior."[178] All this is rooted in the eternal covenant. The rest of the Old Testament is also part of stage zero. During this stage, the atonement is proleptically applied and portrayed in shadows and types. The pre-cross work of God depends on stages 1–3 and foreshadows its completion. This is why it is here termed "zero" stage. Thus, the eternally pledged and future atoning work of Christ secured creation's eventuality (even though it was vulnerable to Sin's possibility) and ensured creation's continuance when it came under the power of sin and sentence of judgment until in the future creation is irreversibly and permanently freed from sin.

---

174. Divine foreknowledge is crucial to the Great Controversy, but the exact way God foreknows is not clear. There is no definitive decision on the particular model of foreknowledge.

175. "The salvation of the human race has ever been the object of the councils of heaven. The covenant of mercy was made before the foundation of the world. It has existed from all eternity, and is called the everlasting covenant. So surely as there never was a time when God was not, so surely there never was a moment when it was not the delight of the eternal mind to manifest His grace to humanity." White, "Spiritual Growth."

176. White, *Patriarchs and Prophets*, 53.

177. "Adam's sin plunged the race into hopeless misery; but by the sacrifice of the Son of God, a second probation was granted to man." Ellen G. White, "Satan and Our Appetites."; White, "The Great Standard of Righteousness."

178. White, "Lessons from the Christ-Life."

Atonement Stage One

The first stage is the answer to evil which Christ accomplishes *in himself*. This is Christ in his incarnation,[179] life, and sufferings, ministry, death, and resurrection.[180] Christ personally engages, in his own incarnate human life, in the battle of the Great Controversy.[181] The achievement of Christ in this stage is understood as infinite in consequence and content. All eternity will be given over to exploring its meaning and effects.[182] What follows is an outline of the main achievements. Within the seemingly impossible disadvantage of a fully fall-affected human nature (but never a fall-infected human mind or will),[183] Jesus overcomes the power of sin, the flesh, the world, and Satan.[184] Jesus answers all of Satan's accusations against God and vindicates God's character, law and government.[185] He reveals the depths of God's love to all intelligent beings and secures beyond any possibility

---

179. "For her [Ellen White] the entire incarnation is one phase (among several) of atonement." Wood, "The Mighty Opposites, Part 1," 701. "It was not alone His betrayal in the garden or His agony upon the cross that constituted the atonement. The humiliation of which His poverty formed a part was included in His great sacrifice. The whole series of sorrows which compassed humanity Christ bore upon His divine soul." Manuscript 12, 1900 in White, "Ellen White Comments," 6:1103.

180. The temptations, Gethsemane, and the Cross are seen as the peak "make or break" battles: White, *Prophets and Kings*, 701. Concerning these, John Woods notes, "These events are each moments when the destiny of the world hung in the balance." Wood, "The Mighty Opposites, Part 1," 702.

181. The incarnation was so "that He might work out in His own life the mysterious controversy between Christ and Satan." White, *Fundamentals of Christian Education*, 379.

182. "What a sacrifice is this! Who can fathom it! It will take the whole of eternity for man to understand the plan of redemption." Manuscript 21, 1895 in White, "Ellen White Comments," 7a:481. The incarnation and Christ's atoning sacrifice "will be the employment of the powers of the redeemed through the ceaseless ages of eternity." White, *Selected Messages*, 3:187.

183. The nature of Christ's humanity is a long-standing unresolved debate within Adventism. Is Christ like Adam before the fall (unfallen nature) or after the fall (fallen nature)? Traditionally the accent has been on the latter position. Recent representative positions either follow the older view or attempt to affirm a mediating position between the two. See *Seventh-day Adventists Believe*, 53–60; Dederen, "Christ: His Person and Work," 164–165; Whidden, *Ellen White on the Humanity of Christ*; Zurcher, *Touched with Our Feelings*.

184. "This should be the Christian's consolation. Christ, as man's representative, has overcome the world, the flesh and the devil." White, "Last Talk with the Disciples."

185. Manuscript 128, 1897 in White, "Ellen White Comments," 7a:470. Christ came to "vindicate every precept of the holy law." White, "Christ's Attitude to the Law."; White, *Testimonies*, 8: 207–8.

of doubt the allegiance of unfallen worlds.[186] Jesus offers himself as a substitutionary atoning sacrifice for the sin of the world, conquers death by resurrection, and achieves salvation for humanity.[187] As our representative, Christ recapitulates Adam and humanity's journey, but this time he reverses the outcome. He also reveals a journey that is the polar opposite to Satan. Christ did not grasp onto divine power and privilege but gave his life for the salvation of his enemies, while Satan grasped after God's power in order to rise above and rule all others, and in the end even attempted to kill God.[188] The all-powerful God paradoxically wins the Great Controversy as a weak, vulnerable human being in an act of death and apparent failure. God defeats the mystery of evil by the far more profound and category-breaking "mystery of godliness." Christ's victory is perfect and everything thereafter builds on it. However, it is restricted to Christ alone. In regards to everyone else, it is an "in principle" victory. It is Christ's achievement but not our possession. This necessitates further work (stages) to realize evil's defeat within the wider cosmos.

Atonement Stage Two

The second stage is Christ working out his victory *in humanity* by the Spirit's work within the ministry of the church through the preaching of the gospel

---

186. "Through Christ's redeeming work ... Satan's charges are refuted, and his character unveiled. Rebellion can never again arise. Sin can never again enter the universe. Through eternal ages all are secure from apostasy. By love's self-sacrifice, the inhabitants of earth and heaven are bound to their Creator in bonds of indissoluble union." White, *Desire of Ages*, 26.

187. "When He offered Himself on the cross, a perfect atonement was made for the sins of the people." White, "The Only True Mediator." "Justice demands that sin be not merely pardoned, but the death penalty must be executed. God, in the gift of His only begotten Son, met both these requirements. By dying in man's stead, Christ exhausted the penalty and provided a pardon." Manuscript 50, 1900 in "Ellen White Comments," 7a:470.

188. "The holy angels were horror-stricken that one who had been of their number could fall so far as to be capable of such cruelty. Every sentiment of sympathy or pity which they had ever felt for Satan in his exile, was quenched in their hearts ... [Christ's death] was such a heinous crime ... [it] severed forever the last tie of sympathy existing between Satan and the heavenly world." White, *Spiritual Gifts*, 3:183–84.

of the kingdom.[189] Every person's mind and heart is a battleground[190] and conversion marks the dramatic transition from one kingdom to another.[191]

Personal conversion (justification and the new birth) marks the point at which the defeat of evil is inaugurated in an individual's life even though it is not completed. While in this stage, the emphasis may seem to have shifted to the Spirit and the church. In reality, this earthly work takes place under and within the ongoing priestly intercessory work of the heavenly Christ.[192] This stage is entirely built on the first stage of incarnation, cross, and resurrection. In this second stage, people are by faith incorporated into Christ and his first stage accomplishments. His substitutionary death frees sinners and his representative victory is recapitulated in the lives of believers. This is spiritual warfare understood as new battles in the ongoing Great Controversy in which the outcome of the War has now been decided by Christ's victory. It is fought in the ministry of the church.[193] Everyone who receives and reflects Christ disproves again Satan's accusations and vindicates the character and ways of God.[194]

---

189. This includes Christ's ascension, enthronement as High Priest, Pentecostal giving of the Spirit, ongoing intercession, the work of the Spirit in convicting, converting, transforming believers, and empowering the church for mission. "The church is to conduct an aggressive warfare, to make conquests for Christ, to rescue souls from the power of the enemy. God and holy angels are engaged in this warfare." White, "Young Men as Missionary Workers."

190. "He should see how this controversy enters into every phase of human experience; how in every act of life he himself reveals the one or the other of the two antagonistic motives; and how, whether he will or not, he is even now deciding upon which side of the controversy he will be found." White, *Education*, 190.

191. In conversion "the power of Satan is broken. Man is brought into sacred unity with Christ." White, *Our High Calling*, 89.

192. "As our Mediator, Christ works incessantly . . . striving by His Spirit to win them from Satan's service." White, "Lessons from the Christ-Life." "Christ as high priest . . . immortalized Calvary." White, *Selected Messages*, 1:343.

193. "Sin has extinguished the love that God placed in man's heart. The work of the church is to rekindle this love. The church is to cooperate with God by uprooting selfishness from the human heart, placing in its stead the benevolence that was in man's heart in his original state of perfection." Letter 134, 1902 in White, *Welfare Ministry*, 14. This work includes preaching the gospel, teaching, healing, prayer, relieving suffering, worship, and holy living.

194. "To disprove Satan's claim is the work of Christ and of all who bear His name. It was to give in His own life an illustration of unselfishness that Jesus came in the form of humanity. And all who accept this principle are to be workers together with Him in demonstrating it in practical life." White, *Education*, 154.

Atonement Stage Three

The third stage is Christ consummating his work *in all creation*.[195] This is the final cosmic universalizing of Christ's previous work. This is still built on the incarnation, cross, resurrection, and intercessory work of Christ. To this, Christ now *adds* the work of final judgment and elimination of sin.[196] This judgment work is very extensive and operates in further stages. These are: 1) a pre-advent investigative judgment; 2) the Second Advent itself; 3) a post-advent judgment (millennial Judgment); and 4) a final execution of these judgments in which sin, death, evil, sinners, fallen angels, and Satan himself are permanently annihilated. The final judgment process works in a logical manner. The pre-advent judgment concerns the relationship of all professed followers of God. During this heavenly work Christ completes the spread of the gospel on earth. This splits humanity into two camps, which harden in loyalty or opposition. Probation then closes for humanity. Christ returns to reward, resurrect, and glorify his saints. This is then followed by the post-advent or millennial judgment. This judgment concerns the wicked. While open to angels and unfallen worlds, it is conducted by Christ and the saints. All of the history of sin, from its entrance to Christ's return, is examined. All questions are explored and answered.[197]

This final judgment process is crucial to the Great Controversy theodicy.[198] Other theological worldviews view judgment as primarily about human salvation or rewards and punishment. For the Great Controversy, the judgment is essential to completely finalize Christ's victory and vindicate God. Throughout history, God's dealings with humanity have been characterized by numerous judgments or "mini-covenant lawsuits."[199] That is, open judicial proceedings in which the facts about God and creation can be seen and understood prior to the subsequent salvation or punishment. The

---

195. This includes the pre-Advent judgment, the sealing of the saints, the close of probation, the Second Advent, translation of the living, resurrection of the dead, glorification of the saints, the Millennial Judgment, the final extermination of death, sin, sinners, the recreation of the physical world and God coming to dwell permanently on earth. For an excellent introduction see Moskala, "Toward a Biblical Theology of God's Judgment," 138–65.

196. "Ellen White is careful not to replace intercession with judgment. The eschatological phase of work is *added* to the prior phase." Wood, "All Must Appear," 644.

197. Webster, "The Millennium," 934–36.

198. See MacPherson, "Theodicy," 457–76.

199. The ubiquitous presence and importance of the covenant lawsuit is traced in Davidson, "The Divine Covenant Lawsuit Motif in Canonical Perspective," 45–84. See also the many examples given in Shea, "Biblical Parallels for the Investigative Judgment," 1–30.

final judgment process is the last and final divine covenant lawsuit in history to finalize the Great Controversy. In a sense, all of history has been a vast cosmic lawsuit and not simply a cosmic war. History is a political-legal-ideological battle between God and Satan over the deepest issues of the divine administration. It cannot be settled by theoretical claim and counter-claim but only by the practical demonstration and accumulation of evidence from both sides in history. Satan via his accusations has put God on trial and God has put sinners and their rebellion on trial. Such a cosmic controversy and lawsuit must finish with a judgment. This judgment exposes and brings to light every issue and every actor within the contest.

As with all judgment, it is not for the purposes of informing God. Instead, it is the divine means of informing and healing creation. If the origin and continuation of sin and suffering was due to the mystery and wilful mystification that sin, and Satan presents to the created mind (not to mention the enslavement to those who embrace it), then only by a thoroughly meticulous unveiling and exposing of sin and Satan, in the light of a contrasting revelation of God's righteousness, can sin and evil cease to present any risk to created intelligences. Nothing is hidden. The entire history of the Great Controversy is open to view. Everything vindicates God. The centerpiece is the incarnation, suffering, atoning death, and resurrection of Jesus. God could not have done any more than he did. It is confirmed by evidence and demonstration that indeed sin was unjustifiable. This comprehensive, vast, open, collectively-engaged judgment overcomes (and heals) the limitations and vulnerability of a finite creation in a way that engages and respects the psychological and social needs of creation. Creatures need time (a thousand years is given) to think, discuss, explore, and process. After this, the universe is now completely informed and secure in truth. Sin will never arise again. The judgment reveals the true results of the atoning sacrificial suffering work of Jesus.[200]

The Millennium[201] also gives the final conclusive reconfirmation that God is just and right. After being bound to a lifeless earth for a thousand years Satan and his angels are briefly released to work among the recently

---

200. "The angels ascribe honor and glory to Christ, for even they are not secure except by looking to the sufferings of the Son of God. It is through the efficacy of the cross that the angels of heaven are guarded from apostasy. Without the cross they would be no more secure against evil than were the angels before the fall of Satan. Angelic perfection failed in heaven. Human perfection failed in Eden, the paradise of bliss ... The plan of salvation, making manifest the justice and love of God, provides an eternal safeguard against defection in unfallen worlds, as well as among those who shall be redeemed by the blood of the Lamb." White, "What Was Secured by the Death of Christ."

201. For an overview of the Adventist view of the Millennium see Webster, "The Millennium."

resurrected wicked. Instead of repentance Satan immediately tries to organize the wicked into another rebellion. The wicked willingly co-operate.

At this time, God displays before all the wicked (human and angel) a panorama that displays the main events in the Great Controversy, including the fall of Satan and the selfless suffering and sacrifice of Christ. Along with this, each individual in their own minds recalls all the opportunities God gave them and how God tried to win them to the right. Satan views all this vast history. The truth is so powerful that he can no longer deny it. He finally and freely confesses the righteousness of God and the justness of his impending destruction.[202] The wicked also confess with him. "With all the facts of the great controversy in view, the whole universe, both loyal and rebellious, with one accord declare: "Just and true are Thy ways, Thou King of saints.""[203] This is very important. The problem of evil is universally acknowledged to be resolved—by all parties! It is not by philosophy or theory or argument but by demonstration and history. This *free* confession of God's goodness by creation, both righteous and unrighteous, is based on the incontrovertible evidence. God has not resolved the problem of evil by power or force. God has so conducted himself that he has enabled the universe to freely come to the truth.[204] Amazingly, not long after this confession Satan regathers himself and attempts one last frenzied attack on God.[205] The wicked, however, turn on him in hatred.[206] This is the final and now redundant evidence God is in the right. Sin is incurable. There is nothing God can do to help Satan or the wicked. The only remaining option of eternal destruction is now seen to be just and even merciful. God then eliminates sin, sinners, evil and suffering forever. Only one reminder of sin is left—the scars on Jesus—a testament to God's suffering, sacrificing, unselfish love.[207] God is love.

202. White, *The Great Controversy*, 670.

203. White, *The Great Controversy*, 670–71.

204. "Truth is omnipotent, but it does not work in the human agent in opposition to the human will. Here is the turning point of freedom and responsibility." White, "The Abiding Trust."

205. White, *The Great Controversy*, 671.

206. Satan "endeavours to inspire them [the wicked] with his own fury and arouse them to instant battle. But . . . [none] acknowledge his supremacy. His power is at an end. The wicked are filled with the same hatred of God that inspires Satan; but they see that their case is hopeless . . . their rage is kindled against Satan" White, *The Great Controversy*, 671.

207. The universe is not kept safe by the threat of an eternal hell: White, *The Great Controversy*, 674. Instead, the permanent humanity of Jesus and his scars function as an eternal assurance to the once fallen human race. See White, "The Treasure of Truth Rejected."

SUMMARY AND CONCLUSION

This study is now in a position to summarise the way the Great Controversy processes the emergence of evil as a problem by a progression through three stages and its resolution by a threefold atoning process.

The Mystery of Evil

The Great Controversy theodicy operates from the metaphysically necessary and *a priori* presupposition that evil is an inherently inexplicable mystery. God alone can truly know and understand what evil or sin is. It is the unthinkable, irrational act of a finite contingent-free creature refusing to trust its own creator by instead turning inward towards itself. It is selfishness in a cosmos designed for love. It is contingent creation seeking to become morally autonomous and independent of its Creator. Evil is inexplicable, yet it arose. Evil confounds human reason, yet precisely by separating from divine wisdom and Law, it is also self-seducing and self-justifying. This first step involves the hard-to-understand and irrational but deliberate act of self-deception and self-seduction by Satan which becomes the launching pad for the deception and seduction of others.

The Mystification of Evil

Following on from this is the intentional mystification of evil by its first advocate, Lucifer/Satan. By giving himself over to self-seduction and wilful self-deception, Satan *mystifies* the mystery of evil by presenting it as a "rational" action, a superior philosophy, and a necessary political alternative. Sin is presented as freedom. Its enslaving nature is denied. Divine law and rule is presented as evil. This "freedom" from God is acclaimed as a good that is arbitrarily repressed. Satan obfuscates and denies the irrationality of the first level of evil. He invents a concocted pretence of rational justification. Disturbingly, owing to the mystery of evil, it cannot be initially seen for what it is. These first two levels together make for the doubly-confounding nature of evil. First, evil's origins are a confounding mystery. Second, the resulting justification of evil by Satan's deceptive arguments mystifies and further confounds the truth. So an artificial level of ideological deception is overlaid on an intrinsically ontological mystery. This renders evil doubly difficult to adequately counter simply by argument and reason.

The Multiplication of Evil

The first two stages develop into the third stage of the multiplication of evil. Evil metastasizes throughout creation. Evil can be multiplied and become a movement because it has been mystified and presented as a form of liberation. As it multiplies it spreads to other minds and becomes a movement. This spread gives the appearance of truth. In convincing others, it ceases to appear to be the idiosyncratic idea of an individual. Those within it become committed to it and enslaved to it.[208] This moral evil brings creation under the curse of death and decay and produces natural evil. The loss of human dominion to Satan means he has direct access to the earthly physical realm.

The first level of evil is the inexplicable birth of sin. The second level of evil is its articulation as an ideology and its spread as a virus of the heart and mind. Without this second level, sin never leaves the mind of the first apostate and cosmic war never develops. Here sin is conceptually weaponized as deception. It becomes an ideology capable of spread. The third level of evil is evil's enmeshment as a constitutive element of the spiritual, mental, psychological, social, political, and even physical dimensions of reality. Moral evil becomes natural evil and socially structural evil. All levels of earthly creation are thrown into conflict with each other as well as with God. The first stage is the origin of Sin. The second stage is the origin of the Great Controversy. The third stage is the origin of Cosmic War in a pain-filled fallen creation. Sin and controversy ground warfare.

The Story of Evil is Also the Story of Satan

In the Great Controversy theodicy, these stages are not theory. They are played out in the personal experience and history of Satan. First, with the *Mystery of Evil*, Satan wilfully deceives himself. Evil emerges existentially, concretely, personally, and practically in Satan as he turns toward himself. Evil becomes larger than Satan alone but it cannot be understood apart from him and it is forever linked to him. The architect of evil and evil co-arise in the same event. Second, in the *Mystification of Evil*, Satan develops an intellectual ideology of lawlessness largely through accusation and lies by which he justifies himself. This ideology of transferable intellectual ideas enables his experience to spread and obscures what is really happening. Over time this original ideology mutates into numerous conflicting variations as seen in the almost endless philosophies and religions in the world. Third, there

---

208. These three levels are replicated and recapitulated in each sinner. We all choose to unjustifiably sin. We all mystify and obfuscate our sin. We all spread sin and evil.

is the *Multiplication of Evil*. By means of the mystification of sin, Satan is able to head a public, cosmic, social, political movement amid both angelic and human community. Humans are both willing co-participants and entrapped victims. He wields profound power and influence over them but the multiplication of human evil is also self-chosen and self-perpetuating.

Atonement as the Reversal of Evil

Undoing Satan's power involves rescuing sinners from the state of enslavement, exposing Satan's mystification of evil, and unveiling the inexplicable and unjustifiable nature of evil itself. This requires a comprehensive atoning work that completely restores every dimension of creation. All of this must be done without compromising God's character, law, or creation's free will structure, even though it was the location of evil's emergence. God's atoning work undoes all three levels of evil. God counters and overcomes the mystery of evil by a greater mystery of godliness. God does the inexplicable in giving himself for his enemies at the cost of infinite suffering to himself. God counters Satan's mystification of evil by giving a perfect revelation of himself in Christ. By means of his extensive atoning work, Christ rescues creation from the spread and enslavement of evil. The final judgment completes the resolution of the Great Controversy, ends the cosmic war, eliminates sin and sinners, and restores creation. A metanarrative of divine love resolves the problem of evil to the universal admission of all creation.

Chapter 4

Comparative Analysis of Boyd's TWT and the Great Controversy Theodicy

It is now possible to examine the Great Controversy Theodicy in the light of Boyd's Trinitarian Warfare Theodicy in order to more fully understand how the Great Controversy works as a theodicy. This involves an internal comparison between related warfare theodicies before an external comparison between them and the wider field of theodicy is made in chapter 5. An internal comparison between similar theories offers a closer analysis than is possible when looking at unrelated theories. This study's interest is in wrestling with issues of inner coherence before engaging in an external evaluation. There is also the desire to identify areas of weakness. This is not a general comparison, rather a focus on the specific way cosmic warfare theodicies respond to the problem of evil. Our interest is in the inner logic of cosmic warfare views. This will be shown to revolve around how both theodicies deal with the question of risk

EXTENDING THE FREE WILL DEFENSE

The earlier examination in the first three chapters highlights that warfare theodicies work by building on the basic free will defense and furthering it by the idea of cosmic war. This furthering is to ameliorate the free will defense weaknesses by constructing an extended free will theodicy that can deal with these limitations or criticisms. This extending of the free will defense is to help it answer questions like Mark Scott's five essential questions for a theodicy.[1] Warfare theodicies use the free will defense to explain Scott's first question about the origin of evil but go beyond it. Evil is not simply a generic metaphysical risk. Cosmic warfare theodicies go further and name the specific originator of evil as Lucifer/Satan, and that recognizing this is crucial for a proper understanding. The cosmic figure of Lucifer is essential for a more expansive explanatory theodicy.[2] Scott's second question concerns the nature or ontology of evil. Free will as a defense to the logical problem of evil often ignores this question. Use is often made of the theory of privation to discuss evil's ontology. Evil is not a thing but a privation of the good: God only makes good. Cosmic warfare theodicies accept this but want to emphasize other aspects of evil's ontology, i.e., the Great Controversy idea of "mystery of evil." The third question about the kind of problem evil poses cannot ignore the modern shift from logical to evidential problems of evil. The free will defense is most successful against the deductive logical form. This success led antitheists to formulate the evidential version. The free will defense struggles with the evidential version, which accepts the fact that free will is a logical possibility but asks instead what actual reasons God could have for allowing the actual degree and amount of evil in the world, not simply its possibility. The cosmic warfare theodicies acknowledge the problem that the evidential argument poses to the free will defense and is, at least in the case of Boyd, an attempt to offer an extended free will theodicy commensurate to the evidential problem of evil. The cosmic warfare theodicy response to the fourth question is linked to the third. Because the problem of evil is the evidential argument, the reason for evil must be more than free will, even though it retains freedom as central. The cosmic warfare theodicy, in contrast to the minimizing-of-evil-tendency within greater good theodicy, does not hold back. It recasts the problem of evil, not as the abuse of free will which supposedly contributes to a greater good, but as the emergence of a vast cosmic war. It accepts the factual premise of the evidential argument that gratuitous evil is real. While theodicies often resist admitting to the ostensive gratuity and pointlessness of so much evil, the cosmic warfare theodicy embraces it as exactly what would be expected if cosmic war is actually what sin unleashes. The reasons given for God's permission are similar to the free will defense but

---

1. See the Introduction. The five questions concern 1) the origin of evil; 2) the ontological nature of evil; 3) the kind of problem evil poses; 4) the divine reason for evil; 5) the end of evil. Scott, *Pathways in Theodicy*, 64.

2. Satan's status as a cosmic and primordial figure gives his abuse of freedom cosmic and primordial explanatory power. Satan also helps the cosmic warfare theodicy address the issue of natural evil, long considered a major limitation of the free will defense.

they have been recast within a cosmic framework. God had cosmic goals. Rejection of them leads to cosmic consequences. Finally, the fifth question about the "end of evil" is unclear in the free will defense. In the cosmic warfare view, it can be identified and named as the ability to win a cosmic war. The precise details of the exact nature of the war and how it is ended differ but there is agreement on the fact that war is what is happening and it must be dealt with.

THE ROLE OF "RISK"

Examining Scott's five questions for theodicies reveals that the majority of the questions (i.e., the first four) deal with framing and defining how evil's permission and emergence is understood. The other major issue is then how evil is eliminated and dealt with (question five). Basically, this concerns evil's conception and its committal, its beginning and its end. Both the possibility and elimination of evil can be helpfully, although not exclusively, understood as the need to account for and deal with "risk."[3] The centrality of the idea of risk, the benefits it produces, the tensions it introduces, and the need to deal with these, all profoundly shape cosmic warfare theodicies. The idea of risk is the very thing that enables these theodicies to initially deal with the problem of evil. God took a risk evil would eventuate—and it did. Risk also places pressure on a cosmic warfare theodicy to deal with the gravity of that risk. Why would God risk so much? Is it worth it? Can God contain the risk? Free will can get a theodicy off the ground but it cannot land it.

This is most clearly seen when the questions Boyd's six theses are designed to wrestle with are examined. Boyd's questions augment Scott's third question on exactly how evil is a problem to a free will-based warfare theodicy, and his fifth question on how risk and evil are overcome. The first two of Boyd's theses, TWT1 (love must be freely chosen) and TWT2 (freedom implies risk), set up the free will defense by spelling out its key implication as risk. The rest of the theses (TWT3–6) are about detailing and dealing with the risk inherent in contingent creaturely love. The main problems Boyd counters can be grouped together under five questions, four of which are specifically aimed at the issue of risk. Behind all of these questions is the foundational, deeper question: *Can we trust a risk-taking God,* particularly his wisdom, character, and ability?[4] In Boyd's work, this macro-question is explored and given definition in the following five questions.

3. "God is a risk-taker if he endows his creatures with libertarian freedom; otherwise not." Hasker, "Does God Take Risks," 219, see also Helm, "Does God Take Risks," 229.

4. Boyd, *Satan*, 158.

The first set of questions can be described as the *"win it"* or *"victory"* questions. God has undertaken a creation project with the risk of cosmic war; can he win the war if it eventuates?[5] Can God guarantee that he will finally win against evil? Will his victory be permanent and eternal or will risk still be an ongoing part of the future? Will evil potentially arise again after victory?[6] In Boyd's case these questions are intensified due to his open theism. If God does not know the actual future, except as probabilities, how can he (and we!) know that he will win? How can we know that he will achieve his aims to a degree that is sufficient to justify the risk he has undertaken in creation?

Closely related is the second set of questions to do with *"value"* or the *"is it worth it"* questions. Is the risk worth it? Is free will worth it? Is it worth all the pain and suffering? The question is asked if God has miscalculated and wagered too much on love and freedom.[7]

There is the third issue of *"how long"* or the *"duration"* question. Why must the risk go on for so long? How long is too long? This questions the wisdom of allowing a risk with extreme duration.[8]

The fourth question is the *"why others"* or *"influence"* question. Why has God allowed persons to have the power over other persons?[9] Why is the risk not individual? Why does someone's wrong behavior affect another? Why is one agent's existence at the mercy of another agent's choice?

The fifth major question is not directly about risk but about how God currently deals with evil. This is the issue of God's intervention and its apparent arbitrariness. This is the *"arbitrariness"* or *"why help some and not others"* question?[10] God appears inconsistent. Since God has power, why does he not use it more often and more consistently?

All of these issues stem from limitations or questions about the free will defense. Allowing that the free will defense does appear to show there is no necessary contradiction between the existence of God and evil, the questions have shifted to the more evidential problem of evil-styled objections about the scale of the risk in the magnitude of suffering and evil. For both Boyd's warfare theodicy and the Great Controversy theodicy to be successful, they must establish their ability to deal with risk-orientated objections

---

5. Boyd speaks of the need to "address the issue of how God can guarantee to win a war if he can never be ensured of winning each or any particular battle?" Boyd, *Satan*, 145–46, 155.

6. Boyd, *Satan*, 179, 191.

7. Boyd, *Satan*, 169, 173–77.

8. Boyd, *Satan*, 179.

9. Boyd, *Satan*, 163–64.

10. Boyd, *Satan*, 185.

to the free will defense. Dealing with risk is therefore at the heart of understanding each cosmic warfare theodicy.[11] Here their distinctive defining arguments are displayed and here can be seen their points of weakness and tension. By now it is apparent that while freedom and its risk is central to the cosmic warfare task, the risk is not simple or singular. It involves a number of different elements. The questions about risk concern three elements: its emergence, its continuance, and its elimination (see Table 6). Each element has a different set of questions associated with it. The discussion of risk around these three elements is diagrammed below. The questions are particularly brought out by the evidential problem of evil. These elements will guide the discussion. How do cosmic warfare theodicies deal with all three of the elements of risk? The answer to this will reveal the heart of how the two theodicies work as a specific category and reveal the different and distinctive approaches of each. It will also reveal weaknesses and areas of problem. This will provide the basis for the final comparison in the next chapter of the Great Controversy theodicy with the wider field of theodicies.

Table 6: Elements in the Problem of Risk-Associated Freedom

Emergence of Risk (*Origin/Permitting of Evil*)	Continuance of Risk (*On-going Allowance of Evil*)	Elimination of Risk (*Abolition of Evil*)
Why did God permit/allow evil?	Is the value of the risk worth the cost (scale of suffering and evil)?	How and when will evil end?
Was evil a possibility or necessity? (What probability?)	Why does evil affect others (esp. the innocent)?	How is it that the redeemed will no longer be able to sin?
Why did evil arise?	Why does evil continue so long?	How can we be sure that evil will not arise again?
How could evil arise from good?	Why are divine interventions so arbitrary (or absent)?	
How could evil spread?		

11. For a discussion of risk and no risk versions of providence, see Tiessen, *Providence and Prayer*.

A SUB-THESIS: COSMIC WARFARE WITH OR WITHOUT COSMIC CONTROVERSY

In exploring these elements of risk the central thesis for this chapter and thus an important sub-thesis of this study will now become clear. War and conflict form a crucially important role in cosmic warfare theodicies, but the exact *nature* of the conflict and how it is conceptualized have profound implications for the entire theodicy. In broad terms, cosmic warfare theodicies tell us that an exalted being, Lucifer/Satan, through an abuse of freedom, is at war with God and has drawn angels, humanity, and, in some respects, nature itself into this rebellion. Both Boyd's TWT and Seventh-day Adventism's Great Controversy theodicy see the necessity of invoking cosmic war by a cosmic being, not simply free will, to answer the evidential argument from evil. Evil, pain, and suffering exist because this life is a cosmic warzone. Freedom abused escalates to war and stopping short of this by only detailing an abuse of human free will is incomplete. There is a great deal of overlap in how the two warfare models describe cosmic war but key differences emerge between the two when a comparison is made of how this war is understood or what the nature of the conflict is.

The first difference is in the preferred *mode* of analysis and explanation: Boyd's theodicy relies on a particular *metaphysics* of love while the Great Controversy theodicy relies on a specific *metanarrative* of love. The second difference arises out of the first. Boyd's theodicy, based in a metaphysics of love, centers on the ability of the metaphysics of *love* and *freedom* to account for cosmic war. In contrast, Adventism's Great Controversy theodicy, based in a metanarrative of love, works on the ability of a politicized cosmic moral controversy involving *love, law,* and *freedom* to account for cosmic war.

This second difference is between a "bifocal" (love and freedom) and a "trifocal" (love, freedom, and law) framing of the cosmic war. The third difference naturally flows from this and concerns the *levels or layers of explanation* that arise from the different modes of analysis/explanation. Boyd's metaphysical approach gives rise to a free will defense within a cosmic warfare theodicy. This generates two distinct explanatory levels. The Great Controversy metanarrative approach yields a free will defense within a cosmic warfare theodicy which is itself within a broader cosmic controversy theodicy.[12] This generates three levels of explanation. The presence or absence of a defining role for controversy over divine law accounts for the difference between Boyd's bifocal theodicy and the Great Controversy trifocal theodicy. This difference in levels of explanation can be pictured thus:

---

12. Our later conclusion will modify and sharpen the exact relationship between free will, cosmic warfare, and the Great Controversy.

Boyd's *Trinitarian Warfare Theodicy*
FWD ⟶ TWT
Adventism's *Great Controversy Theodicy*
FWD ⟶ CWT ⟶ GCT

The Great Controversy incorporates within itself both free will and cosmic warfare. This means it has three layers to its explanation. Boyd's theodicy only has two layers. The free will defense by itself is a singular layer of explanation. Certain implications would seem to follow. Having fewer levels within a theodicy places a greater burden to explain challenges using only those levels. However, having a greater number of levels, and especially if the levels are of differing but complementary kinds (i.e., metaphysical vs metanarrative), would theoretically mean a richer explanatory potential. It should be noted that it is not simply a matter of adding justificatory patterns as explanations but of adding explanatory levels.[13] Of course each level must be logically and coherently interrelated, as merely adding levels carries the risk of increasing the potential for a contradiction between levels. But if additional levels are integrated and correspond to each other, then a deeper level of response (and potentially resolution) to the problem of evil and more explanatory power is possible. This does not adjudicate which warfare theodicy is optimal, but it does encourage us to see if the Great Controversy theodicy might possess additional options of response in some areas. That remains to be demonstrated or discounted. At this point, it will help to summarise the difference between the two theodicies as a critical sub-thesis. The crucial difference in theodicies is that Boyd's theodicy is a *cosmic warfare without a controversy* while the Great Controversy theodicy is a *cosmic warfare based in a specific controversy*. How significant this sub-thesis is and to what degree it effects how the question of risk is dealt with will occupy much of this chapter. This will prepare for the final chapter in which it is detailed how the Great Controversy resolves the problem of evil amid the wider context of other theodicies.

---

13. For example, we could add the natural law pattern to the free will pattern to enhance its explanatory power. However, if we placed natural law and free will within a process context or a cosmic war context, we would be changing the levels of explanation, not merely adding a justificatory pattern.

Metaphysics versus Metanarrative

The first key difference concerns the preferred mode of analysis and explanation. Both cosmic warfare positions contain metaphysics and have a metanarrative (Boyd's metanarrative does not have the idea of cosmic controversy), but they predominantly rely on one or the other of these in order to construct their theodicy. Boyd mines his worldview in order to give explicit and detailed metaphysical answers. The narrative element plays a lesser subsidiary role in his theodicy.[14] It is at the level of metaphysics that the theodicy is dealt with. In contrast, the metaphysics of the Great Controversy are latent, implicit, and often undeveloped. Its metanarrative is richly developed and drawn upon in order to deal with the problem of evil, often bypassing or replacing metaphysical explanations with alternative or complementary narrative ones. Metaphysics at times plays a preliminary and preparatory role for the real level of explanation which is the narrative.[15]

Boyd's theodicy arises out of his bifocal analysis of the metaphysics of libertarian freedom and contingent love. This is most clearly in his six theses. He then applies these theses to the biblical claims about Satan. Satan serves as the exemplar or paradigm of the risk of contingent freedom giving rise to sin and cosmic warfare.[16] In the Great Controversy a metanarrative detailing the trifocal abuse of freedom, controverting of divine love, and rejection of divine law forms the matrix out of which arises its theodicy. Satan abuses freedom, controverts and rejects divine law and love, offers an aggressive alternative, and initiates cosmic warfare and controversy. While Boyd's metaphysics are primarily concerned with the mechanics of creaturely freedom/love, the Great Controversy as a theodicy combines that concern for creaturely freedom/love with an emphasis on a public contesting of divine love and law (also interchangeably understood as divine character and government). Accordingly, Boyd's metaphysics of freedom and love account for the possibilities of cosmic war while the Great Controversy's metanarrative of freedom, love, and law account for cosmic war *and cosmic controversy*. In Boyd's theodicy, *freedom* and *love* alone account for war. In the Great Controversy theodicy, *freedom*, *love*, and *law* together

---

14. This is highlighted by Pyne and Piske's telling criticism: "Readers who choose this book by title may be disappointed by Boyd's limited discussion of Satan." Pyne and Piske, "Review of *Satan and the Problem of Evil*." 113. Satan is more a paradigm exemplar than a narrative character.

15. Cosmic warfare theodicies may benefit from each other; see Davidson, "Cosmic Metanarrative," 102–19, for Adventist openness to Boyd's work.

16. See again especially the summary in Boyd, *Satan*, 205.

account for the controversy.[17] The presence or absence of a central role for law is a distinguishing feature. In order to aid this discussion, a comparative summary of the two cosmic warfare responses to risk will be shown in the following two diagrams. Table 7 outlines how Boyd's Trinitarian Warfare theodicy deals with risk.

Table 7: Boyd's TWT Resolution of Risk and the Problem of Evil[18]

Elements in the Problem of Risk-Associated Freedom		
Emergence of Risk (*Origin/Permitting of Evil*)	Continuance of Risk (*On-going Allowance of Evil*)	Elimination of Risk (*Abolition of Evil*)
Boyd's Trinitarian Warfare Theodicy uses a *"Metaphysics of Love"* to deal with these Risk Elements (key features outlined below)		
TWT 1 *Love entails freedom* TWT 2 *Freedom entails risk*	TWT 3 *Risk entails moral responsibility* TWT 4 *Moral responsibility is proportionate to the power to influence* TWT 5 *The power to influence is irrevocable*	TWT 6 *Power to influence is finite*
Cosmic War Begins *Free Will Defense*	Cosmic War is Contested *Spiritual Warfare / Atonement via Christus Victor*	
Libertarian freedom (*Covenant of non-coercion*)	Compatibilist freedom (*Divine Intervention permissible on spent freedom*)	

Boyd's six theses roughly correspond to the three areas of risk (emergence, continuance, elimination). A libertarian free will defense explains evil's emergence but recourse is then made to compatibilist freedom to account for evils elimination.

17. This illustrates the "levels of explanatory layers" argument made earlier. Boyd is focused on the contingency of creaturely love, whereas the Great Controversy theodicy assumes this (one layer) and takes that same contingency as controverting the propriety of divine love/law (extra layer).

18. For specific details of Boyd's view outlined in this diagram see chapter 2.

Comparative Analysis of Boyd's TWT and the Great Controversy Theodicy

Below is Table 8 which summarises how Seventh-day Adventism's Great Controversy theodicy deals with risk.

Table 8: The Great Controversy Theodicy Resolution of Risk and the Problem of Evil[19]

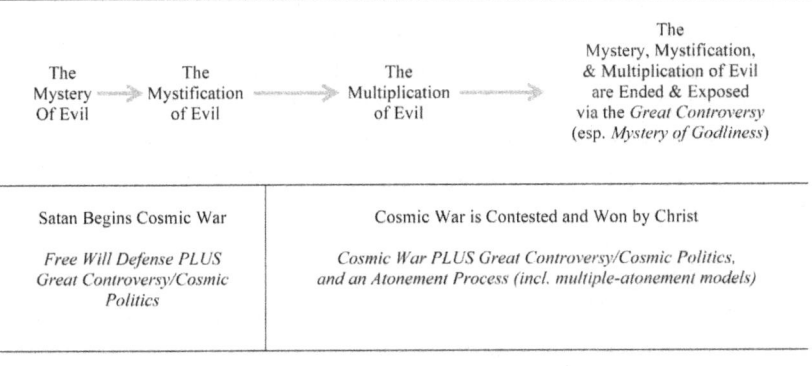

While chapters 2 and 3 of our study were largely analytical and descriptive, this chapter is critical and evaluative. This study so far has largely been summative: in order for cosmic warfare theodicies to work, they must simultaneously balance the need for *risk-associated freedom* in order to account for evil, with the requirement to manage and eventually eliminate the risks associated with freedom (either by a metaphysics of love or a metanarrative of love). This study now moves to a critical evaluation of how this risk balancing act puts tension on cosmic warfare explanations. In each of the

---

19. For specific details of Adventism's Great Controversy Theodicy outlined in this diagram see chapter 3. For a discussion of the modified form of libertarian freedom as Soft or Virtue Libertarianism see later in this chapter.

three stages (emergence, continuation, elimination) evil's riskiness threatens to escalate into a recalcitrant and uncontainable element. Most of this is traceable to particular concepts of freedom.

PROBLEMS WITH RISK AND LIBERTARIAN FREEDOM

The free will defense assumes a libertarian understanding of free will. Both Boyd and the Great Controversy assume standard libertarian understandings of freedom. While this understanding may be adequate for a defense against the logical problem of evil, is it adequate for the needs of a theodicy in which the explanatory demands are higher? We will look at critiques of Boyd's work that suggest it is not. This then has implications for the Great Controversy view for two reasons. First, the Great Controversy theodicy shares structural similarities to Boyd's theodicy on this very issue. Second, at this metaphysical level, the Great Controversy theodicy reveals its underdevelopment and a lack of philosophical reflection. Thus, as will be shown, at this most foundational level both cosmic warfare theodicies face issues of adequacy and coherence unless their account of freedom is clarified.

Libertarian freedom stands in contrast to compatibilist freedom. Compatibilist freedom is so-called because it affirms the compatibility of human freedom and divine determinism. In compatibilism, all that is required for freedom is that someone does something voluntarily (unforced); that is, they do what they want or desire to do.[20] What they want or desire, however, is not determined by them but by other secondary factors or causes. God may therefore determine certain outcomes by the use of or control of secondary causes. In this understanding, it is the person who performs the actual action, not God, even though, given the chain of causation or providential circumstances, they could not do otherwise. In contrast, libertarian freedom is usually understood as possessing either one or both of the following characteristics. First, agents possess the *power of self-determination* as opposed to determination by external or secondary factors (be it natural processes, divine control or otherwise). External factors may influence but not determine. This means the ultimate and final explanation for the choice is with the agent.[21] The second characteristic is the *"power to do otherwise"* also known as the power of contrary choice or alternative possibilities. When facing alternative possibilities a person who chooses A rather than B

---

20. "Freedom of inclination," according to Bruce A. Ware, *God's Greater Glory*, 80.

21. Also called the "sourcehood approach," that is, the agent is the source of their own actions not some other cause or agent; Timpe, *Free Will in Philosophical Theology*, 8. See also Timpe, *Free Will: Sourcehood and Its Alternatives*.

could, nevertheless, under the same causes and circumstances, have chosen B if they so willed.[22] Plantinga's free will defense affirms both elements but emphasizes the second element, "the power to do otherwise." When confronted by a moral situation in which one course of action is right and the other is wrong, the person can choose either. He terms this *morally significant freedom*.[23] In Plantinga's account, it is the power to have done morally otherwise which gives freedom its particular moral significance and distinguishes these choices from free choices which have no moral significance.[24] Of these two definitions for libertarian freedom the second one ("power to do otherwise") is the dominant one.[25]

Advocates of a Great Controversy theodicy affirm either one or both understandings of libertarian freedom. Asscherick opts for the definition of "self-determination."[26] John Peckham speaks of the "power to do otherwise."[27] Unhelpfully, many other Great Controversy advocates often fail to define freedom any further than simple expressions such as "free choice" or "free moral agency."[28] It is assumed that such terms will be understood by all and there is little discussion or awareness of the range of options. Context and wider theological commitments indicate that the freedom is, nevertheless, libertarian and not compatibilist. Gregory Boyd also accepts the two commonly expressed understandings of libertarian freedom. Boyd states that "we must possess the power to do otherwise" and "we must be able to *determine ourselves*" in relation to God and morally responsible actions.[29]

Having established that the two cosmic warfare theodicies use standard concepts of libertarian freedom there is a need to ask the question 'what then is the issue'? What is the problem? The problem lies in a tension that exists between the two components that make up libertarian freedom. Simply put, if freedom is the 'power to do otherwise' then the possibility of evil seems to be an eternal possibility.[30] After all, if creatures are only free

22. Also called the "alternative possibilities approach." Timpe, *Free Will in Philosophical Theology*, 8.

23. Plantinga, *The Nature of Necessity*, 166. Plantinga, *God, Freedom and Evil*, 29–30.

24. For example, a trivial non-moral alternative possibility would be whether to eat with chop sticks or with knives and forks.

25. Timpe, *Free Will in Philosophical Theology*, 8.

26. Asscherick, *God in Pain*, 144. "By freedom we here mean the power of self-determination . . . the self is the ultimate cause of its own choices."

27. Peckham, *The Love of God*, 112–14.

28. See Cairus, "The Doctrine of Man," 208, 209; John M. Fowler, "Sin," 232–42.

29. Boyd, *Satan*, 56, 57.

30. Feinberg, "God Limits His Power (Bruce Reichenbach): John Feinberg's

if they have the power to do otherwise, then they must eternally possess this power to potentially do evil, otherwise, they would not be "free." This would mean that God's creation is always at risk and there is an eternal question mark over God's solution to the problem of evil. The potential for another cosmic war would seem to be open-ended and thus God's victory is always provisional. Both Boyd and the Great Controversy are aware of this and seek to assure that sin will not arise again.[31] The Great Controversy is aware of the need for sin not to arise again but seems largely unconscious of the logical tension between the differing conceptions of libertarian freedom. This reveals its lack of philosophical awareness and precision. Boyd is aware, but his answer appears confused and confusing. This suggests that an uncritical use of the free will defense by warfare theodicies may conceal a major theory-threatening contradiction. The free will defense, as normally understood, poses problems for cosmic warfare theodicies, unless it can be redefined adequately.

Issues in Boyd's Discussion of Freedom

What is confusing in Boyd's discussion is that he begins his six theses with libertarian freedom, but ends them with the opposite, compatibilist understanding. An overstated but helpful way of saying this is that Boyd begins an Arminian but ends a Calvinist. In his first two theses he uses libertarian freedom ("power to do otherwise" and "power of self-determination") to show why evil is an unavoidable risk if God chooses to create truly free creatures capable of love (classic free will defense). As freedom is needed for love, God makes a covenant of non-coercion with creation. This means evil cannot be unilaterally eliminated without eliminating the existence of free creatures. How then to tame the risk of evil? This is the importance of Boyd's final thesis which closes down the danger of risk by arguing that freedom is finite (TWT6). Due to the process of character solidification human freedom eventually becomes morally fixed. Boyd asserts that such morally fixed freedom is now to be understood as compatibilist freedom (the exact opposite understanding of his original understanding of freedom).[32] The

---

Response," 125. Add open theism and the problem is compounded; see Ware, *God's Lesser Glory*, 159.

31. "TWT6 also provides a plausible explanation of how it is that the possibility of love entails risk without holding that heaven will be eternally risky." Boyd, *Satan*, 191. "Never will evil again be manifest . . . A tested and proved creation will never again be turned from allegiance to Him whose character has been fully manifested before them as fathomless love and infinite wisdom." White, *The Great Controversy*, 504.

32. "Our libertarian freedom is the probationary means by which we acquire

reason he does this is so that God can intervene on a person's compatibilist freedom in a way that he couldn't if the freedom was libertarian.[33] God is free to violate (or is no longer bound by) the covenant of non-coercion when a creature acquires compatibilist freedom. God is not limited to non-coercive activity, he can intervene if needed. This is how Boyd argues that God can ensure evil's defeat and be certain about the future.[34]

Paul Helseth's Criticisms

More than anyone else, Boyd's most tenacious critic Paul Helseth has seized upon this tension to argue that Boyd's position is untenable and contradictory, and that the God of open theism is an ambivalent, arbitrary,[35] and "capricious being."[36] Helseth makes the following claims. First, the entire coherence of the openness program (and its response to the problem of evil) is jettisoned because God cannot accomplish his goal without violating an essential component of that program, namely, self-determining freedom.[37] Second, if God can sometimes work in a coercive fashion, it makes it much more difficult for Boyd to maintain that the ultimate explanation for evil is free will agents (human or angelic) rather than God.[38] Third, following on from this, this willingness to use coercion "makes it more difficult to rescue God from being tarnished by the problem of evil."[39] This is because if God can actually use coercion then why does he not intervene more often to stop evil and suffering? God's neglect, especially in view of him having no blueprint, appears completely arbitrary with "no rhyme or reason for to his unilateral activity."[40] How decisive is Helseth's critique? It does appear that

---

compatibilistic freedom either for or against God." Boyd, *Satan*, 189.

33. "After God's irrevocable gift of self-determination to an agent is 'spent,' as it were, God is under no obligation to refrain from intervening on the agent's freedom." Boyd, *Satan*, 191.

34. "TWT6 is crucial . . . because it alone allows us to render coherent . . . that the war that God fights in this present age is *not an eternal war*." Boyd, *Satan*, 190.

35. Helseth, "On Divine Ambivalence," 509.

36. Helseth, "God Causes All Things," 45.

37. The willingness of God to violate free agents self-determining freedom "jettisons the coherence of the openness program, then, for it establishes that God cannot accomplish his ultimate purpose without violating a significant component of that purpose." Helseth, "The Trustworthiness of God, 293.

38. Helseth, "The Trustworthiness of God," 295.

39. Helseth, "The Trustworthiness of God," 297.

40. Helseth, "The Trustworthiness of God," 305.

Helseth pinpoints problems with Boyd's TWT, but it remains open as to whether they are fatal or not.

Much of the problem is that Boyd's account of freedom is not consistent, and Helseth has focused on this inconsistency. This is because when Boyd seeks to find biblical support for his case for God's willingness and ability to intervene on human freedom, he chooses the example of Peter's denial of Christ.[41] Before looking at this, it must be pointed out that this inconsistency problem is directly linked to Boyd's open theistic denial of exhaustive definitive divine foreknowledge.[42] This is a crucial point to understand. Boyd's need to maintain his open theism creates tension in his theodicy. The application of open theist assumptions would lead to the conclusion that God cannot definitively foreknow that Peter will deny Jesus and yet Scripture seems to indicate that Jesus knew exactly what would happen.[43] Boyd escapes this conclusion by saying that God knew Peter's character tendencies and orchestrated a lesson in order to teach the apostle about love and servant leadership.[44] In other words, God knew that Peter would deny Jesus because God arranged the events so that things happened exactly as God said. God escapes the general openness of the future by deliberately determining a particular future in this case. This sounds like Boyd's earlier explanation of what happens after a libertarian free agent becomes a compatibilist free agent and thus God can freely use "coercion" and intervene on the person's freedom without violating the no-longer-binding covenant of non-coercion. But this cannot be. The problem is that Peter still possesses libertarian freedom.[45] He has not solidified his character so that it is compatible with divine determination. Proof of this is that Peter eventually changes to a confessor instead of a denier. Theoretically, the covenant of non-coercion should still apply to Peter. This appears to imply, for Helseth, that either all freedom is actually compatible with divine determinism or that God is actually an untrustworthy covenant breaker.[46] Either option is anathema for Boyd. It is this contradictory conclusion that stems from

---

41. See the discussions in Boyd, *God of the Possible*, 35–37; Boyd, *Satan*, 130–33.

42. Boyd notes that "it is difficult to account for fulfilled prophecy unless we assume that the Lord can at times intervene to ensure that particular acts would occur." Boyd, *Satan*, 184.

43. Matt 26:34; Mark 14:30; Luke 22:34. Jesus' statement reveals knowledge of what Peter will do, how many times he will deny, and the activities of a rooster. This doesn't seem like a likely statement based on Peter's general character tendencies but a foreknowledge of future events.

44. Boyd, *God of the Possible*, 35–37.

45. Helseth, "The Trustworthiness of God," 295.

46. Helseth, "The Trustworthiness of God," 295.

Boyd's use of (a still libertarian freedom-possessing) Peter as an illustration, upon which Helseth's critique rests. Helseth suggests that the only way out for Boyd is that either God can foreknow the future contingents (thus denying his open theism) or that God knew he would remove Peter's self-determining freedom and ensure he denied Jesus (thus denying God's commitment to loving non-coercion).[47] In other words, Boyd can escape by the Arminian path of full foreknowledge or a Calvinistic-style path of consistent divine determination but he can't keep his open theism.

What is to be made of Helseth's criticisms?[48] Helseth implies that Boyd is employing a hard "coercive" form of compatibilism,[49] but Boyd is clear that God does not directly coerce the will.[50] Any failure to intervene is due to God respecting the metaphysical limits free will places on him.[51] Boyd is clear that Peter freely acted out of his then-current freely formed character.[52] Peter wasn't forced to deny Jesus. The circumstances were the context, not the cause. When he invokes it, Boyd's compatibilism is "soft" like Helseth's own Calvinism. Additionally, for Boyd, God may or may not have even orchestrated the situation. Boyd appears to equivocate on this point. At times, he seems to imply that God did orchestrate events,[53] and at other times he states that we don't know if God needed to, implying that he may not have.[54]

---

47. Helseth, "The Trustworthiness of God," 297. Boyd must either concede God can know the future or that God knew he would "orchestrate circumstances that would *compel* Peter to betray Jesus, *in which case God forced Peter to sin*." Helseth, "The Trustworthiness of God," 295–96. Italics mine.

48. Helseth also claims Boyd's God is arbitrary because he has no singular blueprint for each evil or each divine intervention. However, Boyd's neo-molinism allows him to say that God already has set responses to every contingency that might arise, see, Boyd, "Response to Paul Kjoss Helseth," 70. In effect, God has multiple blueprints, but he does not yet know which one to use.

49. Helseth, "The Trustworthiness of God," 293, 297. "Soft" coercion is working compatibilistically with agents who have established their own characters. "Hard" coercion is compelling agents to do what they possibility would not do if the power to do otherwise was still true of them.

50. "God cannot meticulously control the free will of agents" nor can he "revoke" it." Boyd, "God Limits His Control," 191. "One thing God cannot do, by definition, is meticulously control or unilaterally revoke a free will once given." Boyd, "God Limits His Control," 192.

51. "When God fails to intervene, it is precisely *because* "the self-determining freedom of wicked moral agents is irrevocable," and "To the extent that God gives humans and angels say-so, he by definitions limits his own unilateral say-so." Boyd, "Response to Paul Kjoss Helseth," 70.

52. Boyd, "God Limits His Control," 194.

53. Boyd, *Satan*, 131.

54. Boyd, *God of the Possible*, 36.

However, it should be noted that the principle of orchestrating the situation is never rejected.[55] Thus, while it is difficult to make a hard version of Helseth's critique stick, a soft version seems to remain. It appears on one side of Boyd's equivocation that somewhat fortuitously events happened as God surmised, and he did not orchestrate anything. Here Helseth is wrong in this specific case. God determined nothing except to "predict" and redemptively work with Peter after the denials. Events opportunely happened as surmised. But on the other side of the equivocating, God needed to intervene and orchestrate to ensure that a pressure situation developed in order to make certain Peter denied Jesus (in keeping with the earlier prediction and for the purposes of humbling discipline of the apostle). Things didn't happen as God hoped and so he had to make things happen. Here Helseth's criticism holds some weight. The problem is that even in the first version of events the principle of orchestration is not rejected, it just didn't need to be acted on. Ultimately, Peter could not have done otherwise. Either he fortuitously and freely did so as "foreseen" or God ensured the situation was such that Peter would deny. This seems to be an elimination of libertarian freedom's "irrevocability." The whole point of the criticism is that Peter's freedom was still libertarian and thus off-limits for any determination. Boyd can argue that Peter's character was solidified enough (i.e., compatible enough) for God to foreknow and ensure this. True. But then isn't everyone's character solidified enough in this sense for God to foreknow and even determine everyone? What then of open theism? We are back to the start.

It is not that Boyd's model can't work in all cases. Boyd gives examples such as God ending someone's freedom by terminating their life, examples include Ananias and Sapphira (Acts 5:1–11), King Herod (Acts 12:20–23), the Canaanites, and the Flood.[56] The problem is that these interventions are fatal for the agents. None of these examples help explain God's ability to predict the behavior of non-executed agents (like Peter). As it stands, Peter threatens to be the exception that would bring down the rule. It may be too absolute a claim to say, as Helseth does, that this problem is completely fatal for Boyd. But we can say that this part of Boyd's theory is too ill-defined and has too many unanswered questions, and inconsistencies, to carry the weight it does. Either God foreknew Peter's actions, contra open theism, or God determined someone's actions, contra libertarian self-determinism and the power to do otherwise. The coherence of Boyd's account of taming

---

55. Interestingly, his latest version of Peter's denial has no mention of orchestrating or squeezing. Just an affirmation that it is not hard to imagine a God with perfect knowledge being able to know what Peter would do in such a situation. Boyd, "God Limits His Control," 194.

56. Boyd, *Satan*, 185.

risk is thereby called into question. Can risk-elimination be achieved while postulating a contradictory theory or violating a foundational assumption? This area needs to be revisited by Boyd. Risk theodicies are risky.[57]

Satan as Exemplar or Contradiction?

This is not the only point of tension in Boyd's formulation of his six theses and the rest of his theodicy. Boyd claims that Satan is the paradigm for his six theses. Satan bridges theoretical propositions and actual reality by functioning as the exemplar of the theses.[58] The problem is that Satan's ongoing existence appears to be a counter-example or another exception to the way Boyd formulates parts of the six theses. How so? In Boyd's explanation of the six theses, an agent's libertarian freedom is only for a probationary period of time until the agent's character is morally settled in a particular direction. Once this time is up God may intervene on the now compatibilist agent (although not on the individual's will) and by providential means determine the individual's actions if he desires.[59] The problem here is that Satan has obviously settled his moral character long ago on the side of evil and rebellion. This should mean that God is free to intervene on Satan and apparently determine him as he sees fit or even to stop him. The covenant of non-coercion no longer applies to Satan. So why does God tolerate Satan? Why doesn't God exert compatibilist control over Satan, for example, to guarantee Satan only does evils that work for the greater good? God could theoretically eliminate gratuitous evil in Satan's case. In fact, wouldn't God have a duty, let alone a motive, to constrain Satan

Boyd does have a way to escape this conclusion. He argues that part of the balance between the irrevocability (TWT5) and finitude (TWT6) of a free agent's moral and social influence is their "quality of freedom." An agent's quality of freedom is the scope of their influence (ability and potential for good or ill) and the temporal duration of that influence. This quality is dynamic and conditioned by at least five factors: 1) The ongoing influence of God; 2) Our original constitution; 3) Our previous decisions; 4) Other agents and their decisions; and 5) Prayer.[60] The first factor of God's ongoing

---

57. In contrast to Boyd, Ellen White affirms that Jesus foreknew Peter's denial, even down to his thoughts, but also that it could have been otherwise! She even describes what would have happened if Peter accepted the predicted warning; see White, "Peter's Fall."

58. Boyd, *Satan*, 205–06.

59. Boyd, *Satan*, 185. Boyd even speaks of "coercive power."

60. Boyd, *Satan*, 191–205.

influence doesn't help as Satan is no longer open to the saving influence of God (the third factor, Satan's previous decisions, reinforces this point). There is no reason for God to tolerate his continuance. The fifth condition of prayer doesn't help explain Satan's ongoing existence. Believers pray for his defeat. This leaves the second (original constitution) and fourth (other agents) factors. The original constitution refers to the agent's created nature, its temporal potential, their mental and physical capabilities, and potential roles intended by God. All of this accounts for the agent's moral and social ability to make an impact on the flow of history for good or evil. Boyd suggests that if Satan has the "capacity to corrupt the cosmos for billions of years" it is because he had the same temporal capacity to bless it.[61]

This argument implies that while Satan's character is morally settled and spent, the temporal potential of his freedom has not yet been spent, and this is why God cannot or will not intervene to stop Satan. This does not seem satisfactory. After all, many humans of great influence and ability suddenly die and clearly do not exercise their full temporal capacity. Why is Satan's temporal capacity so inviolable? It could be explained that the curse of death means our physical potential (which is underneath any temporal endurance) is vulnerable to mortality in a way Satan is not.[62] Even if this way out is acceptable, why should temporal capacity for influence continue when the moral character is clearly settled for evil? Is God held hostage to a measurable duration of time linked to Satan's temporal capacity, regardless of how vast his moral evil is, before he can end Satan's reign of terror? Is God left watching the clock tick down? Irrevocable temporal potential, even though not eternal, strikes one as an arbitrary metaphysical constraint when removed from character and morality. God naturally must allow creatures to possess temporal existence, but it makes more sense as a dynamic potential rather than a set capacity that God must wait to expire. God's acts of judgment seem to support this as they are linked to morality rather than to metaphysics. Boyd's mention of "billions of years"—a figure well beyond any of the Bible's own—seems to exacerbate the sense of divine miscalculation and the enormity of the risk. It also makes for dismal eschatological prospects. God can't end things until Satan has exhausted his apparently massive temporality. Of course, the situation becomes utterly farcical if Satan has immortality. God would be waiting forever! Help is at hand as God could confine Satan to hell. But this only reintroduces the problem in a different

---

61. Boyd, *Satan*, 182.

62. Other human agents (the fourth factor) can cut short other human potential by their actions (e.g., murder, etc.). But, of course, humans can't kill Satan. But God cuts short humans' potential—why not end Satan's? Surely, it would help reduce evil and suffering.

guise. Now the question becomes: Why hasn't God already put Satan in hell?[63] My sense is that Boyd has not thought through the interrelationship of all these things and would likely need to make significant adjustments to his theory were he to do so. What they would be is hard to tell.[64] There is one other possible alternative for Boyd. This is the fourth factor, where quality of freedom is affected by other agent's influence and actions. Boyd uses this factor to illustrate how one agent can diminish another agent's freedom by a negative, destructive influence or, conversely, one agent can enhance another agent's freedom by positive influence. How this might add duration to Satan is not clear. Do evildoers enhance and believers diminish Satan's physical durability? This seems unlikely. This is really another variation of one's constitution. I doubt Boyd would take this approach. It makes more sense to understand that other agent's cooperative actions can enhance or extend the influence of Satan across communities and over time but not his own physical duration. This concept of influence is more in line with cosmic controversy, to which this study now turns.

This discussion highlights the plausibility of the sub-thesis for this chapter. The concept of cosmic warfare benefits from having cosmic controversy as an additional layer of explanation. In contrast to Boyd's Satan, the Great Controversy theodicy, drawing on the explanatory level of metanarrative and controversy rather than the metaphysics of war, offers a different kind of answer. Satan has raised accusations against God that will not go away with his destruction. These accusations go to the heart and foundation of God's rule and concern his character, law, and government. Destroying Satan does not eliminate the deceptive power of his lies, for these have spread to other agents. Considering Satan's claim that God's justice eliminates mercy, destroying Satan could appear to reinforce rather than disprove this claim. Additionally, God does not want the universe serving him from fear. Premature destruction could bring about that very state of affairs. Therefore, the timing of the elimination of Satan is linked to the exposure of his lies and a comprehendible vindication of God.[65] Such lies can be completely discredited only when it is shown that all advocates, and especially the chief advocate and epitome of the ideology of lawlessness, are without excuse or justification. Divine wisdom holds off until the great controversy can be resolved without possible doubt or prevarication. With the cosmic controversy settled, the cosmic war is ended. Here the reasons for

63. Of course Boyd has moved to an annihilationist perspective and no longer believes in an eternal hell. This option is no longer available to him.

64. There are many loose ends in Boyd's eschatology and anthropology and we lack the information to really understand his position.

65. White, *Great Controversy* 498–99.

God permitting evil and cosmic war to continue are different to and uncontemplated by Boyd. The Great Controversy theodicy reflects the complexity of politics more than the mechanics of metaphysics. There is a powerful analogical this-worldly plausibility to this argument. Numerous political, philosophical, ideological claims make for appealing ideas that are only realized as bankrupt once they have been demonstrated as failures in practice.[66] The temporal capacity to influence is directly linked to the perception of plausibility. Once an idea is discredited, it loses viability and existence. God does not need to abide by a temporal measure of time (although God is constrained by the conceptual limits of his creatures and the slow-moving contingencies of history). What God needs to do is expose and discredit all elements of Satan's alternative in a way that creation can grasp and accept. Only then will evil's temporal potential evaporate. Satan's temporal capacity is linked to his (multiplication of) lies, not to the natural longevity inherent in his nature or to the simple baseline talent he was originally gifted with (although that talent has greatly contributed to the complexity and time needed in exposing him).

Complicated by Angels

Boyd's position on Satan, freedom, and risk is further complicated by his thoughts about angels. Boyd suggests that there is even now a "certain class of angels whose destiny is not yet resolved for or against God."[67] He implies that angels, who have been given charge over human beings and nations, can still become evil or irresponsible and that this accounts for a lot of suffering and evil.[68] To put this into perspective, Boyd appears to have Satan falling at least 500 million years ago,[69] and yet 500 million years later Boyd implies that some angels are still vulnerable to rebellion. The questions multiply once more, each with the effect of undermining his theodicy project by amplifying the sense of risk gone wrong. How long does it take for an angel to settle their character? If angelic character is not settled after millions of years what hope is it that it ever will be? Why is it that God can still lose angels after such a long period? Has God not been able to counter Satan

---

66. Communism could be an example of this.
67. Boyd, *Satan*, 180.
68. Boyd, *Satan*, 166.
69. Boyd, "Evolution as Cosmic Warfare," 143, fn 38. This allows Boyd to use Satan as an explanation of natural evil—not simply as case-by-case satanic manipulations of nature to cause disastrous events—but as the cause of structural changes to nature's laws.

effectively—even post-incarnation and -cross?[70] One wonders how often different groups of angels have fallen and rebelled. And more worryingly, if there have been multiple falls then how many more will there be? Can God ever get things under control if he has not been able to after 500 million years? These issues are well beyond the issue of the free will defense and are directly related to particulars of Boyd's theodicy.[71] Add to this Boyd's comments (or are these merely rhetorical?) that a cosmic war that has gone on for millions of years so far could potentially go for millions more, and one could be forgiven for wondering whether things seem out of God's control or at least that God has seriously miscalculated the cost of freedom. Can we really imagine millions of more years of the current evil? All of this raises again the size, significance, and problem of the risk in Boyd's theodicy, the very questions an evidential problem of evil-style approach raises. Boyd's open theism adds to this concern. Is God's lack of exhaustive foreknowledge one of the reasons for the length of time?

In contrast, the Great Controversy account offers a significantly different explanation. It argues that God let the angelic rebellion fully develop until all angels made a decision and settled their characters for or against God.[72] There was only one angelic fall. At the same time it does acknowledge that even loyal angels, along with unfallen beings, do not immediately have all of their doubts and questions answered. They are still concerned about Satan's charges against God. God does not ignore creaturely concerns. These unfallen beings are still loyal, and over time have had their loyalty more than confirmed by God's actions in the incarnation, cross, and power of the gospel. The fall of Adam expanded the war to earth where God now deals with the controversy and rebellion. The controversy will continue for a comparatively short period of time (thousands of years rather than millions). God allows things to go on as long as is needed to comprehensively answer all questions in the great controversy in such a way that evil and war will never rise again; that, and no more. God acts to bring agents to a decision either for or against him and thus establishes clear time parameters for probationary time.[73] God's three-phased plan of salvation includes a clear

---

70. Boyd could maintain that Psalms 82 is pre-cross and that post-cross angelic desertion is no longer possible, but I am not aware of him making this argument.

71. The most obvious is Boyd's attempt to incorporate the vast ages of the evolutionary time scale into his theodicy. Boyd must move the fall of Satan back to an extremely long period in the past and account for why God tolerated Satan's rebellion and was not able to end it. The time periods involved put an enormous pressure on his six theses.

72. White, *Selected Messages*, 1958, 1:222.

73. White, *Desire of Ages*, 587. Scripture suggests a pattern of limited periods of probationary time: 120 till the flood, 400 years for the Canaanites, 70 years for the

eschatological mission for the church in which all of the world is brought to a decision for or against God and takes a side on the Great Controversy.[74] This is one of the ways God keeps moving things forward, ensuring that evil is ended and Satan's ideology is defeated. All of this is based on God's wisdom and foreknowledge. This clear eschatology stands in contrast to Boyd's open-ended and uncertain eschatology in two ways. One is in regard to length of time and the other regards how God moves the world to its end. In the Great Controversy theodicy risk is foreseen, embraced, planned for, dealt with, and overcome.

Christology and Risk

The need to reduce risk spills over into Boyd's Christology in an interesting way. The metaphysics of Boyd's cosmic war are so risky that Boyd cannot allow Jesus to be subject to them as creatures are. Boyd makes Jesus an exemplar of some parts of his six theses but exempts him from other elements. In a 2002 article, Bruce Ware argued that consistent open theism would mean that since Jesus possessed libertarian freedom he might not have gone through with the cross and, consequentially, God could not have truly foreknown (on Boyd's open theism understanding of freedom) if Jesus would complete the atonement at the cross.[75] The implication is that God "got lucky," and before the events took place, salvation and the cross were all matters of uncertainty. Boyd's answer is interesting. In order to deny vulnerability to this claim he argues that "Jesus possessed compatibilistic freedom,"[76] not libertarian freedom, which is merely the means to the compatiblistic end. As such, "Christ was humanity *eschatologically defined*"[77] or what humanity is supposed to become. Jesus is the end product of eschatology, but he does not undergo the process to get there. In this way Boyd can argue that "Jesus, being God, was never on probation and hence did not possess libertarian free will (with regard to his openness to God)."[78] Thus, Boyd eliminates the risk of Jesus failing and explains how an Open Theist God could foreknow that Jesus would succeed.

Babylonian exile.

74. White, *Testimonies*, 6:19.

75. Ware, "Defining Evangelicalism's Boundaries Theologically," 193–212.

76. Boyd, "Christian Love and Academic Dialogue," 242.

77. Boyd, "Christian Love and Academic Dialogue." 242. "He [Jesus] was the 'already' entering into the 'not-yet.' He was what we shall be when perfected."

78. Boyd, "Christian Love and Academic Dialogue," 242.

Resolving the foreknowledge problem in this manner opens up new questions and problems for Boyd's Christology and theodicy.[79] Skeptics could ask: If Jesus could come into this world with compatibilist freedom then why can't we all? If Boyd answers it is because Jesus is God (and possesses compatibilist freedom[80]) then doubts are raised about whether Jesus' humanity is really like ours.[81] These nagging questions about the legitimacy of the incarnation go deeper and also call into question Christ's victory in the cosmic war. Scripture implies that Jesus *had* to be made like his brothers in *every respect* and that he had to be able to be tempted like us in every respect.[82] Boyd's position is hard to harmonize with this scriptural testimony. If Jesus did not have libertarian freedom then he is unlike Adam (as originally created) or current fallen humanity. Possessing a compatibilist will that was settled in moral righteousness would mean that Jesus did not face temptation at all, or as any human has. He would have been impeccable from birth. He could never do otherwise. This would mean that having undergone no real battle, he has no real subsequent victory to pass on to humanity. In a cosmic warfare theodicy, this absence of personal warfare and internal struggle with temptation and weakness (which is arguably the most significant and intense element of the war for us) in the experience of the savior is devastating. Jesus in his own humanity never personally engages in the same warfare. His "victory" (or more accurately "invulnerability") is purely a result of his metaphysical being (ontological) and not his own historical, existential overcoming. Jesus is from birth the "end" God is aiming for, but he never goes through the "means" to the end. He is not the means to the divine end. What then is? Our effort? How coherent is it for someone to be the end-goal of a process but who has himself never experienced or undergone that process? How helpful is a Jesus who keeps himself at arm's length from the warfare creatures cannot escape? Wasn't the incarnation so he could for fight for us as one of us? This Jesus is untouchable due to his divinity. His humanity—one can smell the scent of Docetism—is in danger

---

79. See Bruce Ware's questions in response to Boyd's statements in Ware, "Rejoinder to Replies," 255.

80. This seems to imply God is not free.

81. This compatibilism would presumably be due to a set character. Was Jesus then born with a fully formed character? If so, it could only be his divine character, not a humanly developed one. How then is Jesus truly "man"? No human has ever had or could have this. It would make Boyd's Christ analogous to the Jesus of early apocryphal stories who was able to speak from birth. Naturally, all children must learn to speak, and likewise all children must acquire character. Exempting Jesus from this is exempting him from basic humanity.

82. Heb 2:14–18; 4:14–16.

of being an external shell. This is atonement by nature, not by submission, faith, grace, and redemptive achievement.

Here the difference between Boyd and the Great Controversy theodicy is most clearly seen. In stark contrast, the Great Controversy asserts that Jesus assumed a genuine humanity[83] including the risk of failure and eternal loss.[84] It affirms that Jesus was on probation.[85] And that Jesus' temptations were a genuine and frightful reality.[86] This means that Jesus engages in a genuine struggle with temptation and fights Satan in our vulnerable flesh without compatibilistic invulnerability.[87] This means that Jesus' victory over Satan is complete, total (and extraordinary), and transferrable by him to humanity.[88] Jesus can recapitulate his victory in his people by means of his grace both forensically and effectively. It also means that he has effectively, within himself, answered every question in the Great Controversy. It is the enormity of this risk and the magnitude of the victory that makes for an eternity of praise, study, wonder, and exploration. This conflict is not the clash of power (i.e., Jesus' inherently invulnerable will-power versus satanic power as in Boyd's Christology) but the clash of character developed over time, vindicated truth, demonstrated love, and merited grace against evil, lies, temptations, deceptions, hostility, and selfishness. At the central point

---

83. Seventh-day Adventism has had an ongoing debate between those who believe Jesus took something like the human nature of Adam before the fall while others maintain that Jesus took something like the nature of Adam after the fall. The book *Seventh-day Adventists Believe*, 54, offers a semi-official mediating position in which Jesus is unique and his nature bears similarities to Adam's fallen and unfallen conditions.

84. Jesus "came with such a heredity to share our sorrows and temptations, and to give us the example of a sinless life . . . [God] permitted Him to meet life's peril in common with every human soul, to fight the battle as every child of humanity must fight it, at the *risk* of failure and eternal loss." White, *The Desire of Ages*, 49.

85. "He was a free agent, placed on probation, as was Adam, and as is every man." White, "Sacrificed for Us." "For a period of time Christ was on probation." White, "Christ Glorified."

86. White, "Sacrificed for Us." "The temptations to which Christ was subjected were a terrible reality." White, "Against Principalities and Powers." "Had He failed in His test and trial, He would have been disobedient to the voice of God, and the world would have been lost." White, "Christ Glorified."

87. "Many claim that it was impossible for Christ to be overcome by temptation. Then He could not have been placed in Adam's position; He could not have gained the victory that Adam failed to gain. If we have in any sense a more trying conflict than had Christ, then He would not be able to succor us. But our Savior took humanity, with all its liabilities. He took the nature of man, with the possibility of yielding to temptation. We have nothing to bear which He has not endured." White, *Desire of Ages*, 117.

88. White, "In What Shall We Glory?," Through his blood "Jesus has brought moral power to combine with human effort, whereby we may obtain the victory." White, "Compassion for the Erring."

of Jesus our two warfare theodicies take dramatically different turns. Boyd closes off all risk from the person of Jesus, whereas the Great Controversy theodicy affirms the most extreme risk in Christ's overcoming of evil. The reason behind these differences lies in the presence/absence of the idea of cosmic controversy and in different views of foreknowledge. Christ cannot win a controversy or war he himself will not enter. Error can only be overcome by truth, not power. In the Great Controversy theodicy God undertakes a foreknown risk. He sees it ahead in his foreknowledge, and then he accomplishes it through an actual history. It is an accomplishment Jesus must achieve, even if God initially knows he will succeed.[89] In Boyd's theodicy, the profound risk of freedom is experienced by creation but God removes himself from ever experiencing it when he becomes a creature (incarnation). God is an outsider to a risk that he himself allows for others. Such a God could not truly feel the suffering of humanity in the experience of temptation for himself or with humanity.[90] In the Great Controversy, God is the resolver, embracer, and sharer of the risk of creaturely freedom and the suffering that it brings to creatures. God feels most deeply in his divine nature and through Christ's divine-human experience the suffering of temptation and risk. This is a powerful element of theodicy.[91] Here in the issue of Boyd's Christology we see most starkly the combined influence of open theism, a predominantly metaphysical account, and warfare without controversy. The Great Controversy theodicy has a controversy that necessitates Jesus undergoing the radical risks inherent in the incarnation in order

---

89. Concerning Gethsemane, Ellen White has this profound passage: "Satan with his fierce temptations wrung the heart of Jesus. The Saviour could not see through the portals of the tomb. Hope did not present to Him His coming forth from the grave a conqueror, or tell Him of the Father's acceptance of the sacrifice. He feared that sin was so offensive to God that their separation was to be eternal." White, *Desire of Ages*, 753. Christ's psychological experience overwhelmed any foreknowledge. Jesus was literally willing to die eternally for humanity.

90. This weakens Boyd's use of cruciform theodicy. Boyd's Jesus is genuinely vulnerable to physical pain and suffering; however, he is not vulnerable to the pain and struggle involved in resisting temptation.

91. Evil is practical and personal for God. The Great Controversy theodicy has a strong *cruciform theodicy*. "Few give thought to the suffering that sin has caused our Creator. All heaven suffered in Christ's agony; but that suffering did not begin or end with His manifestation in humanity. The cross is a revelation to our dull senses of the pain that, from its very inception, sin has brought to the heart of God. Every departure from the right, every deed of cruelty, every failure of humanity to reach His ideal, brings grief to Him . . . Our world is a vast lazar house, a scene of misery that we dare not allow even our thoughts to dwell upon. Did we realize it as it is, the burden would be too terrible. Yet God feels it all. In order to destroy sin and its results He gave His best Beloved, and He has put it in our power, through co-operation with Him, to bring this scene of misery to an end." White, *Education*, 263–264.

to answer Satan's accusations and vindicate God. In Boyd's cosmic war, God must primarily negotiate metaphysical risk and does so by removing himself (in Jesus' humanity) from the danger by means of the power of an invulnerable will. God has set up a state of affairs in creation that he himself cannot or will not assent to. This seems out of character with the way Boyd understands God but seems necessitated by his open theism.

REINVENTING LIBERTARIAN FREEDOM

This study must wrestle with the tension between the libertarian principle of the power to do otherwise and the need for evil to end. If agents always have the power to choose otherwise then how can their moral state ever solidify? Boyd's response to risk highlights the problem.[92] In order to show how evil will end Boyd switches between models of freedom, from a hard libertarianism to compatibilism.[93] The Great Controversy theodicy also needs to deal with this tension but cannot look to Boyd's failed solution. Unfortunately, the Great Controversy hasn't faced the complexities involved and has no consistent theory of freedom to ground its explanation for why God's historical resolution of the Great Controversy will prevent sin from arising ever again. It is philosophically and theoretically undeveloped. Having a practical workable theory is vital for the plausibility and rational coherence of the Great Controversy theodicy. The next section explores models of libertarian freedom that offer the Great Controversy theodicy a way forward.

Soft Libertarianism

Fortunately, there are versions of libertarian freedom which overcome these deficiencies and can enable the Great Controversy theodicy to work in a coherent, consistent and rational manner. These versions are the "soft libertarianism" of Kenneth Keathley and the "virtue libertarianism" of Dean Zimmerman and Kevin Timpe. Kenneth Keathley[94] offers the following description of soft libertarianism which stands between compatibilism (soft determinism) and hard libertarianism. On Keathley's account, soft

---

92. Boyd's open theism makes this tension even more challenging.

93. "A *hard libertarian* argues that, in order for a person to be genuinely free, he must always have the ability to choose the contrary, or must be free from external influences." Keathley, *Salvation and Sovereignty*, 69.

94. Keathley constructs his version of soft libertarianism from the works of Hugh McCann, *The Works of Agency*; T. O'Conner, *Persons and Causes*; and R. Kane, *The Significance of Free Will*.

libertarianism has five tenets.[95] 1) *Ultimate Responsibility*. This tenet argues that ultimate responsibility is more important for freedom than alternative possibilities. Moral responsibility lies with who or what is the ultimate cause of our choices (in this case the agent and not secondary causes, physical causation, or God's all-determining will). What this means is that agents are responsible for a choice they make if it comes from either conscious deliberation or from undeliberated, automatic, or even determined responses which are due to one's character, where that character is a product of previous freely-made decisions. If our self-chosen character *determines* our response, then, because that character has been freely self-chosen by the agent (and not due to another agent or impersonal forces), that determined choice is one we are responsible for. 2) *Agent Causation*. This is implied in the first tenet. The agent is the cause of their own choices. This is in contrast to event causation in which a choice is the result of a previous chain of events or causes (secondary or primary). Agents can "create new thoughts and actions that have no determinative cause outside of the self"; in other words, agents created in the image of God possess "a little citadel of creativity *ex nihilo*."[96] 3) *The Principles of Alternative Possibilities*. Freedom does require that there is, at least some of the time, the power "to do otherwise." Very importantly this principle is only affirmed once the first two are established and also must be understood in the light of tenets 4 and 5. 4) *The Reality of Will-setting Moments*. It is not always necessary for someone to have the power to do otherwise, but it is necessary for that power to be present during choices that shape and form the moral character of the person. These happen at critical junctures in our lives. Will-setting and self-forming situations, choices, and actions shape who we are. Who we are then shapes what choices we make. This means "the relationship between free choices and character is a two-way street."[97] 5) *The Distinction between Freedom of Responsibility and Freedom of Integrity*. The freedom of responsibility refers to the ability to be faced with choices (and understand them) and be responsible and accountable to respond. The freedom of integrity refers to the ability to do what is right. This is freedom properly functioning and capable. A person may be free in that they have responsibility to do what is right but not be free in that they have lost the ability (or integrity) to do what is right. For example, a drug addict may lose their integrity to resist their addiction but they are still responsible for their actions. Likewise, fallen human beings still possess

---

95. The following five tenets come from Keathley, *Salvation and Sovereignty*, 73–79.

96. Saucy, "Theology of Human Nature," 28, quoted in Keathley, *Salvation and Sovereignty*, 75.

97. Keathley, *Salvation and Sovereignty*, 72.

moral responsibly but lack in themselves the power to fully obey God's law. Together these five tenets make up soft libertarianism. This view affirms the power to do otherwise but only within the larger framework of character setting. Keathley's view maintains that "character determines the range of choices rather than a specific choice itself."[98] A fully developed moral character may 'determine' that someone always chooses what is morally right while not specifying which right choice they must choose. The person's freely chosen character is determining the choice and not another agent (God) or a chain of causal events. This is not compatibilism and theological determinism. Soft libertarianism says that a character could have developed otherwise at least in its initial stages during key will-setting moments. The resultant character may initially influence and eventually determine the way a person chooses but the person is still morally responsible because they freely chose that character over time.

Virtue Libertarianism

A strikingly similar view which also accomplishes what the Great Controversy theodicy needs is the "virtue libertarianism" of Dean Zimmerman[99] and Kevin Timpe.[100] Virtue libertarianism recognizes the two major understandings of libertarian freedom (the "power of self-determination," termed "sourcehood" by Timpe, and the "power to do otherwise" or "alternative possibilities") but also recognizes that they possess an asymmetrical and dynamic relationship. Neither on their own suffices as an adequate definition of libertarian freedom. Most important is the recognition that the "power to do otherwise" must not be absolutized. Virtue Libertarianism argues that freedom is intimately connected to character. Freedom has the goal of moral character (virtue). It is not endless moral indeterminism. Created beings, of necessity, possess morally unformed characters, and, therefore, must initially possess *morally significant freedom* or the power to choose morally otherwise. However, all their choices register, shape and form their character. This still-forming-in-process character then begins to shape their choices. Eventually, a final settled moral character is formed. Freedom attains a fixed particular virtuous (or vicious) character. This fixed character still possesses *morally relevant freedom* (the ability to choose between choices that are in-line with one's settled moral character) even if they can no longer exercise morally significant

---

98. Keathley, *Salvation and Sovereignty*, 70.
99. Zimmerman, "An Anti-Molinist Replies," 176.
100. Timpe, "The Best Thing in Life Is Free," 133–51.

choices against their character.[101] This does not mean that freedom changes from libertarian to compatibilist (with its theological determinism). It is still libertarian with regards to the "power of self-determination." But neither is the freedom, once its character is finally formed and fixed, capable of changing to the opposite moral state. The reason is that the "self" that chooses is now a morally settled or morally self-determined-self.[102] The difference to compatibilism is that this "determination" is freely acquired as a result of the free choices the agent made and not due to another determining agent or the determining of someone's internal state by secondary causes. The self (not nature or God) has freely determined its character[103] and that character now determines the moral quality of the choices of the self. This means a choice, where a person cannot do otherwise due to the settled state of their character, is still morally responsible because their history of free choices is what formed their character. Moral responsibility, a crucial component and argument in favor of libertarian freedom, extends to both free choices *and* freely chosen character. Character is an acquired state and requires freedom. This means that creatures must initially possess but do not need to permanently possess what Plantinga called "morally significant freedom" (i.e., a permanent power to morally do otherwise) which would be tantamount to saying that it is impossible to permanently fix moral character. This may sound to some like compromising the free will defense and saying that moral choices have disappeared for those who possess morally settled characters. It is not. This actually rescues the free will defense from its own limitations. Agents with fully formed virtuous libertarian freedom still possess "morally relevant freedom" even though they have moved beyond the initially formative stage of "morally significant freedom."[104] This means an agent with a freely self-chosen and settled character (e.g., a perfected righteous saint), can face real moral situations but be incapable of choosing evil. They do not want or wish to do evil. This "inability" is not due to a lack of freedom but to freedom reaching its God-ordained goal. Such people are not robots but matured saints.

101. "We define a morally relevant choice as follows: a choice is morally relevant if the person is free to choose among at least two options, and at least two of the options, say, A and B, are related such that either A is better than B or B is better than A." Timpe and Pawl, "Incompatibilism," 414.

102. Theologically, we would add that it is only through the enabling grace of God that a truly morally virtuous character can be formed.

103. An Arminian theology would want to affirm that this "determination" only concerns the will's freedom to receive divine grace rather than its ability to produce moral power. The will's ability is totally dependent on divine grace not self. Divine power is necessary, unmerited, but not irresistible.

104. Morally significant freedom is a subset of morally relevant freedom. Timpe and Pawl, "Incompatibilism," 414.

The difference between the Virtue/Soft Libertarianism advocated here and Boyd's switching between types of freedom is that the "ability to do otherwise" remains a constant in Virtue/Soft libertarianism and is not lost or replaced with compatibilist freedom. Even when the redeemed are morally perfect (or the reprobate are morally irredeemable), their moral choices will not be compatible with God determining their choices. The redeemed will not desire to choose evil but they will freely, by enabling grace, make their own choices. Of course, with characters formed after God's own, and perfected and sustained by grace, there is no need for determinism or coercive interventions. This is just as God would have it. Creatures that are truly like him.

RISK AND THE GREAT CONTROVERSY THEODICY

This discussion of how cosmic warfare theodicies deal with risk has focused on Boyd's view and its comparison to the Great Controversy theodicy. It will now shift to the elements of risk more closely related to the Great Controversy theodicy itself. Most of these are connected to the issue of the plausibility of risk-based explanations. The first four questions are about the emergence of risk. The fifth is about the elimination of risk. The objections are 1) the plausibility of creatures rationally evaluating God, 2) the plausibility of creatures morally evaluating God, 3) the plausibility of finite power contesting divine power, then two related objections, 4) the plausible risk of a good perfect creature (Lucifer) choosing to sin, and, 5) the plausibility of a "risky" genuinely free universe never again falling into sin.

Plausibility of Rationally Evaluating God

The first objection, voiced by Richard Rice, is a philosophical one and concerns the structure of rationality and mental independence. There "is something odd," writes Richard Rice, "about the notion of weighing evidence when it comes to God. How could God be the object of impartial inquiry?"[105] Specifically, how would creatures, "whose minds God has made and upholds, know that God hasn't tampered with their minds?"[106] The problem seems trapped in inescapable circularity, because to "determine *if* God is trustworthy, therefore, we must assume *that* God is trustworthy."[107] In other

---

105. Rice, *Suffering and the Search for Meaning*, 85.
106. Rice, *Suffering and the Search for Meaning*, 85.
107. Rice, *Suffering and the Search for Meaning*, 86.

words, we "must have confidence in the structure of reality and in our cognitive processes."[108] While theoretically valid, on a practical level (and the Great Controversy is a practical-historical response) it could be responded that this objection suffers its own plausibility problem. Did such questions occur or occupy angels? Do they trouble humans? Apparently not. Unless one is consumed by the philosophical and paralysed into inaction, it is hard to see this presenting a practical problem to the Great Controversy theodicy. An urgent moral and practical crisis trumps fine-grained epistemological speculations. We could enquire if it was raised by angels but we could never know. Regardless of this, the Great Controversy theodicy suggests Satan's claims and accusations, and the debates that accompanied it were primarily personal, political, moral, and concrete rather than philosophical, metaphysical, and abstract. This objection is about esoteric philosophical discussions that might forestall but hardly eliminate the more tangible passionate all-or-nothing issues raised in the Great Controversy.

Plausibility of Morally Evaluating God

The second objection is similar but concerned with moral epistemology. It is Rice's query about the idea of creatures morally evaluating God. This is a difficult concept, for "it clearly presupposes some independent standard of goodness by which God is judged, and people will question this for a number of familiar reasons."[109] Rice doesn't develop this thought any further except to indicate in a footnote that he is making reference to what is known as the Euthyphro dilemma.[110] Rice then asserts: "If God is goodness itself, the idea of evaluating God's behavior against some other standard of behavior makes no sense."[111] This philosophical objection is partially accounted for by the previous answer (it is not possible to know if it was argued). But there are other limitations to this objection. While it is true that God is goodness itself—cannot this be questioned? And that is precisely what the Great Controversy claims has happened. The whole point of the Great Controversy is that Satan is denying God's law and character (as the standard of goodness) and is advocating an alternative standard. This objection actually tends to support the Great Controversy theodicy and goes to its very heart. When

108. Rice, "The Great Controversy and the Problem of Evil," 53.
109. Rice, "The Great Controversy and the Problem of Evil," 53.
110. Rice doesn't name it as the Euthyphro dilemma but his statement, "Is something good because God says it is, or does God say it is good because it is?," is a classic formulation of the dilemma.
111. Rice, "The Great Controversy and the Problem of Evil," 55, fn 32.

the ground of goodness is called into question then there is no deeper reality to appeal to. This is also why theoretical or philosophical answers won't resolve the issue. When competing *a priori* presuppositions are at issue, there are no deeper premises to adjudicate between them. There is no neutral place to stand. God knows that only actual experience and demonstration will enable creatures to "know" that his contested truth is the actual truth. The dispute must be tested and settled in the arena of history and not simply in the realm of ideas. According to the Great Controversy, even Satan will admit, although reluctantly and non-repentantly, that he was wrong and God was right. An actual definitive moral answer to all the questions will be achieved.

Plausibility of Finite vs Infinite Power

The third objection raised by Rice concerns the plausibility of a finite creature effectively contesting (and doing so with significant success) its own infinite Creator: "The idea of a superhuman agent whose revolt engulfs the entire universe and poses a genuine threat to God's government seems incoherent in light of traditional concepts of divine power and sovereignty."[112] He asks how could a "creature pose a serious challenge to God?"[113] Couldn't God easily defeat opposition? And conversely, wouldn't any rational and intelligent creature (i.e., Lucifer) clearly understand that it is pointless to stand against God?[114] Who would be so foolish? The Great Controversy theodicy would respond by pointing out that Lucifer's revolt is not based in a clash of power but in a clash of ideas. God's infinite power doesn't settle or address these issues. If anything, divine control and determinism are more likely to confirm Lucifer's claim.[115] A fuller answer becomes more apparent in the response to the next objection.

Plausibility around the Origin of Lucifer's Sin

The fourth objection[116] raises the crucial question of how it is that a perfect being in a perfect habitation could sin in the first place. Is this risk plausible?

---

112. Rice, *Suffering and the Search for Meaning*, 84.

113. Rice, *Suffering and the Search for Meaning*, 84.

114. What could any creature hope to gain from contesting God's supremacy—if they know God can annihilate them? Rice, *Suffering and the Search for Meaning*, 85.

115. The concepts of free will and divine self-limitation further help explain the greater potential of finite power.

116. Rice actually presents the fourth and fifth objection as one objection. I am

John Hick maintains it is a "sheer self-contradiction" that perfect creatures would "inexplicably and inexcusably" rebel against God.[117] To imagine otherwise is to "postulate the self-creation of evil *ex nihilo*."[118] Scott even claims that this is "the Achilles' heel" of the free will defense.[119] This is not the generic problem of evil's origin but the concrete problem of Lucifer. The problem can be expressed in the dilemma that if the reason for sin arising is due to a flaw in Lucifer (his nature, intellect, circumstances, or his faculty of the will—rather than his exercise of it) then either he or his environment was not perfect and ultimately God is to blame. If sin is not due to any such antecedent reasons, conditions or causes, then it is without cause and is irrational. How could it rationally eventuate?[120]

This is a very old theological discussion and not unique to cosmic warfare theodicies, although it is more pressing for them considering how much is built on a Luciferian rebellion. Early Church Fathers and medieval scholars tried to resolve this dilemma. Augustine probed the fall of Lucifer at length. In the end he could not settle on a full solution. Peter King summarises Augustine's reflections: "Why did Lucifer turn his will away from God? There is no cause; he had his reasons, namely, his love of himself, but in the end that is just to say that he turned his *voluntas* to himself rather than God. Primal sin is precisely as explicable as any other action—and precisely as inexplicable as well."[121] As such we must stop with the willed choice and not try and follow an infinite regress of explanations.[122] It remains a mystery.[123] Augustine does not address the issue of whether Lucifer's motives were rational or not and, therefore, whether his account of Lucifer's fall is rationally plausible. After all, only a rational creature could be culpable.[124] This is something that Anselm (1033–1109) understands and pursues. "Anselm wants to show that Lucifer was fully qualified as a moral agent and, therefore, could be held responsible for his primal sin—and justly punished

---

splitting them up because the fourth objection stands alone in its own right.

117. Hick, *Evil and the God of Love*, 250.
118. Hick, *Evil and the God of Love*, 250.
119. Scott, *Pathways in Theodicy*, 90.
120. See Pini, "What Lucifer Wanted," 2.
121. King, "Augustine and Anselm on Angelic Sin," 271.
122. King, "Augustine and Anselm on Angelic Sin," 268–69.
123. The later, more explicitly deterministic Augustine speculated that God gave some angels confirming grace and withheld it from others. This simply puts the blame back on God. See Russell, *Satan*, 213. Hick mistakenly thinks this later Augustinian view is part Luciferian accounts of the fall. Hick, *Evil and the God of Love*, 250.
124. "Augustine had sidestepped the issue of Lucifer's rationality." See King, "Augustine and Anselm on Angelic Sin," 274.

for it."¹²⁵ The ensuing medieval discussions tended to argue along either intellectual or volitional explanations. They hoped to clarify the relationship between intellect and knowledge, on the one hand, and will and desire on the other, and whether sin arose in one or the other. Lucifer's primal sin was "the supreme test case for whether intellectualism implies intellectual determinism and whether voluntarism implies irrationality."¹²⁶ Anselm, Aquinas, Scotus, and many other medieval greats weighed in trying to explain the first sin. Hoffman's conclusion is telling: "Voluntarists and intellectualists inevitably arrive at the same conclusion . . . one cannot explain why he sinned rather than not, or why he sinned but the archangels Gabriel and Michael did not."¹²⁷ The mystery of iniquity or evil remains unsolved. Kevin Timpe traces the intellectualist-voluntarist divide in more recent thinkers and comes to the same conclusion: "It looks then as if a Christian account of primal sin cannot avoid all arbitrariness."¹²⁸ Timpe suggests that most libertarian-inclined Christians will find this arbitrariness unsatisfactory but leaves it open "whether or not this amounts to an insurmountable objection to the philosophical respectability of Christian accounts of free will and sin."¹²⁹

Chapter 3 showed that the Great Controversy theodicy response is, rather strangely, to welcome all this as the central affirmation about evil. The general idea of evil's mystery is not unique to the Great Controversy¹³⁰ but what is unique is the welcome embrace and the use it is put to. It functions as the presupposition necessary to help prevent evil's subversion and confounding of reason. Why the self-creation of evil *ex nihilo* is impossible is never truly substantiated by Hick. It is simply asserted. In fact, the very claim of the Great Controversy is exactly what horrifies Hick. Evil was *ex nihilo*.¹³¹ Not abstractly, but in the specific person of Lucifer. The Great Controversy theodicy meets Hick's assertion with an equal counter-assertion. This may be philosophically confronting and controversial but it alone shifts the discussion to solid ground.¹³²

---

125. "This is Anselm's main innovation over Augustine, and it is quite an original accomplishment, among other things anticipating contemporary decision theory." King, "Augustine and Anselm on Angelic Sin," 274.

126. Hoffman, "Theories of Angelic Sin," 283.

127. Hoffman, "Theories of Angelic Sin," 316.

128. Timpe, "The Arbitrariness of the Primal Sin," 255.

129. Timpe, "The Arbitrariness of the Primal Sin," 256.

130. Surin, *Theology and the Problem of Evil*, 52–54, 162.

131. This is not the creation of evil as a thing (ontology) but the choice that gives it historical existence (volition).

132. Boyd sees evil as mysterious because we cannot epistemologically trace all the

Contrary to Hick's and others', the Great Controversy theodicy maintains that it is foolish to think that the problem of evil can be understood ahistorically or without Satan, as if reason (religious or secular), philosophy, or abstraction were a more direct route to the issue. False conclusions will inevitably come from skeptics or theodicts who ignore this. The only way to avoid saying irrational things about evil is to accept its irrationality as well as its historicity. Analysis of the phenomena of evil is not excluded, just prevented from a kind of self-sabotage. Some evils (pl.) are explainable as events in a history, even if "evil" itself (sing.) is inexplicable. Therefore, narrative and history is a richer way of approaching the problem of evil. Gordon Graham argues against "strategies" that speak of evil as costs versus benefits (greater goods). "What is actually required is an account of evil that acknowledges its ineliminably evil character, and at the same time shows how it can be overcome." He then states, "The elements of this idea lie in the structure of narrative, and it is the power of narrative form . . . that illuminates the deficiencies of the alternative we have been considering."[133] World War I or II is not fruitfully explained via metaphysics or deduction. Why think the problem of evil is different? History, narrative, and politics are a much more appropriate and fruitful means, especially if evil is warfare, even cosmic warfare. The Great Controversy theodicy turns this objection on its head.

The Plausibility of the End of Evil's Risk

The fifth objection is similar to the fourth, only it concerns not the origin but the end of evil.[134] The Great Controversy theodicy claims that evil's risk will be eternally eliminated because so much evidence will amass of God's

---

factors that go into an evil event due to the complexity of creation. "Relocating the mystery of evil is, I believe, one of the most distinct features of the trinitarian warfare theodicy." Boyd, *Satan*, 216. He also points out that "Evil is a mystery, but it is not a mystery concerning Yahweh's character." Boyd, *God at War*, 149.

133. Graham, *Evil and Christian Ethics*, 171. Narrative is "central to many areas of thought and reflection, notably the legal and the moral. In fact . . . narrative can determine moral meaning." Graham, *Evil and Christian Ethics*, 175. (The Great Controversy theodicy is a moral-legal controversy). Narrative transforms how we understand evil. Instead of denying evil, ameliorating it, or counterbalancing it as in a cost-benefit framework (the outcome of greater good approaches like Hick's), evil is seen as "horrible acts in the final raging struggle of an evil intelligence that knows itself to be defeated." See Graham, *Evil and Christian Ethics*, 179.

134. "A further question about the coherence of this luciferous theodicy concerns its concept of a morally secure universe." Rice, "The Great Controversy and the Problem of Evil," 53.

love and evil's absurdity that it can never arise again. Knowledge removes ignorance. Rice raises the objection that "this account seems to shift the premise of rebellion from perversity to ignorance."[135] Here is how Rice frames the dilemma: "If sin is a matter of ignorance, we have a basis for confidence in the ultimate security of the universe, but we cannot explain Lucifer's heavenly revolt. On the other hand, if sin is essentially an act of perversity, then we can identify Lucifer's rebellion, but we have no guarantee that some other being will not make an irrational, wholly unjustified, decision to rebel against God in the future."[136] What makes this difficult is that Lucifer rebelled in the very presence of God with a full knowledge of God's character.[137] He seemed to have the conditions needed to be morally secure. The interesting twist Rice introduces is to frame the end of evil as the mirror of its beginning. Whatever explanation is offered for the beginning will be in tension with what can be claimed at the end. Put in terms of this discussion this is suggesting either evil's "risk" is rational or its "elimination" is, but not both. Is the Great Controversy idea of the mystery of evil too robust a concept? Is it a risk that cannot be eliminated?

A full discussion is beyond the scope of this thesis. A few brief points will have to suffice. First, suggesting that ignorance makes sin more explicable faces its own problems. It is true that originally no unfallen creature would know what evil is. All were "ignorant." But finite creatures are ignorant of many things. That is definitional. If being a creature means limited knowledge, then trust in God in all such areas is axiomatic. Failure to trust God's truth itself is "perverse." Such ignorance can be wilful. Intellect and will are hard to separate. Ignorance does not make evil more explicable. And it is unlikely that a perverse will has no "reasons" (regardless of their truthfulness). Original evil is not the mind then the will falling prey to a deception or seduction. Evil is self-deception and self-seduction. It is the

---

135. "Now, if Lucifer could rebel against God with all that he knew of God's character, how can we be sure that in the future ages no other being will do the same? On the other hand, if enough evidence could prevent someone from sinning why was it Lucifer, of all creatures, who started it?" Rice, "The Great Controversy and the Problem of Evil," 53.

136. Rice, "The Great Controversy and the Problem of Evil," 53. Rice's framing echoes the intellectual versus voluntarist debate, with ignorance versus perversity substituting as the polarities.

137. Rice, "The Great Controversy and the Problem of Evil," 53. Earlier Rice noted that the Great Controversy maintains that Satan and his angels could not be offered salvation because unlike Adam and Eve they rebelled while having a full (obviously not exhaustive) knowledge of God's love and goodness. They were not ignorant. Adam and Eve did not know God in the same way. They had the hope of a full revelation winning them back. Rice, "The Great Controversy and the Problem of Evil," 49.

mind-willing and the willed-thinking of an agent. The horns of the dilemma are vulnerable. Rice's division between ignorance/intellect and perversity/will is too tidy. Second, the emphasis of the Great Controversy lands on the relationship (between God and creation) and especially *character* (the moral state of creation) not on mind or will.[138] Character includes both the mental and moral but is not reducible to one or the other. It is too weak a description to say that knowledge or removal of ignorance is what makes the universe safe. The Great Controversy provides knowledge and wisdom based in experience, demonstration, and history. Against the danger of "perversity," creatures individually and collectively will have freely developed, matured, settled, and perfected *characters*. Central to the overcoming of the mystery of evil is the *mystery of godliness* as "incarnation" (God uniting himself to creation) and "Christ in us" (creation being united to God), as revelation to the angelic and unfallen universe. This is not simply "knowledge," this is a structural change in the divine-creature relationship. More than removal of ignorance lies behind the Great Controversy theodicy solution to evil's mystery. Third, it is not merely the mystery of evil but the mystification of evil (which enables the spread of rebellion) that produced cosmic war. At the end of the Great Controversy, all elements of the mystification are disproven. A mystification could never gain traction again. Hypothetically, even if an individual fall "could" take place again, no cosmic war would eventuate. These reflections do not completely remove the dilemma. But the dilemma is not fatal. At worst, God is free to eliminate a truly recalcitrant creature should one arise. The entire universe knows what evil means. As God justly annihilates sinners at the end of the Great Controversy so he could do so again if needed.[139]

Even if these answers don't fully suffice, the Great Controversy theodicy can fall back on divine foreknowledge. God foreknew that the Great Controversy will be eternally successful. It is likely that no-one can totally eliminate theoretical dilemmas connected to evil's origins or its end. This mystery is the strange, illusive challenge to creation, which can be hedged

138. Hence the need for a clearer conception of libertarian freedom, namely, some form of soft libertarianism or virtue libertarianism.

139. Unsurprisingly, the shift to character as an answer raises a new issue. Why didn't Lucifer form a settled mind/character (as the redeemed will)? It could be that, ironically or paradoxically, in so perfect an environment as heaven, where good character is ubiquitous and externally reinforcement, and thus so little tested, that the process of internally setting character is extremely slow. The will thus retained its morally open significant potential for a lot longer than in our current hothouse environment in which moral options are constantly pressing upon us and compelling swift character formation. In this case Lucifer's character formation was still not settled enough to completely and absolutely preclude the as-yet-unencountered possibility of the mystery of evil.

against but not completely prevented, because it must (and can) be cured against only upon its emergence.

CONCLUSION

By undertaking an internal comparison between Boyd's theodicy and the Great Controversy theodicy we found that cosmic warfare theodicies explain evil as the risk based in free will. Risk accounts for the possibility and continuity of evil, however, it is the size, scope, and ability to end risk that is the crux of a viable cosmic warfare explanation. Cosmic warfare theodicies resolve the problem of evil by how they deal with risk. Boyd offers a bifocal explanation using libertarian freedom (free will defense) within a cosmic war model to deal with risk. Evil is a power conflict arising from and operating within the metaphysical structures of love and freedom. The Great Controversy theodicy has a trifocal explanation for risk, using libertarian freedom (free will defense) within a cosmic war that operates within an additional new layer of cosmic controversy. Evil is a political-ideological conflict made possible because of freedom and love but revolving around God's law. These approaches handle the perils of risk differently. Boyd's libertarian metaphysics (and Open Theist denial of exhaustive definitive foreknowledge) require him to equivocate between models of freedom, and he ends up relying on (the incompatible model of) compatibilist freedom to resolve libertarian risk. This is one of a number of other serious internal tensions in Boyd's attempt to resolve the issue of risk. The Great Controversy theodicy relies on metanarrative instead of metaphysics to resolve the hazards of risk. Victory in a cosmic controversy is not based in metaphysical constraints but in winning the controversy. Nevertheless, the Great Controversy theodicy needs a metaphysical model of freedom that is in harmony with its metanarrative and avoids the equivocation between incompatible models of freedom as seen in Boyd's approach.

This chapter identified Soft or Virtue Libertarianism as models of freedom that the Great Controversy metanarrative could utilize to round out its theodicy. This chapter also looked at objections to the Great Controversy theodicy based in questions about the plausibility of its account of the emergence of evil. It was found that these objections failed to consider elements of the Great Controversy which offer adequate responses so that none of these objections prove fatal.

Chapter 5

Modelling the Great Controversy as a Theodicy

In this chapter, how the Great Controversy theodicy resolves the problem of evil and an outline of the Great Controversy metanarrative as a working theodicy in response to the evidential problem of evil will be put together. How the Great Controversy progressively resolves the wider theodicy issues at issue will be outlined. In so doing, a pattern emerges where solutions to problems are often partial or unsuccessful and uncover new problems which, in turn, require more comprehensive and fuller solutions to arrive at an adequate solution:

Problem 1 > solution 1 = problem 2 > solution 2 = problem 3 > solution 3

The process is not necessarily endless. The endpoint is not a perfect theodicy that can answer all issues and faces no more challenges (impossible when dealing with the vast problem evil presents to us) but to reach a point where solutions stop generating new theory-defeating problems. In dealing with the final problem (problem 3), we will present two different "modelings" of the Great Controversy which show how it can successfully deal with major problems for theodicy. The various modelings presuppose (and hopefully demonstrate) the unity and coherence of the underlying metanarrative. The structure of the argument for chapter 5 is outlined in Table 9:

Table 1: Structure of Argument in Chapter 5

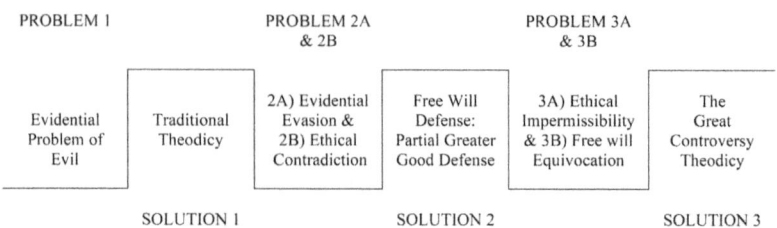

For context, it is helpful to briefly re-cap the initiating challenge of the Evidential Problem of Evil (problem 1), and the response of traditional theodicy (solution 1). The traditional greater good defense is found to be a false start and fails as a solution in two major ways. One is its questionable denial of the reality of gratuitous evil. This external evidential or factual problem of the denial of gratuitous evil will be called the problem of "evidential evasion" (problem 2A). The other more important failure is the fatal ethical contradiction and incoherence in traditional theodicy. Traditional theodicies rely on consequentialist ethics even though theism is ethically deontological. This internal theoretical contradiction between theological and theodicy ethics will be called the "ethical contradiction" problem (problem 2B). Among the most pointed criticisms of traditional theodicies' ethical inconsistencies are those made by anti-theodicy. In response to these criticisms, a free will defense, understood as a "Petersonian" partial greater good defense, offers a promising initial cosmic-warfare-friendly response to the evidential problem (solution 2). This free will response is foundational for the Great Controversy Theodicy, although the Great Controversy goes beyond it. This "solution 2" is partially successful but incomplete and eventually falls short in the face of new objections (problem 3A and 3B). There is a new external evidential problem. While Solution 2 shows that evil can be gratuitous, on its own it struggles to ethically account for *the amount and scale of gratuitous evil*. The question then becomes: Are creation and free will really worth all the evil? This is a version of Boyd's "worth it" question. This will be called the "ethical impermissibility" problem (problem 3A). The other problem is a new internal theoretical problem. The idea of libertarian freedom can account for the "fact of evil" in terms of its origins and initial permission but not for the continuation of evil mentioned above (i.e., scale of evil) nor more importantly for the end of evil. This is a version of Boyd's "win it" question. Boyd attempted to resolve this problem by equivocating between different models of freedom, one model of freedom to explain the origin of evil and a different one to explain its end. This internal theoretical problem will be called the "Free will equivocation" problem (problem 3B). It involves arbitrarily switching between models of freedom in order to answer the "win it" question. The Great Controversy theodicy (solution 3) will be shown to resolve problems 3A/3B.

PROBLEM 1 (EVIDENTIAL PROBLEM OF EVIL) AND SOLUTION 1 (TRADITIONAL THEODICY)

In Chapter 1 it was shown how the evidential argument frames the problem of evil trilemma in such a way that theists are faced with the hard choice between a strongly "evident" factual premise (gratuitous evil exists) or the widely held theological premise (an omni-God only providentially permits evil for a greater good). One can affirm either reality but one cannot affirm both. What gives this argument power is that both premises seem obvious to the theist and skeptic. Theists have typically accepted the way antitheists have framed the evidential argument and offer a range of greater goods (free will, soul-making, higher harmony, natural order, divine glory etc.) as explanations for evil.

Formulating Theodicies: The Full Greater Good Defense (Solution 1)

These various greater goods detail the *parts* of a traditional theodicy and *what* makes them work. But this study is interested to see *how* they work. To do this theodicies will be formulated below. All of these greater goods are expressions of the *full greater good defense*.[1] This means the greater goods are *subsequent* to the evil (GGSUB), that is, the evil is necessary to achieving the greater goods. The evil is the means to the good.

$$\text{Evil/Suffering }_{(NECESSARY)} \longrightarrow \text{Greater Good }_{SUBSEQUENT}$$
or
$$\text{Evil }_{(NEC)} \longrightarrow GG_{SUB}$$

A good example is John Hick's soul-making theodicy. His entire theodicy is teleological in structure. The greater good end is what justifies the evils in the often-harrowing soul-making process. Evil and suffering are the means to the end but they are outweighed by the good of the end.

$$\text{Evil/Suffering }_{(NECESSARY)} \longrightarrow GG_{SUBSEQUENT\ (E.G.\ SOUL\text{-}MAKING)}$$
or
$$\text{Evil }_{(NEC)} \longrightarrow GG_{SUB\ (S\text{-}M)}$$

---

1. See chapter 1 for a comparison between full and partial greater good defenses.

However, because of dysteleological evils (evil or suffering that is soul-crushing) this theodicy, as it stands, does not work. Evil is clearly not outweighed in many cases. To rescue the justificatory pattern of soul-making, Hick needs to add another eschatological element—an afterlife with further opportunity in the form of the doctrine of "universalism." This ensures that everyone eventually perfects their soul and that any evil experienced along the way is finally outweighed and compensated. Thus, Hick's theodicy works as follows:

$$\text{Evil}_{(NEC)} \longrightarrow \text{GG}_{SUB\,(S\text{-}M)} + \text{Universalism}$$

Felix Culpa is another classic greater good defense.[2] Plantinga's felix culpa was examined earlier. In Plantinga's version libertarian free will provides the occasion for the fall. However, it is the fall into evil itself and not free will that brings about and necessitates the greater good of incarnation and atonement.[3] Free will could have continued without sin and thus without atonement. That is why free will is not included in the formulation. Free will is present, along with many other factors (e.g., Molinism, allusions to Satan, Natural Order), in Plantinga's description. For felix culpa to work one could even utilize a compatibilist account of freedom to account for the evil. Indeed, the Calvinist versions of Jonathan Edwards's and Paul Helm's do exactly that. Plantinga's version looks like this:

$$\text{Evil/Felix Culpa}_{(NECESSARY)} \longrightarrow \text{GG}_{SUBSEQUENT\,(E.G.\ INCARNATION/ATONEMENT)}$$
or
$$\text{Evil/FC}_{(NEC)} \longrightarrow \text{GG}_{SUB\,(INC/AT)}$$

Calvin's and Edwards's versions of felix culpa keep the same basic greater good structure but also differ from versions like Plantinga's and Milton's.[4] The greater good is defined more broadly as the divine glory revealed and manifested to creation. This goes beyond the incarnation and atonement to include the necessity of a display of justice, wrath, and eternal punishment

---

2. Felix culpa advocates include John Milton, Gottfried Leibnitz, John Hick, and Paul Helm. Diller, "Are Sin and Evil Necessary," 87–88.

3. "This theodicy, then, like all greater good theodicies, purports to show why all evils are necessary to a greater good that God aims to achieve." Peterson, "Christian Theism and the Evidential Argument from Evil," 184. Peterson points out that sin/evil is not necessary to the great good of incarnation but only to that of atonement. Diller, "Are Sin and Evil Necessary," 184–85.

4. With free will Plantinga and Milton are libertarians while Edwards and Helm are compatibilist.

in hell. The (Calvinistic/Edwardian) divine glory defense (DGD), in effect an expanded felix culpa, looks like this:

$$\text{Evil}_{\text{(NECESSARY)}} \longrightarrow \text{GG}_{\text{SUBSEQUENT (E.G. FULL DISPLAY OF GOD'S ATTRIBUTES)}}$$
$$\text{or} \quad \text{Evil}_{\text{(NEC)}} \longrightarrow \text{GG}_{\text{SUB (DGD)}}$$

Common to all these full greater good theodicies is the necessitating of evil. Evil and suffering have instrumental value and purpose in being the necessary means to the greater good. Evil is never gratuitous. God's meticulous providence ensures all evils serve a good purpose. What ultimately justifies everything is the outcome. The greater good outweighs evil. These are all teleological in shape.[5]

THE PROBLEMS OF EVIDENTIAL EVASION (PROBLEM 2A) AND ETHICAL CONTRADICTION (PROBLEM 2B)

These traditional greater good theodicy solutions (solution 1) have two major problems (problem 2A & B). These are the external problem of "evidential evasion" (problem 2A), and the internal problem of "ethical contradiction" (problem 2B). The first problem is a non-fatal but very unsatisfying response while the second is more serious and reveals a fatal contradiction. Problem 2A of "evidential evasion" will first be considered. This evidential evasion is the observation that greater good attempts to explain evil end up "evading" the reality of gratuitous evil. The evidence for gratuitous evil appears axiomatic, while the evidence that all evils (including gratuitous evils) work to a greater good is elusive and lacking. Theism admits as much by appealing to skeptical theism and claiming that while it cannot show a greater good for such evils, nevertheless no-one can claim that there are not other unknown/unknowable greater goods which could explain this. At best this creates a frustrating intellectual deadlock in which theism is unable to show from reality that the evidence supports its position, but it is still able to insulate this failure from acting as a decisive disproof or disconfirmation of its position by means of skeptical theism. The debate ends up inconclusive but weighted in the skeptic's favor. Considering the evidential problem of evil is an inductive argument from evidence in terms of plausibility and probability and not about proof, this is a telling undermining of the theist

---

5. Some modern theists add skeptical theism to their greater good theodicies. Evil is necessary for general and specific greater good, but what the actual specific greater good is that justifies a particular evil is unknown to us. And, being limited finite beings, we have no reason to think that we can necessarily know what it may be.

position.⁶ The evidential problem of evil appears to be sustained to the degree that the factual affirmation of gratuitous evil is more likely than not to be true.⁷ The restricted theism of the evidential problem of evil seems to fail the correspondence test⁸ only to escape or "evade" this total theory failure via unknown/unknowable greater goods of skeptical theism. This is a Pyrrhic kind of victory.⁹

Formulating the Partial-Greater Good Defense (Solution 2A)

Theism requires a different approach. Help comes by recalling the distinction already made between two different versions of the greater good approach in chapter 1. Traditional theodicies, outlined above, use the full-greater good defense. This is what most people think of when they use the term "greater good." Following Michael Peterson's work the alternative partial-greater good defense was identified. This approach marks a genuine break with traditional theodicies. These two approaches are opposites. In the full-greater good defense, the greater good is *subsequent* to evil (GG-SUB). In the partial-greater good defense, the greater good is *antecedent* to the evil (GGANTE). As such, this good is good, in and of itself, and does not require the evil. Its connection to evil is indirect, it only gives rise to the possibility of evil or arises simultaneously with the evil, without causing or necessitating the evil. Evil may, therefore, be gratuitous. The reality and substantial evidence for gratuitous evil is not denied. There is no need for

---

6. William Rowe highlights the strain skeptical theism puts on the credibility of theism. He notes that if "human and animal life on earth were *nothing more than a series of agonizing moments from birth to death*, my friends' [Daniel Howard-Synder and Michael Bergmann] position would still require them to say that we cannot reasonably infer that it is even likely that God does not exist . . . [but] surely there must be some point at which the appalling agony of human and animal existence on earth would render it unlikely that God exists." Rowe, "Is Evil Evidence against Belief in God?" 26. Rowe believes the current amount of evil is at that point.

7. Hence some theists engage in the "Moore Switch." This strategy admits evil invalidates belief in God but other Christian evidences turn the argument back in favour of belief. Johnson, "Calvinism and the Problem of Evil: A Map of the Territory," 51. Here theism survives despite its theodicy! A theodicy able to affirm the evidence for gratuitous evil is preferable.

8. On the "Correspondence Theory of Truth" see Craig and Moreland, *Philosophical Foundations*, 135–42.

9. Michael Peterson objects to the apparent moral implications of skeptical theism where we "literally have no idea whatsoever whether the life of Mother Teresa was better or worse on the whole, and made a better or worse contribution to the goodness of the world overall, than the life of Saddam Hussein." See Peterson, "Christian Theism and the Evidential Argument from Evil," 186.

evil to be explained by reference to God's ordaining, willing, or necessitating it. The partial-greater good defense understanding of free will (solution 2A) is what the Great Controversy presupposes, and resolves problem 2A.[10] There is a risk that comes with free will and that risk is the possibility of evil, including gratuitous evil.[11] This can be formulated as:

$$GG_{ANTECEDENT\ (E.G.\ FREE\ WILL)} \longrightarrow Evil_{(RISK)}$$
$$or \quad GG_{ANTE\ (FW)} \longrightarrow Evil_{(RISK)}$$

A Petersonian partial-greater good defense version of the free will defense (solution 2A) thus successfully deals with the problem of "evidential evasion" (problem 2A). Gratuitous evil is part of the risk that attends the greater good of creatures who have free will. There is no need to evade the evidence for gratuitous evil because the factual premise of the evidential argument from evil is not denied. In fact, if evil arises, gratuity is to be expected. This is accomplished by modifying the theological premise of the evidential argument, from a God of the absolute exercise of omnipotence in meticulous providence and control of all events, to that of a self-limited omnipotence engaging in general providence.[12]

ANTI-THEODICY AND THE PROBLEM OF ETHICAL CONTRADICTION (PROBLEM 2B)

More challenging than the issue of evidential evasion is the problem of ethical contradiction (problem 2B). Anti-theodicy brings out this problem.

10. Not all uses of free will in theodicy are partial-greater good defenses. Plantinga's felix culpa theodicy uses free will but in a full greater good defense. This is in contrast to his free will defense. Diller therefore asks which Plantinga is right: "In a free will theodicy it is the permission of evil that is essential to the greater good that God intends, in the felix culpa theodicy it is the evil itself that is essential to the greater good. Evil is made reasonable as a functional good." Diller, "Are Sin and Evil Necessary," 95–96.

11. While free will is a clear example of a partial-greater good, there are few other contenders for this category of partial-greater goods. Other possible contenders are John Feinberg's "Integrity of Humans Defense." See chapter 6 of Feinberg, *The Many Faces of Evil*. Another is Shenk, *The Wonder of the Cross*. Interestingly, both are theologically deterministic.

12. Peterson has long argued that the strength of the factual premise should motivate theologians to revisit the theological premise of meticulous providence. The reason being is that "[A]s long as the principle of Meticulous Providence is accepted, responses to the evidential argument will be driven in the predictable directions of either Skeptial Theist Defense or Greater Good Theodicy, neither of which are prepared to admit that the world would have been better without the evil in question." Peterson, "Christian Theism and the Evidential Argument from Evil," 187.

Toby Betenson outlines six major moral objections anti-theodicy has with traditional theodicies.[13] They are that 1) "Theodicy demonstrates a stark moral insensitivity"[14]; 2) "Theodicy adopts too detached a perspective"[15]; 3) "Theodicy exhibits an irremissible moral blindness"[16]; 4) "Theodicy uses the wrong moral theory"; 5) "Theodicy treats people as mere means, not ends in themselves"; and 6) "Theodicy adds to the evils of the world."[17] This studies chief interest is in the fact that all of these objections share a basic foundational objection that cannot be ignored and which this analysis reveals is a problem endemic to traditional theodicy. The root objection that drives anti-theodicy and calls greater good theodicies into question is revealed in objections 4 and 5. It is the problem of ethics for theodicy. Betenson's fourth objection is that "Theodicy uses the wrong moral theory." Theodicy seems to work off an "unrestricted utilitarianism"[18] and instrumentalist approach to evil.[19] Evil is the instrumental means to achieving the good. What matters is the outcome or consequence. This violates the deontological principle in Romans 3:8 of not doing evil so that good may come. When this moral theory is applied to people it becomes the fifth objection where "theodicy treats people as mere means, not ends in themselves." This is violating a basic principle that people have value in and of themselves and should not

---

13. Betenson's claims should not go unchallenged. Some of his points are overstated or do not apply universally to all theodicies, even traditional ones. We addressed some responses to anti-theodicy in the first chapter and found that anti-theodicy is not always entirely convincing and has its own limitations.

14. The moral insensitivity is in how it downplays horrific suffering and evil as something that can be outweighed by a greater good or when explaining its necessity it is compared to minor suffering (like going to the dentist). In this way evil/suffering is trivialized. Betenson, "Anti-Theodicy," 57.

15. "There is something monstrous about an utterly objective and impersonal moral machine, calculating the costs of innocent suffering against the benefits of greater goods." Betenson, "Anti-Theodicy," 58. The purely dispassionate/abstract theorising of theodicies is troubling.

16. Anti-theodicy objects to the idea that we should be "open-minded about the possibility that horrendous evils, such as the holocaust, could be justified by appeals to greater goods" because to do so is to fail to acknowledge the reality of suffering and evil and to fail to lend a voice to the cries of the innocent sufferers (hence "irremissible moral blindness"). Betenson quotes Surin (who is paraphrasing Adorno): to be "open-minded when confronted with these morally surd realities is to have lost any possible accordance with the truth." Betenson, "Anti-Theodicy," 59.

17. Betenson argues that the previous five points reveal morally bad practice, and in so doing they add to the evil in the world. Additionally, theoretical detachment may render one oblivious to the constant need to counteract evil. Betenson, "Anti-Theodicy," 62. And, if everything serves a good end then why intervene to stop evil?

18. Betenson, "Anti-Theodicy," 60.

19. Betenson, "Anti-Theodicy," 61.

be used to another's ends.[20] Building on the problem that theodicy uses the wrong moral theory, Betenson outlines a dilemma that gets to the heart of the problems for traditional theodicy. He formulates the following argument (Betenson uses Hick's Soul-making theodicy as his example):

1. If traditional theistic ethics is true, then consequentialism is false.
2. If traditional theodicies (such as the "Soul-Making Theodicy") are true, then consequentialism is true.
3. Therefore, either the traditional theistic ethics is false, or traditional theodicies are false.[21]

Theology and theodicy are in ethical conflict. This is the problem of "ethical contradiction" (problem 2B). Christian theism is ethically non-consequentialist or deontological.[22] Theodicy is consequentialist. Betenson states that "My dilemma forces these theists to resolve this inconsistency; either abandon consequentialist theodicies, or abandon non-consequentialist ethics, you cannot have both."[23] Which way should the theist go? What this dilemma does do is undermine the option of skeptical theism. Even if there is an outweighing greater good that requires evil, this would not be permissible because the ethical reasoning behind the theodicy is theologically suspect. There is nothing for skeptical theism to rescue. "Clearly, there are two very obvious ways we can resolve this dilemma: reject consequentialist theodicies, or reject traditional theistic ethics."[24] His closing comments in his *Philosophical Compass* article are damning. Theodicies must make it that evil is not fundamentally at odds with belief in God. "Yet, in responding to

---

20. This problem was more evident in theodicies of the past. Betenson notes the more recent "patient-centered" approaches of Eleonore Stump and Marilyn Adams in which any goods that justify suffering must be a benefit for the sufferer. Betenson, "Anti-Theodicy," 61. Even so, Betenson faults them for retaining a "consequentialist justification via compensation." Betenson, "Anti-Theodicy," 61.

21. Betenson, "The Problem of Evil as a Moral Objection to Theism," 71.

22. For evidence that Christian theistic ethics are non-consequentialist and deontological, see McNaughton, "Is God (almost) a Consequentialist?," 265–81; Chappell, "Why God Is Not a Consequentialist," 239–43. See also Craig and Moreland, *Philosophical Foundations*, 446–59, Christian ethics are either deontological or virtue ethics; Craig and Moreland, *Philosophical Foundations*, 458. Shenk argues that Boyd's warfare theodicy is deontological: see *The Wonder of the Cross*, 105. Adventism is deontological; see, Kis, "Christian Lifestyle and Behavior," 675.

23. Betenson, "The Problem of Evil as a Moral Objection to Theism," 71.

24. Betenson, "The Problem of Evil as a Moral Objection to Theism," 83. Betenson ventures that "I suspect the former is the better option, but I will not argue for this here." He then adds that "this is the response of the 'moral anti-theodicists.'" The Great Controversy theodicy would agree with anti-theodists.

the problem of evil by constructing a justification of God's permission of terrible evil, theodicies think the morally unthinkable, they sanction the unsanctionable, they justify the unjustifiable; theodicies render "ok" what should not be rendered "ok." In short, "Theodicies mediate a praxis that sanctions evil."[25] Betenson makes a good point but illogically overstates things while doing it. The problem with the ethical contradiction between theism and traditional theodicy is not that evil is fundamentally at odds with belief in God, as if all belief in God and all theodicies are vulnerable to his analysis and succumb to the problem he highlights. The problem is that the existence of evil is fundamentally at odds with particular theodicies and particular beliefs about God, specifically those in which God's action of permission is based on requiring and necessitating evil to produce good. It is those specific theodicies that justify the unjustifiable. Free will theodicies and cosmic warfare theodicies, for example, possess a different belief about God and his permission of evil and thus a different theodicy which may not be vulnerable to this problem.[26] What is clear is that a new solution is needed that that avoids the fatal "cold" of the evidential problem of evil or the fatal "cure" of consequentialism theodicies.

Resolving Ethical Contradiction through the Doctrine of Double Effect (Solution 2B)

Deontological theism needs a theodicy that is ethically consistent to avoid the ethical contradiction. The partial-greater good defense version of the free will defense resolves the problem of evidential evasion and also goes a long way to resolving this problem of ethical contradiction (Problem 2B). To demonstrate this, use will be made of the ethical concept of the "Doctrine of Double Effect" (DDE). This will prove important for articulating the way the Great Controversy theodicy resolves the problem of evil.[27] The DDE

---

25. Betenson, "Anti-Theodicy," 64. The last quote is taken from Trakakis, *The End of Philosophy of Religion*, 28–29.

26. Diller notes the comparison between free will and felix culpa defenses. "Unlike a free will theodicy, in a Felix Culpa theodicy God desires evil as a means to his good purposes. This move has a dangerously distorting moral and theological impact." Diller, "Are Sin and Evil Necessary," 96. The moral distortion is implying that God is functionally equivalent to a utilitarian or moral consequentialist. Diller also asks, "Moreover, should we not resist a theodicy which would attempt to explain the source of the evil in a way that would make the emergence of evil rational or sensible." Diller, "Are Sin and Evil Necessary," 96.

27. Maintaining deontologically consistent reasoning is crucial to the success and viability of the Great Controversy theodicy.

refers to a form of deontological ethical reasoning undertaken by a moral agent when faced with a moral dilemma. The doctrine or principle aims to show that "it is permissible to cause a harm as a side effect (or 'double effect') of bringing about a good result even though it would not be permissible to cause such a harm as a means to bringing about the same good end."[28] DDE is a valuable instrument and principle of moral reasoning that is common in discussions of medical and military ethics but also applies in other areas.[29] The principle is not uncontroversial but enjoys widespread appeal and use.[30] It should be noted that the assumption in this discussion is not that God is subject to the DDE in a way that creatures are, but that as a deontological principle, DDE is consistent with the God who is the source of right and wrong.[31] The DDE serves to show God's moral and rational consistency and this vindicates his actions. His actions align with the best moral reasoning which itself aligns with God's character. The Great Controversy theodicy (a partial-greater good defense) demonstrates this truth. The DDE is not so much a singular principle as a series of moral conditions that must be upheld in a moral dilemma where harm or evil may result from our actions. The four conditions are:

1. The act itself must be morally good (or at least indifferent).
2. The agent must not positively intend the bad effect.[32]
3. The good effect must be produced directly by the action, not by the bad effect (the evil must not be the means of the good).[33]

28. McIntyre, "Doctrine of Double Effect."

29. The first clear, explicit appearance of DDE is in Thomas Aquinas's discussion about self defense, in which he says that it is permissible to harm a person in self-defense because harming the person is not the goal, it is a side effect of the effort to protect oneself. Aquinas, *Summa Theologica* (II-II, Qu. 64, Art.7)

30. David Oderberg notes that the DDE is, despite criticisms and difficulties, "a keystone of sound moral thinking" without which much ethical reasoning "would remain nothing but a high ideal with little consistent applicability." Oderberg, "The Doctrine of Double Effect," 324. Everyday examples include whether to drive a car knowing it causes pollution or whether a doctor should give an antibiotic knowing that it will cause a rash, etc.

31. We are not arguing that God has moral obligations to something outside himself. God is simply true to himself. For a discussion of various issues such as the ethics of divine obligation, the Euthyphro Dilemma, etc, see Evans, *The Problem of Evil*, 133–96.

32. "If 'avoiding evil' means anything, it means, first and foremost, that one may never intend evil, whether as means or as end. One may, however, *permit* or *tolerate* it." Oderberg, "The Doctrine of Double Effect," 326–27.

33. The conditions, DDE2 and DDE3, rule out evil as means or ends "A plausible presumption in action theory is that he who wills the end also wills the means." Oderberg, "The Doctrine of Double Effect," 326. With DDE3 a person "must, at most, only

4. The good effect must be sufficiently desirable to compensate for the bad effect.[34]

These will be referred to as *DDE1* or "Lawful condition," *DDE2* or "Intention condition," *DDE3* or "Means/Ends condition," and *DDE4* or the "Proportionate condition." There are a number of well-known scenarios in the literature illustrating the exercise of the DDE. A doctor who opposes abortion may, nevertheless, believe it permissible to allow an abortion to occur in the case of a pregnant women who needs to have a hysterectomy in order to remove an immediate life-threatening cancer.[35] The goal is not the abortion, although it will occur due to pursuing the intended goal of saving the mother's life. Another common scenario is that of administering pain relief drugs to terminally ill patients which may have the side effect of hastening death. One does not intend the hastening of death, rather only the relief of pain. Many other examples are drawn from medical and military situations.[36] Other much-discussed scenarios include sacrificing one's life to save others versus suicide,[37] and killing in self-defense versus the pre-emptive killing of someone who intends to kill you.[38]

In order for an act to qualify as permissible, the action must not violate any of the DDE conditions. The first three conditions are clear deontological principles. The last condition could be (mis)read as a consequentialist principle but needs to be understood deontologically.[39] A consequentialist reading would misunderstand the DDE principle as seeing the outcome as solely justifying the action. This would in fact render the first three conditions unnecessary. On the proper deontological understanding, DDE4 only comes into play when the other conditions have been satisfied. In other

---

foresee that he will or may cause (or allow) the evil effect." Oderberg, "The Doctrine of Double Effect," 327.

34. For other articulations of the DDE see the *New Catholic Encyclopedia*, 1021; Sulmasy, "The Use and Abuse of the Principle of Double Effect," 87.

35. In carrying out the hysterectomy, the doctor would aim to save the woman's life while merely foreseeing the death of the fetus. Performing an abortion, by contrast, would involve intending to kill the fetus as a means to saving the mother. McIntyre, "Doctrine of Double Effect."

36. See the distinction between the strategic (or tactical) bomber versus the terror bomber in Oderberg, "The Doctrine of Double Effect," 326.

37. McIntyre, "Doctrine of Double Effect."

38. McIntyre, "Doctrine of Double Effect."

39. The DDE4 condition can be mistakenly read as "disguised consequentialist judgment" but the "clause in no way requires one to compare good and bad states of affairs in order to judge the overall balance of good over evil. All it says is that there must be a proportionate reason for causing the evil effect." Oderberg, "The Doctrine of Double Effect," 327.

words, no moral wrong in itself is being committed by taking the action but the action still has consequences. This leads to the question: is this morally allowable action also a permissible action, given there is a serious unintended side effect? One can only evaluate this by looking to see if the goods it produces are sufficiently proportionate to the harm or evil that eventuates as a by-product of the action. On this understanding of the fourth condition, the outcome itself does not justify the action or nullify the first three conditions, but it may serve to confirm its permissibility or prohibit its occurrence.[40] The prohibition may be due to the lack of value or worth or gain or likelihood of the good. In this way, the proportionality condition functions in a manner subsidiary to the deontological. The good gained by the action may be trivial and minor in comparison to the harm it produces and thus impermissible. Consequences don't in themselves determine right or wrong, but they may serve to reveal the wisdom or worth of an action.[41]

Use of the Doctrine of Double Effect (DDE)

The applicability of the DDE to theodicy has been noted by others, although it is surprising that there has not been greater use made of it. Examples of explicit reference to the DDE in theodicy discussions include Porkoli's and Haj'jari's suggestion that Milton uses double-effect reasoning in his theodicy of *Paradise Lost*.[42] Jeremy Evans, referencing Bruce Reichenbach's Natural Law theodicy, says that "there is a double effect from human participation in a lawlike natural order."[43] In mind here are the natural evils which people suffer from (examples given include diseases, sickness, disasters, birth defects, as well as the fact that the fire which helps us cook can also burn us) which are the results of the natural order we are part of. Evans quotes Reichenbach as saying that these "are the by-products made possible by that which is necessary for the greater good."[44] It appears in Peter Byrne's

---

40. "But DDE is first and foremost a doctrine about what we *may* do, in other words it is a doctrine of permissibility." Oderberg, "The Doctrine of Double Effect," 327. We can make further decisions within that sphere of permissibility, we may do either what is advised or what is admirable. We may "take a more elevated course of action than simply doing what we are allowed." Oderberg, "The Doctrine of Double Effect," 327. But all of these decisions are only made if something is permissible.

41. "For a consequentialist, all that matters is the weighing of out-comes. For the defender of DDE, *what matters is the relative importance of the reasons* for taking a proposed course of action." Oderberg, "The Doctrine of Double Effect," 327. Italics mine.

42. Porkoli and Haj'jari, "Double-Effect Reasoning in Paradise Lost," 18.

43. Evans, *The Problem of Evil*, 11.

44. Reichenbach, *Evil and a Good God*, 101.

discussion and critique of Paul Helm's deterministic-style theodicy.⁴⁵ Gwen Griffith-Dickson includes it in her discussion of the problem of evil and her referencing of Trau's free will defense. She states that theodicy issues "can be considered with the doctrine of 'double effect.'"⁴⁶ The DDE has been used by Alexander Pruss and Heath White to alleviate the challenges theological determinism has in dealing with the problem of evil. Their discussion will be returned to later.⁴⁷

Applying the Doctrine of Double Effect (DDE)

This study will now apply the DDE to theodicies. Doing so clarifies a number of things. It provides deontological proponents a structured way of evaluating the ethical permissibility/impermissibility of their own theodicies and also of other theodicies. It serves to show that there are a class of theodicies that make the same criticisms that Anti-theodicy makes of traditional theodicy, without falling prey to the same criticism. These deontologically consistent theodicies resolve the problem of ethical contradiction (this includes the free will defense structure of the Great Controversy theodicy). If Hick's soul-making theodicy is taken as an example (see Table 10), it can be seen that under a DDE analysis his theodicy violates multiple conditions. It might pass DDE1 (God acts to create a soul-making environment). But it violates DDE2 and especially DDE3, as God positively intends that suffering and evil will take place (contra DDE2) and they function as the means to bring about soul-making (contra DDE3).⁴⁸ Soul-making also spectacularly fails DDE4 in the form of dysteleological evils where many souls are crushed rather than made. To counterbalance this, Hick opts for souls having additional chances for soul-making in the afterlife and asserts the heterodox doctrine of universalism. Both of these are theologically problematic. Regardless of this, given that DDE2 and 3 are violated, the action is ethically impermissible. And because this is a deontological ethical construct, simply overweighing the evil by good consequences does not justify intending the evil.

Table 10: Hick's Soul-Making Theodicy and the Doctrine of Double Effect

---

45. Byrne, "Helm's God and the Authorship of Sin," 193–204.

46. Griffith-Dickson, *The Philosophy of Religion*, 326–27. J M Trau has also published under the name J M Zwerner.

47. White, "Theological Determinism and the 'Authoring Sin' Objection," 78–95; Pruss, "The First Sin: A Dilemma for Christian Determinists," 187–99.

48. Note: Violations of DDE1–4 are underlined and bolded in italics in the diagrams.

Plantinga's felix culpa fails in a similar manner (Table 11). The action of God creating a world in order to produce incarnation and atonement necessitates God not only ensuring evil arises (contra DDE2) but also that the evil is the means to the production of the greater good (contra DDE3).

Table 11: Plantinga's Felix Culpa Theodicy and the Doctrine of Double Effect

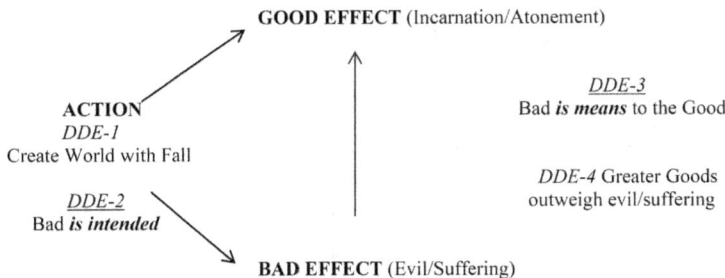

The divine glory defense (Table 12), like felix culpa, violates DDE2 and 3. God appears to need evil and the reprobate in order to accomplish his ends. God intends the fall and evil (DDE2). The good effect is completely dependent on the evil. Divine glory defense determinism also strengthens this evaluation. One could also argue that DDE4 is also violated in regards to the wicked.

Table 12: The Divine Glory Defense and the Doctrine of Double Effect

The DDE and the Free Will Defense

If the free will defense is foundational for the Great Controversy theodicy, then the use of the partial-greater good defense version makes a significant difference when evaluated by the DDE (see Table 13). The divine action is good (DDE1). Evil is not intended, although it is foreseen as a risk, and the risk is permitted (DDE2). It is important to note that it is only the risk of evil, and not evil itself, which is the double effect. This is very significant, as critics of the DDE sometimes raise the objection that intention and foresight are too close together to be separated. In this criticism, DDE2 is collapsed into DDE3 with foreseen effects counting as intended means. DDE proponents reject this. However, even if this criticism was accepted, the most that can be said is that God intended the *risk* of evil, not the evil itself, although he foresaw the emergence of evil. God foresaw that a responsible, accountable free will agent caused and intended evil. This act cannot be traced to God's action, intention, or causation, only his permission.

Table 13: The Free Will Defense and the Doctrine of Double Effect

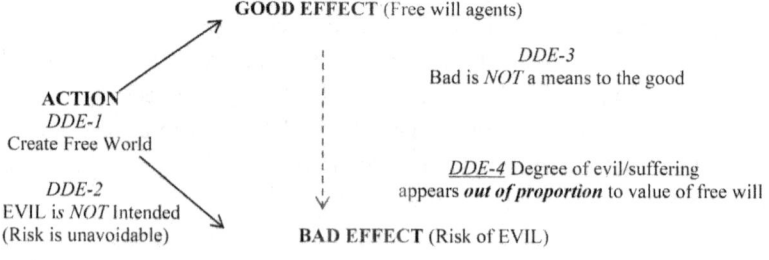

THE PROBLEM OF ETHICAL PERMISSIBILITY (PROBLEM 3A). IS CREATION WORTH IT?

The DDE has its own dual effect. It shows that a partial-greater good defense version of the free will defense avoids ethical contradiction and resolves problem 2B (that is, it does not violate DDE1–3,) but unfortunately, in doing so, it reveals a new problem (see Table 13). It faces a real problem with DDE4, the "proportionate condition." Is a free creation (based on the necessity of permitting the possibility of gratuitous evil) actually worth it? This is another way of saying is the "risk" worth it? This is the problem of "ethical impermissibility" (problem 3A), the problem of the value of creation in face of the scale of evil. This is the evidential problem of evil returned. Is good worth the risk of evil? Is creation morally permissible but proportionately questionable?[49] The free will defense is clearly not enough. Continuing to maintain creation for the sake of the abstract value of freedoms when evil and suffering are concretely overwhelming it seems morally cruel and rationally foolish. Offering only a minimal deontologically consistent defense, in which God is justified and within his rights to preserve a freedom-enabling creation state, but ignoring the sheer magnitude of the effects, leaves the impression that God is unfeeling and callous (questioning God's omnibenevolence). In this case, the logical win is a moral loss. Gratuitous evil not being in itself an argument against God does not mean that any amount of gratuitous evil is justified. Does a Petersonian partial-greater good defense answer the evidential problem of evil according to the logical letter but fail its ethical or evidential spirit?

The problem is complicated further. Because a partial-greater-good appeals to an antecedent good (free will creation) to justify the divine permission of evil, it cannot be appealed to on its own to explain subsequent extreme evil. To do so is to transform it into a full-greater good (GGSUB). Such a move ends up back in a consequentialist ethical position in violation of key theological and deontological norms. So, while the free will defense helps to explain the divine permission for evil's origins, it needs some other help to account for subsequent ongoing evil. It needs practical theodicy, it needs eschatology, it needs expanded theism. It needs a fuller story. It needs all of this to be integrated together. It needs a narrative theodicy like the Great Controversy, though the Great Controversy theodicy must itself avoid retreating to ethical consequentialism in order to answer this reoccurring issue of value or worth.

---

49. The same could be said of the natural law defense, which is often combined with the free will defense.

Resolving Ethical Permissibility and the Doctrine of Triple Effect

To respond to the problem of ethical permissibility (3A) this study will run the Great Controversy theodicy through the moral matrix of the DDE. In doing so, use will be made of an expansion of the DDE called the "Doctrine of Triple Effect" (DTE). Before doing so it will be noted how theological determinists have attempted something similar.[50] In the book *Calvinism and the Problem of Evil*, several authors attempt to read and validate deterministic-style theodicies through the Doctrine of Double Effect (DDE). Alexander Pruss, a Catholic Philosopher and non-Calvinist, broaches DDE as a way of conducting theodicy for a deterministic theology.[51] The reason to appeal to DDE is because in Thomistic determinism "creaturely free actions are determined by God's causality and not by any finite causes."[52] This appears to make God violate the deontological principle (or DP), where DP stands for the "the basic ethical principle that one may not do evil that good may come of it."[53] God appears to determine and intentionally cause the first sin. This discussion's interest is not in how Pruss helps the Thomist or determinist but that in his discussion he looks at how other deterministic and non-deterministic theologies might utilize DDE.[54] He does this because all Christians face the issue of God's permission of sin (he has the first sin particularly in mind).[55] He outlines how different theologies can argue a story of God intending an initial set of conditions that lead to sin, but that God in fact intended those initial conditions for a reason independent of the fact that they bring about sin.[56] For example, he argues Open Theists and exponents of Simple Foreknowledge could argue that initial conditions for freedom are good reasons independent of the fact they lead to sin.[57]

---

50. If the DDE/TDE is able to help the vastly more difficult challenges theological determinism faces with the problem of evil then such an approach may prove even more effectual when used in a non-deterministic setting.

51. Pruss looks at Thomistic and Edwardsian Calvinism versions of determinism.

52. Pruss, "The First Sin: A Dilemma for Christian Determinists," 188.

53. Pruss, "The First Sin: A Dilemma for Christian Determinists," 188.

54. The deterministic theologies he has in mind are Edwardsian Calvinism and Thomism; the non-deterministic theologies are Molinism, Simple Foreknowledge, and open theism.

55. "For all Christians hold that God at least permits sin to happen. A theodicy for that permission is needed, and it seems that the theodicy will need to make reference to the goods to which the sin will be a means." Pruss, "The First Sin: A Dilemma for Christian Determinists," 190.

56. Pruss, "The First Sin: A Dilemma for Christian Determinists," 191.

57. He notes that "in these two stories, it is the great good of significantly freely acting well that is involved in the theodicy, rather than just the good of significant

He mentions that the Edwardsian compatibilist might say that God has a reason to produce the initial conditions which are intrinsically valuable independent of the fact they necessitate sin. What these are is not clear. Pruss, not being a Calvinist himself, simply leaves these as hypothetical possibilities.[58] He mentions that Molinists may argue the same except the initial conditions "do not necessitate sin, but they counter-factually imply it."[59] While these explanations work as far as they go, Pruss argues that they are problematic as Christian responses because they do not use Adam's sin as *felix culpa*, "a sin that happily leads to the great goods of redemption." Pruss regards use of felix culpa as essential because it "seems plausible that any theodicy faithful to the Christian tradition will have to make use of the valuable consequences of sin," but he notes the sketches he gave do not make such use.[60] Instead, they reply on initial conditions (free will, natural order, etc.) and not the goods of redemption. He then notes that "this highlights an apparent tension in the Christian tradition between DP and standard Christian theodicies."[61]

Pruss then suggests a way of incorporating felix culpa into these sketches without violating the DP.[62] In constructing this alternative way Pruss significantly modifies felix culpa so that it is not the same as the full greater good version (i.e., Plantinga's version) which we have been examining. Due to such modification, his discussion is a significant advance on Plantinga. What interests us is the structure of Pruss's version. He argues that God has a divine reason R for producing the initial conditions that is independent of them leading to sin or the valuable consequences of sin (redemption). These initial conditions R have a defeater. There "is a defeater S for these reasons: the fact that sin *might* (open theism, simple foreknowledge), *would* (Molinism), or *must* (Edwards) result."[63] However, felix culpa, the great goods of redemption, acts as a defeater-defeater for S. Pruss explains it in such a way as to avoid violating DP. "God does not, then, produce

---

freedom." Pruss, "The First Sin: A Dilemma for Christian Determinists," 191.

58. One Calvinist-compatibilist possibility is the "Integrity of Humans Defense" of John Feinberg; see *The Many Faces of Evil*, 165–91; 388–90.

59. Pruss, "The First Sin: A Dilemma for Christian Determinists," 191.

60. Pruss, "The First Sin: A Dilemma for Christian Determinists," 191.

61. Pruss, "The First Sin: A Dilemma for Christian Determinists," 191.

62. This is another way of saying we mustn't engage in consequentialist reasoning.

63. Pruss, "The First Sin: A Dilemma for Christian Determinists," 191. Italics mine. I see these differences as significant and would argue that not all use of DTE is equal. The necessity ("must") of the Edwardsian approach calls into question to what extent the evil is unintended. The Great Controversy theodicy use of the DTE is preferable to the deterministic use.

the initial conditions in order to produce the great goods of redemption. To do that would be to intend sin as a constitutive means to these great goods. Rather, God recognizes these great goods as a defeater to a defeater to R, and what God intends are the goods in R such as orderly initial conditions, freedom, etc."[64] The structure is as follows:

Table 14: Pruss's Felix Culpa as a Triple Effect

Act	Double Effect	Triple Effect
Reason *(R)* →	Defeater *(Sin)* →	Defeater-Defeater *(felix culpa)*

Pruss observes that this is structurally like Francis Kamm's "triple effect" story of the party (here termed as the Doctrine of Triple Effect or DTE).[65] In brief, Kamm argues that you might want to throw a party, but there is a defeater in that it will create a mess. However, the guests are the kind of people you can expect to help you clean up. You don't hold a party with the intention of having people clean up. Your intention is the party but the clean-up is a defeater-defeater to the mess a party might bring.

Modeling the Great Controversy Theodicy through Double/Triple Effect

The DDE has helped vindicate the free will defense as deontologically consistent but also shown that the free will defense on its own fails the fourth condition of proportionality (DDE4). Will the Great Controversy theodicy, which builds on the free will defense but goes beyond it, maintain deontological consistency while resolving disproportionality? When the Great Controversy theodicy is modeled using the DDE, it corresponds to Kamm and Pruss's "triple effect" (see Table 15). God's divine act is to create a good and free creation. This is good in itself and his intention for doing so is independent of the evil that may arise or the redemption that may ensue. This act has a defeater. A good free creation risks the possibility of evil as cosmic war/cosmic controversy. Nevertheless, by means of conducting a cosmic

---

64. Pruss, "The First Sin: A Dilemma for Christian Determinists," 192.

65. Kamm, "The Doctrine of Triple Effect," 21–39. "Kamm, in one characteristically intricate discussion, explores the superiority of a doctrine of triple effect and argues that an unintended side effect of one intended action may be a means to another legitimate and intended outcome, thus rejecting the view that one intend the means to one's intended end." Coady, *Morality and Political Violence*, 140.

Modelling the Great Controversy as a Theodicy

controversy in response to evil, which respects and preserves the freedom of a good creation, God can redeem creation.

Table 15: The Great Controversy Theodicy as a Triple Effect

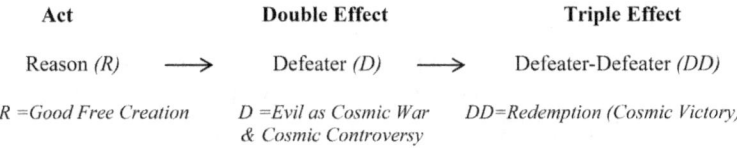

In this model, God does not operate consequentially. God is not creating in order to produce a fall into sin or evil. This good creation is valuable in and of itself but it is also worth undertaking, even in the face of great evil, because this good creation is redeemable. Redemption (and specifically a redemption that solves the cosmic controversy) removes the defeating potential of failing the fourth condition of "proportionality." Even if evil *temporarily* arises, creation maintains its worth and value by being *permanently* redeemed from evil. This resolves problem 3A of ethical impermissibility. Creation is good and rational. It is not self-defeating. If the Great Controversy theodicy is formulated it becomes apparent that it follows the DTE structure that Pruss uses but also highlights the different way various "goods" operate (Table 16).

Table 16: Great Controversy Theodicy "Good's" and Triple Effect

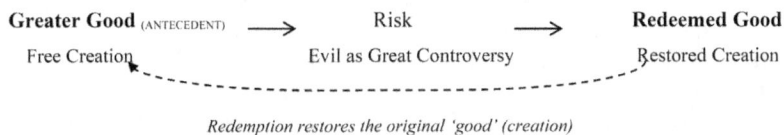

Redemption restores the original 'good' (creation)

The Redeemed Good Defense

In this formulation, a "free creation" is a partial greater good defense (a good antecedent to evil) and the good of redemption is in service to the antecedent good of creation. This contrasts to full greater good defenses (i.e.,

Plantinga's felix culpa, the divine glory defense) in which evil is necessary to achieve subsequent "greater goods." In the Great Controversy theodicy, redemption is occasioned (not necessitated) by evil occurring in the antecedent good it seeks to recover. Therefore, redemption is a "great good" that restores an earlier "greater good" but it is not itself the "greater good." It is restorative of the antecedent good. Thus, in terms of justificatory patterns, the Great Controversy theodicy combines a partial-greater good version of the free will defense with a supplementary "Redeemed Good Defense."

The Great Controversy theodicy is very clear that God did not ordain evil in order to achieve a greater good.[66] The original purpose or ends of creation were not a means to evil or redemption. Instead, it is the reverse. Redemption is a means back to the original ends or purpose. The plan of salvation was to "restore in man the image of his Maker, *to bring him back to the perfection in which he was created . . . that the divine purpose in his creation might be realized—this was to be the work of redemption.*"[67] Evil is what defeats God's purpose. Redemption restores it. Evil is not instrumental to redemption. Redemption is instrumental to the original purpose.[68] This brings us to the relationship between creation and covenant.[69] God knew the risk involved in a free creation and he foresaw evil's actual emergence. Divine deliberation about creation, therefore, involved deliberation about risk and evil in the form of redemption. Creation and covenant go together.[70] What this means for this discussion of DDE/DTE, is that God's "Act" of Creation is in fact a dual act. God acts to create but simultaneously within that act he covenants to redeem creation. Creation's risk necessitates redemptive covenant, redemptive covenant guarantees creation. God is, from all eternity, the God who covenanted to be the Father who gives himself

---

66. God had foreknowledge of the future of sin and "*allowed* matters to develop and work out. [but] He *did not work to bring about* a certain condition of things" and instead planned to meet it with redemption; see White, "The Mystery of God." Italics mine.

67. White, *Education*, 15,16. In the end "*All that was lost by sin has been restored . . . God's original purpose in the creation of the earth is fulfilled* as it is made the eternal abode of the redeemed." White, *The Great Controversy*, 674. Italics mine.

68. God's "purpose that the longer man lived the more fully he should reveal this image—the more fully reflect the glory of the Creator." White, *Education*, 15. Had man never fallen he would "have *fulfilled the object* of his creation, more and more fully [he would] have reflected the Creator's glory." White, *Education*, 15.

69. By "covenant" we are talking about the divine covenant to save humanity, also known as the everlasting covenant or covenant of mercy.

70. "The salvation of the human race has ever been the object of the councils of heaven. The covenant of mercy was made before the foundation of the world. It has existed from all eternity and is called the everlasting covenant. So surely as there never was a time when God was not, so surely there never was a moment when it was not the delight of the eternal mind to manifest His grace to humanity. White, "Spiritual Growth."

in his Son and Spirit for our creation *and* redemption.[71] Creation is built on Christ's sacrifice. The Great Controversy theodicy postulates *Felix Creatio* via *Felix Soter*[72] (a fortunate creation through a blessed Saviour) and not felix culpa. The "Redeemed Good Defense" is based in a *"Felix Soter"* theodicy.[73] God doesn't require or use evil as a means to an end, God freely becomes the means to restoring an end we lost and don't deserve.

The risk of a free creation, therefore, becomes a risk to God. Creation could not proceed unless God was willing to open himself up to personal risk, to vast suffering, and even to sacrifice himself for a hostile creation.[74] If God was not willing to redeem a creation that would fall then while his initial act of creation would still be a good act (satisfying DDE1–3), it would not be wise nor permissible because that creation would be destined to be defeated by evil. A non-redeemed or non-redeemable creation fails the "proportionate condition" (DDE4). Evil would be an undefeated-defeater. This is not so much a matter of evil outweighing good, it is more a matter of evil defeating good.[75] It would not be rational for God to engage in self-defeating behavior.[76] But if God is willing to sacrifice himself for creation then even evil cannot defeat this great good and the "proportionate condition" (DDE4) is satisfied and problem 3A is resolved. Of course, one may object that evil does defeat the purpose of creation in the case of the lost.[77] But this is not a sustainable objection, as even in this, God is rightly

---

71. "God gave His only begotten Son to die for mankind. How could He have given more? In this gift *He gave Himself*. 'I and My Father are one,' said Christ. By the gift of His Son, God has made it possible for man to be redeemed and restored to oneness with Him." White, "Words of Admonition Elmshaven." Italics mine.

72. Or *"Felix Salvator."*

73. "Redemption was not an afterthought, a plan formulated after the fall of Adam, but an eternal purpose, *suffered* to be wrought out for the blessing, not only of this atom of a world, but for the good of all the worlds that God had created." White, "The Plan of Salvation." Italics mine. Here we have redemption as an eternal purpose (covenant and creation are counterparts), as a great good and blessing for the universe, but also that as a response to evil it is "suffered" to be permitted. Redemption reveals God's character in a supererogatory manner.

74. See White, *Education*, 263–64.

75. Even the language of "defeat/victory" corresponds to warfare theodicy, whereas "outweighing" corresponds to greater good theodicy.

76. Having no redemption would be inconsistent with God's compassionate character. Deliberately not offering redemption, so as to ensure there are reprobates who may be eternally punished in order to display divine glory, is even worse on Great Controversy theodicy grounds.

77. This is not the case. God freely and non-coercively offers the lost salvation. Their rejection is not a defeat for themselves but not God because he willed that they be allowed that choice.

maintaining his commitment to a *free* creation (God is not determining any to be lost), and God offers them salvation (it could be otherwise for the lost). God defeats evil in the cosmic war; therefore, no one needs to be defeated by evil. There is no necessity nor intention. Therefore, creation is worth it. This is true from creation's perspective for many reasons. Creation is a good within itself. Evil, as a cosmic controversy, is only a risk, not a necessity. The risk is not inevitable, but it is foreseen. God prepares for the risk by covenanting himself. The period of evil and suffering is limited in time. The special way God conducts himself in this cosmic controversy means redemption is offered for the fallen, and evil and risk will be permanently eliminated. From God's perspective, despite the suffering he experiences, creation is worth it.[78] From both the Creator's and creation's perspectives the negative side effect of risk and evil is proportionate to the act of God creating a redeemable creation. All of this is deontologically consistent. Ethical impermissibility is resolved without introducing ethical contradiction.[79] This is shown in the following diagram (Table 17) which brings together the many elements of the Great Controversy Theodicy discussed in chapters 3, 4, and 5 to reveal how its ethical structure works.

---

78. "The compensation for this sacrifice is the joy of peopling the earth with ransomed beings, holy, happy, and immortal. The result of the Savior's conflict with the powers of darkness is joy to the redeemed, redounding to the glory of God throughout eternity. And such is the value of the soul that the Father is satisfied with the price paid; and Christ Himself, beholding the fruits of His great sacrifice, is satisfied." White, *The Great Controversy*, 652.

79. Because both skeptics and traditional theodicies operate on consequentialist reasoning they end in a stalemate over whether evil outweighs greater goods or vice versa. The Great Controversy theodicy obviously rejects this kind of ethical reasoning. It would ask, how can evil or good be turned into a unit of measurement and then compared or weighed? Moral actions must be evaluated against a moral standard, not in terms of quantities. Due to this it is wrong for skeptics to say that God should not create because some will suffer. What this actually means is that the mystery of evil, even by its mere potential, should be granted a veto on God's actions. Evil triumphs over God and good. This gives an inexplicable thing (evil) an unjustified ontological status in which it is allowed to become metaphysically ultimate and determinative. Not creating due to this objection would have God conceding ethical ultimacy to evil's effects. This is unthinkable. It is "un-deontological." This does not mean God ignores evil. But he faces evil from the ground of his own ultimacy and goodness.

Table 17: The Deontological (non-Consequentialist) Ethical Structure of the Great Controversy Theodicy

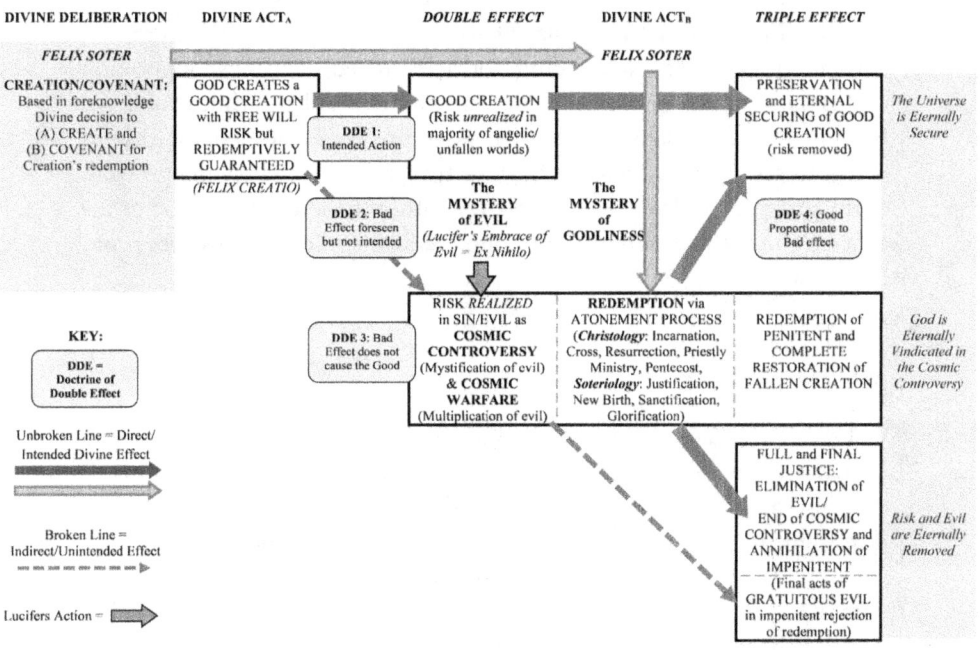

THE ISSUE OF EQUIVOCATING THEORIES OF FREEDOM (PROBLEM 3B)

Having established a Great Controversy Theodicy that is ethically consistent with its own theology (resolving "ethical equivocation"), and that can answer the question of whether creation is "worth it" in the face of the scale of evil (resolving "ethical impermissibility"), it is now time to turn to the final major challenge. Can the Great Controversy theodicy answer the "victory" or "win it" question if it maintains the idea of the open-ended risk inherent in libertarian freedom which is so essential to the free will defense? Risky freedom can account for evil's origins but resists the idea of evil's end (eternal libertarian freedom implies endless risk). Chapter 4 revealed Boyd's unsuccessful attempted to resolve this problem by equivocating between different theories of freedom. This is the "free will equivocation" problem (problem 3B) in the face of the "win it" question. The Great Controversy theodicy needs to resolve the "win it" question without engaging in equivocating theories of freedom. In chapter 4 we foreshadowed "virtue libertarianism" as a way out of this problem. In this section, it will be shown that virtue libertarianism can be incorporated into the Great Controversy theodicy in a way that is consistent with its storied/narrative nature (the particularities of the story should not be flattened), and how application of this theory resolves the free will equivocation problem, while avoiding a fall into consequentialist ethics. By looking at a recent attempt by Richard Shenk to resolve this issue, it will show that this is ultimately the problem of the place of theological anthropology within theodicy. At the end of the chapter a modelling of the Great Controversy theodicy that resolves problem 3B will be shown.

Shenk's Theodicy

Richard Shenk attempts to form a theodicy by offering a larger theory of freedom, placed within a Cross-focused framework, as a effective way of addressing the problem of evil. While Shenk's sympathies are with theological determinism, he is very keen to avoid ethical consequentialism.[80] Shenk's work builds upon earlier discussions of the changing nature of human freedom in Christian theology. Timpe and Jenson sum up the three stages to human free will in theological anthropology.[81] These are the progression from *status integritatis* (also called *status naturae elevatae* or *status iustitiae originalis*) through to *status corruptionis* to the *status gloriae*.[82] The *status integritatis* refers to the pre-fall state in which humans were able to freely sin or not sin. *Status corruptionis* is the post-fall state in which fallen humans are freely able to sin due to sin's effects but they are not able to refrain from sinning. The *status gloriae* refers to the post-glorification state in which the redeemed are able not to sin and are not able to sin.[83] There are libertarian and compatibilist versions of both. There is also a fuller version going back to Augustine and frequently used by Reformed theologians in which humans were 1) pre-fall *posse peccare/posse non peccare* (able to sin/able not to sin); then 2) post-fall *non posse non peccare* (not able not to sin); then 3) regenerated *posse non peccare* (able not to sin); and finally 4) glorified *non posse pecccare* (unable to

---

80. Shenk, *The Wonder of the Cross*, 106.
81. Timpe and Jenson, "Free Will and the Stages of Theological Anthropology."
82. That is, the state of integrity (state of elevated nature/state of original justice); the state of corruption; and the state of glory, respectively.
83. Timpe and Jenson, "Free Will and the Stages of Theological Anthropology," 235.

sin).[84] This four-stage rendering is more complete than the three stages. Shenk builds on this theological anthropology in constructing his theodicy. Shenk's thesis argues that God is taking Creation through the various stages of freedom in order to arrive at his ultimate aim of creation possessing "conforming freedom." This is a final eschatological form of freedom where creatures will "be as free as God in respect to evil" and thus "perfectly and permanently free from evil and suffering."[85] With this conclusion Shenk is able to answer *how* God's people will persevere in heaven when they did not in the garden of Eden.[86] The "how" is seen in the progression within the various eras. Shenk says that each stage of freedom develops because of a Creation-Crisis event. The Creation event begins with "Unfettered Freedom."[87] This is a form of "perfect" freedom but which is not fettered or tied to God's perfection.[88] Interestingly, Shenk also maintains that this is a "freedom *decreed* to defect from perfection in time."[89] God intends this freedom to defect, although God does not cause it to defect. This defection is due to the crisis event of the fall. This leads to the second stage of "Forfeit Freedom" in which people are enslaved to disobedience. Shenk sees this era and the following era as more similar to compatibilist freedom. Then follows the Creation-Crisis event of the Cross and the Church, which opens up the possibility of "Penultimate Freedom." This is a kind of "now-not-yet" freedom in which people experience both the struggle of "forfeited" and a taste of "conforming" freedom. Finally, following the Crisis and Creation events of the final judgment and the new heavens and new earth, God's elect enjoy "Conforming Freedom."[90]

---

84. Timpe and Jenson, "Free Will and the Stages of Theological Anthropology," 233. See Augustine, "A Treatise on Rebuke and Grace," Chapter 33, 485.

85. Shenk, *The Wonder of the Cross*, xvii, 11, 157–87.

86. Shenk, *The Wonder of the Cross*, 158–60.

87. Also called "defectable" or "defective" freedom. Shenk, *The Wonder of the Cross*, xviii.

88. Shenk sees it as similar to libertarian freedom, where creation is free to choose for or against God. Shenk, *The Wonder of the Cross*, 170.

89. Shenk, *The Wonder of the Cross*, xviii.

90. Shenk's conforming freedom shares structural parallels and similarities to virtue libertarian freedom in which freedom has reached its goal of virtue. Shenk, *The Wonder of the Cross*, 250–53.

Table 18: Shenk's Four Stages of Freedom and the Three Creation-Crisis Events

Unfettered Freedom	Forfeit Freedom	Penultimate Freedom	Conforming Freedom
	Creation & Fall	Cross & Church	Judgment & New Creation

Shenk's argument is that God uses "Evil and Suffering" to overcome "Evil and Suffering" and that this is the necessary way evil is overcome. He is clear that God cannot achieve this by force. God must use this historical process so that creation can develop conforming freedom. God creates creation with a freedom liable to fall, so that he can move them to a freedom invulnerable to falling. Shenk tries to bridge theological determinism[91] and free will approaches, libertarian and compatibilist versions of freedom. He wants to affirm theological determinist style theodicies like the divine glory defense[92] but without its consequentialism,[93] and to utilize the idea of free will but without the libertarian free will defense. It is a difficult balancing act. He wants to be able to answer why creation can begin free and liable to evil but end up free and yet unable to do evil. This is part of the "win it" or "victory" question. He does this without the idea of libertarian risk. In a sense, he offers a reformed version of Boyd's tactic of moving between different kinds/definitions of freedom. Shenk equivocates between models of freedom. Given the diversity of freedom-states that a theodicy must account for, how can such equivocation be avoided?

It is an open question whether Shenk's theodicy manages to maintain determinism and completely avoid consequentialism.[94] This will not be explored directly here, although a later critique will raise questions about its successfulness. His argument is a sophisticated and substantial advance on previous deterministic theodicies with much to adapt and admire, especially in his Cross-centeredness.[95] Shenk is especially helpful to the Great Contro-

---

91. "I am proposing that those who understand God's will as determinate in all things are correct." Shenk, *The Wonder of the Cross*, 159.

92. Shenk, *The Wonder of the Cross*, 158–60.

93. Shenk, *The Wonder of the Cross*, 105–6.

94. Such questions are raised by Simon Oliver in the "Foreword," in *The Wonder of the Cross*, xi.

95. Shenk, *The Wonder of the Cross*, 246, 249. The improvements seem to be linked to his willingness to play, even in a limited way, with libertarian-style freedom, and clarifying metaphysical constraints on divine power. He is in effect modifying determinism.

versy theodicy in two ways. First, his predominantly theological rather than philosophical response is one friendly to the Great Controversy narrative approach. Second is his attempt to correlate an ethically non-consequentialist theodicy onto the dynamics of theological anthropology and freedom. This is exactly what the Great Controversy theodicy seeks to do.

Applying Virtue Libertarianism to Theological Anthropology to Resolve Problem 3B

If virtue libertarianism is used as the Great Controversy theodicy understanding of freedom and is mapped onto the stages of theological anthropology and the question of evil, we arrive at an alternative model compatible with cosmic warfare views. As Shenk and others have argued, there are four eras or stages with freedom progressing through each stage. Important events lie behind the changes in each era. But most significantly, unlike Shenk and Boyd, there is only one model of freedom.

Shenk recognizes problems with both libertarian and compatibilist versions of free will when tackling evil and that neither of them, as they are, properly describes freedom in all eras.[96] The Great Controversy theodicy agrees with this perception but while Shenk opts for differing kinds of freedom, the Great Controversy theodicy offers a singular parsimonious theory of freedom that coherently accounts for all eras and various states of freedom (and kinds of beings whether angelic or human, something Shenk struggles with, as will be shown later). This parsimony suggests but does not establish superiority. At the least, virtue libertarianism avoids problematic and needless equivocations regarding the nature of freedom. The following diagram (Table 19) depicts the states and stages of freedom in the Great Controversy theodicy utilizing virtue libertarianism:

---

96. Shenk, *The Wonder of the Cross*, 158–60.

Table 19: The Four Stages and Six States of Freedom

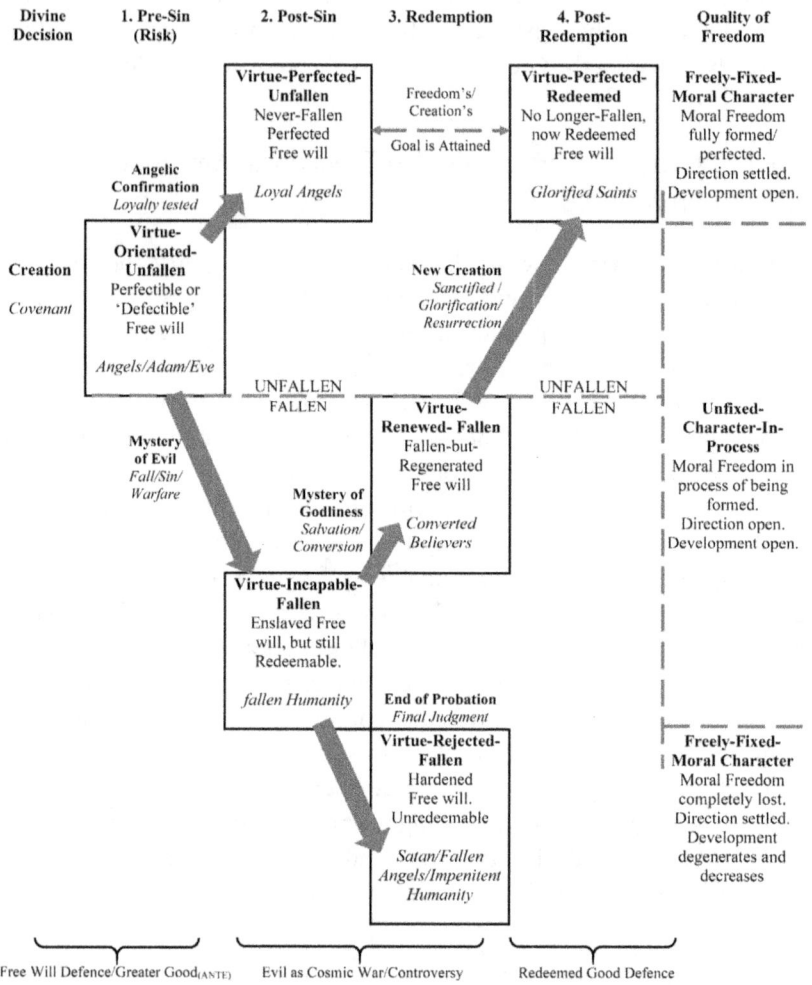

Like Shenk, the Great Controversy theodicy argues that God cannot instantaneously create beings with perfected freedom, nor will he use force or coercion. Creatures can be both perfect and yet able to fall. But unlike Shenk, the Great Controversy theodicy shows that evil is not necessary for perfected freedom.[97] The never-fallen angels experience the test between

---

97. "Man was created a free moral agent . . . he must be subjected to the test of obedience; *but he is never brought in such a position that yielding to evil becomes a matter of necessity.*" White, *Patriarchs and Prophets*, 331; see also White, *The Great Controversy* 492–93. Italics mine.

good or evil in the first stage of the cosmic controversy, but they resist evil, and are confirmed in their character and have their freedom perfected in virtue.[98] As with Shenk's theodicy such freedom is perfect yet morally mutable. But in contrast to Shenk the origin of evil is not described as decreed[99] nor is freedom described as completely unfettered to God's character. The "virtuous" nature of even immature libertarian freedom could be understood as "weakly" or "resistibly" fettered to God's character, but fettered nonetheless, and as much as is possible.[100] Freedom from the beginning is deliberately orientated to virtue by God.

Table 20: Comparing the Eras/Stages of Freedom in Shenk and the Great Controversy Theodicy

	Stage 1	Stage 2	Stage 3	Stage 4
Shenk's Stages of Freedom	Unfettered Freedom	Forfeit Freedom	Penultimate Freedom	Conforming Freedom
Proposed Stages and States of Freedom in the Great Controversy Theodicy	Virtue Orientated (*unfallen*)	Virtue Incapable (*redeemable*) Virtue Rejected (*irredeemable*)	Virtue Renewed	Virtue Perfected (*never fallen*) Virtue Redeemed (*once fallen*)

Like Shenk, each era happens due to some creation or crisis event, but there are more of these events in keeping with the larger narrative the Great Controversy theodicy operates with. The co-joining of "covenant" with creation makes clear that the danger is foreseen from the beginning. The fall is given more definition as the "mystery of evil" leading to the larger ideas of controversy and warfare. The problem of evil (intrinsic only as risk) to creation is overcome by a greater mystery, that of the saving "mystery of godliness." The acceptance or rejection of salvation settles freedom in either virtue or vice, which is finally confirmed by judgment or glorification. Freedom is

---

98. It is also possible that some angels' characters were already fixed before the testing. The test revealed and reinforced the established character.

99. "In the judgment of the universe, God will stand clear of blame for the existence or continuance of evil. It will be demonstrated that the *divine decrees are not accessory to sin*. There was no defect in God's government, no cause for disaffection." White, *Desire of Ages* 58. Italics mine.

100. "God made man ... with *noble traits of character, no bias towards evil* ... high intellectual powers ... *strongest possible inducements* to ... obedience." White, *Patriarchs and Prophets*, 49. Italics mine.

capable of both moral direction (to good or evil) and development within each direction. The openness of direction is not endless, eventually character attains a definite moral state, and development is only endless when freedom is coupled with virtue, otherwise it eventually degenerates and ends in self-destruction. The Great Controversy theodicy can learn from Shenk's approach but only with important modifications. Central would be a change to his idea of evil as a "subordinate-metaphysical-necessity." By this Shenk means that God does not cause or author evil, however, because creation is finite it is inevitable that evil will result.[101] This concept is helpful only if it is understood to describe the *risk* of evil and not evil itself. Risk is necessary. Evil is not.[102] Risk, not evil, is the subordinate-metaphysical-necessity that accompanies God's choice to create free creatures.

Shenk, Angels, Satan, and the Cosmic Controversy Perspective

Another key difference between Shenk's theodicy and the Great Controversy theodicy is the role and place of angels and Satan, and the nature of the warfare God must fight. When these are factored into the discussion an increased strain on Shenk's model is seen. Shenk's whole thesis operates on the assumption of the marginality of Lucifer/Satan, the angels, and their fall, to the overall storyline of Scripture and to theodicy. If angels (unfallen, fallen, Lucifer to Satan, demons) are significant, then, as will be shown, Shenk's approach is incomplete. It fails to tell the whole story. This is the main Great Controversy criticism of Shenk's view. His view has much to offer but fails because it neglects to seriously incorporate vital evidence. A number of issues result from this neglect. If evil and suffering are necessary for the production of conforming-freedom and necessary for God's plan, then how is it that some angels appear to have conforming-freedom without passing through the preceding stages? Some angels never fall. This appears to show that God can produce conforming-freedom without suffering and evil. Shenk acknowledges this. Non-defecting angels indicate that human sin is not a subordinate-metaphysical-necessity but only an accidental necessity.[103] In this scenario, unfettered freedom did not *have* to fall. But if this is so, then why would God decree evil? If God decreed what was not

---

101. God is a metaphysical necessity. Evil is not. But because God desires creatures with conforming freedom he subordinately needs evil as part of the process to achieve that.

102. The Great Controversy theodicy might need to say that, given God's foreknowledge of risk-eventuating-in-evil, such evil was *contingently inevitable*, inevitable once such contingencies are known and permitted. But "inevitable" is different from "necessary." Many angels, for example, did not fall.

103. Shenk, *The Wonder of the Cross*, 287.

subordinately necessary, then Shenk's theodicy would seem to end up in ethical consequentialism (God decreed it because it would bring the greater good of conforming-freedom) which Shenk is at pains to avoid.

Realising this problem, Shenk argues that it is impossible to know what angelic freedom was like, and so no one can say it was libertarian like Adam's.[104] Shenk is not really agnostic on this, however; when he does try and address the issue, he sides with theological determinism and the compatibilist freedom approach of Augustine, Luther, and Calvin, in which angels fall because *God did not give them persevering grace*.[105] In this view, God is not responsible for this sin. The angels freely chose what they desired. However, non-determinists would point out that they did so only because God has complete control over the secondary causes which ensured that particular desire and choice. God purposely and intentionally ordained their exact choice, and so his decision is the ultimate reason they fell. Amazingly, after laboring so hard to avoid the consequentialism of a greater good approach, Shenk resorts to that very approach. Shenk ends up with a divine-glory-defense-style argument for angelic sin. "*We do know that for his own glory*, God could have created some angels with a freedom that permitted them to defect and created others who could not defect."[106] Shenk seems to embrace the consequentialism he resists. What Shenk gains in his theodicy for humans he loses in his comments on angels.

The difficulties deepen if Shenk's view of that particular fallen angel, Satan, is probed. In a footnote, Shenk wonders about how Satan fits in. He asks, "Of what need does God have of Satan?"[107] It would seem God needs to

---

104. Shenk, *The Wonder of the Cross*, 288–89. Shenk argues that angels are totally different from humans, especially in regards to freedom. But there is no reason to assume complete difference, especially in regards to angels lacking free will. One should not even assume that because they are not explicitly described as being in the image of God that they don't bear some image of God. After all, angels are termed the "sons of God" just as humans are (Job 1:6; 2:1; 38:7). Angels are spirits in a similar way to God being Spirit and humans having a spirit (John 4:24; 1 Cor 2:10–11; Heb 1:7, 14; 12:9, 23). Angels are clearly moral beings, else they could not fall or be holy. They clearly possess personhood and will. All this becomes more significant when we remember that humans were made a little lower than the angels (Ps 8:4–6). It would be odd if those higher than us lacked such a basic feature as freedom of will. Shenk's musings on angels seem to calculated to remove the problem angels pose for a theodicy that has no necessary place for them.

105. Shenk, *The Wonder of the Cross*, 288. Contrast this to: "Nothing is more plainly taught in Scripture than that God was in no wise responsible for the entrance of sin; that there was *no arbitrary withdrawal of divine grace*, no deficiency in the divine government, that gave occasion for the uprising of rebellion. Sin is an intruder, for whose presence no reason can be given." White, *The Great Controversy*, 492–93. Italics mine.

106. Shenk, *The Wonder of the Cross*, 289.

107. Shenk, *The Wonder of the Cross*, 290. Notice the deterministic language of necessity.

kick off the progression of eras so he can eventually arrive at a conformingly free (human) creation. Shenk says that "God's Story minimally requires Satan theologically; Satan has a purpose in God's Story theologically, or he would not appear." He confesses he doesn't know the answer. But he ventures one. "Could it be that God's plan required that evil not begin with humanity and that it not ever be impersonal?" He also asks, "Is personified evil a kind of mercy to God's human wilful-creatures?"[108] There are two discomforts with this. First, is the recurring drift to consequentialism. Shenk starts using instrumental language to describe Satan, even suggesting a "personal" Satan may be a "mercy." This sounds like a strange Luciferian twist on felix culpa. Satan is a kind of *Felix Tentator* (fortunate tempter) producing a *Felix Temptationem* (fortunate temptation). God is using, even needing, Satan/evil to produce good (The end justifies the means?). Shenk could avoid this if he offered a similar theodicy for angels as he does for humanity. But that is a problem. Angels don't experience the four stages of freedom. So, what place do angels have, and what value are the stages for them, when they do not participate in them? The second problem is broader. The Great Controversy theodicy would argue that Shenk dramatically underplays Scripture's perspective on Satan. When evil is discussed neither Satan nor cosmic warfare is marginal.[109] Satan may not be all-prevalent in Scripture, but he appears in major story-defining moments in the Scriptures narrative of evil and suffering. The serpent of Genesis chapter 3 brings sin and suffering into the world and starts the whole story rolling. Satan is crucial to the story of Job's suffering (Job 1 & 2). The entire ministry of Jesus, his wilderness temptations, exorcisms, healings, teachings, the sin-solving-Cross (John 12:27–33; Col 2:13–15), his death-defeating resurrection, (Heb 2:14, 15), as well as the ministry of the church (Eph 6:10–20), and especially Revelation, with the end of sin, suffering, and death (Rev 12 & 20), are all predicated on the essential importance of defeating Satan. Shenk's claims are unpersuasive. How can Shenk develop an adequate theodicy of evil when Satan, the power behind evil, is marginalized? Shenk speaks often of God's need to fight evil but it is cast more as a fight against a subordinate-metaphysical-necessity rather than the scriptural account of a fierce conflict with principalities and powers. All of this is an argument in favor of a cosmic warfare theodicy.

---

108. Shenk, *The Wonder of the Cross*,

109. This is not to discount that the predominant scriptural focus is evil as human sin. But for the importance and unavoidability of angels and Satan to evil in Scripture, see, Boyd, *God at War*; Boyd, *Satan*; Tonstad, *Saving God's Reputation*; Graham, *Evil and Christian Ethics*.

THE DUAL RISK OF FREEDOM

It is advanced here that the Great Controversy theodicy, with its idea of cosmic controversy, combined with a theory of virtue libertarianism, better handles Scripture's testimony concerning humanity (theological anthropology), angels, Satan, and evil, and thus better responds to the problem of evil. The Great Controversy is a fuller theodicy. But something else is at work. The placement of virtue libertarianism within a Great Controversy metanarrative reveals deeper elements to freedom and evil, and highlights what is another unique emphasis and distinct element of the Great Controversy theodicy. Freedom is not just a volitional risk; it is also a *cognitive* and *collective* risk. Usually, freedom's risk is restricted to the volitional potential for evil based in the libertarian definition of freedom as the power "to do otherwise." This volitional approach is very rarely expanded in theodicy discussions to include the intellectual component to freedom.[110] In contrast, the Great Controversy holds it as essential for theodicy to consider freedom's power as volition and *intellectual* ("the power to think and to do"[111]), as well as individual and collective, and all are equally essential to understanding evil. Risk is not restricted to the moral bivalence of volition. Risk is more than that. Risk concerns the will (freedom to choose and act) and mind (freedom to think and say). It is volitional-*intellectual*. In view here is not the non-culpable possibility of cognitive mistakes which is an innocent part of finite creaturely limitation. Instead, freedom's deeper risk lies in the profound power of intellectual revolt. It encompasses the potential for mutinous ideas, seditious philosophy, and subversive politics. In theodicy, risk is not often explored as hostile independent thought, political subterfuge, and organized ideological opposition. Sin is not only the mysterious act of perverse wilful volition, it is also the wilfully perverse assertion of a mind justifying itself and condemning its creator. In the Great Controversy, freedom's risk is evil-as-cosmic-controversy. The Great Controversy theodicy theory of freedom could more accurately be termed, Cognitive Virtue Libertarianism, bringing together the inseparable elements of moral character, intellect, and volition, all of course necessarily existing in a social or communal context. I doubt most theists would object

---

110. The exception to this is medieval and modern discussions of evil's origins. But even here, the exploration of the intellectual dimensions of freedom is limited to demonstrating the plausibility of the seemingly irrational claim that an individual perfect being (i.e., Satan), in a perfect environment, would choose evil. Once this is answered (or often seen as unanswerable) any follow-up construction of theodicy proceeds without a key role for the intellectual risk of freedom.

111. White, *Education*, 17.

to this in principle, but it is telling that theists do not pursue this fact and instead rely on philosophical and metaphysical explanations as the key to the heart of theodicy.

This helps confirm the earlier observation in chapter 4 as to why Boyd has a warfare theodicy but no controversy. He is restricted to the metaphysics of volition and lacks the intellectual dimension of the war. How was Satan able to convince himself and so many others to rebel? How does evil spread, reproduce, mutate, acquire new justifications, and prove so resilient for so long? This is largely left untouched or undeveloped. This then makes it harder to answer how sin and warfare can be ended. In a non-deterministic context, this must be answered with more than assertions that evil will end by recourse to raw power and control on God's behalf. Shenk rightly has a historical process which majors in transformation of the volition state but regrettably neglects the intellectual side. Shenk's process tackles subordinate-metaphysical-necessity but not deeply conceptualized rebellion. But humans (and I would argue angels) are free, cognitive beings with minds, opinions, and thought processes. None are infinite or all-knowing, and so all creatures are challenged by great questions and must work through them. This also means that in the long-term God cannot deal with these intellectual controversies and doubts by sheer force or by using an endless "trust-but-don't-question-or-think" approach which evades answers. In doing this, God would disregard the temporal psychology of his own creation. These things can only be answered by demonstration and evidence. God's process in response must deal with both the minds of individual beings and the collective mind of creation (hence a special atonement-vindication process is needed by God, not simply to save creation, but to also answer the political attack). To do this the actual issues which lie behind evil's power and spread must be identified and addressed. For the Great Controversy theodicy, this intellectual element is not a lesser issue or secondary adjunct to the issue of depraved volition. These are the inseparable dual dimensions of freedom and evil. Free will as volition is not enough. Warfare is not enough. There is a need to understand the generating, sustaining power of ideological *controversy*. There is a need for a bigger concept of risk and then a broader means of dealing with that risk. The Great Controversy theodicy needs a theory of freedom that adequately accounts for risk, and particularly the kind of risk that makes sense of the vastness of evil as cosmic war and controversy. At the same time, it must be capable of accounting for the non-endlessness of evil and risk, and their cosmic resolvability, all the while avoiding the problem of equivocating between conflicting ideas of freedom. A cognitive-virtue-libertarianism successfully meets these needs and helps commend the Great Controversy as a substantial theodicy.

CONCLUSION

This chapter has laid out how the Great Controversy theodicy works at resolving the problem of evil in its evidential form. The Great Controversy theodicy is able to resolve the evidential argument by successfully dealing with self-defeating internal contradictions and perceived unlikelihood due to an apparent disparity with external evidence. To do this the Great Controversy theodicy makes a decisive break with traditional approaches to theodicy. It rejects the full-greater good defense and builds on a distinct version of the free will defense which affirms the evidence for gratuitous evils and is ethically congruent with a Christian deontology. This particular free will approach is a crucial departure from traditional theodicy and succeeds in avoiding the traditional failings but is not completely successful as it generates some new problems (ethical impermissibility and free will equivocation). It is at this point that the distinctive elements of the Great Controversy theodicy help take the free will defense beyond its limitations and produce a more comprehensively coherent theodicy. The Great Controversy theodicy succeeds by both rescuing and going beyond the free will defense. A modeling of the Great Controversy theodicy demonstrates that it is able to use a version of the doctrine of double effect to rationally show how it is ethically permissible for God to permit evil in a non-consequentialist manner. The Great Controversy theodicy does not retreat to a full-greater good defense but employs a "redeemed good defense" (a deontological extension of the non-consequentialist partial-greater good defense) based in a "*Felix Soter*" theology. In this a sacrificial Saviour makes possible a risky world. This is in contrast to felix culpa, in which a fallen world makes possible the great goods of a savior. A complementary modeling also shows that a singular model of freedom (a Great Controversy theodicy version of virtue libertarianism which is sensitive to the metanarrative of cosmic controversy and thus places equal emphasis on volitional and intellectual-cognitive elements of the free will) avoids equivocating between models of freedom and at the same time can account for the emergence and ending of evil, without compromising the achieved ethical consistency. The Great Controversy theodicy, therefore, expands the notion of free will as a defense into a theodicy of cosmic warfare, and beyond that into a broader theodicy of cosmic controversy, by employing specific and self-consistent ethical and volitional theories.[112] It is the making explicit of these expanded elements which enables the metanarrative of Great Controversy to function as an effective response to the problem of evil, especially in its evidential form, within the discipline and conversation that is theodicy.

---

112. A K. Anderson developed a typology for theodicies based on when they resolve the problem of evil within the divine narrative. The four are the Protological (e.g., Plantinga's free will defense deals with creation), the Christological (e.g., Dorothee Soelle focuses on Christ), the Enestological (this means "here and now," e.g., Griffin's Process theodicy), and the Eschatological (e.g., Hick's afterlife dependent Soul-making theodicy). Anderson suggests a theodicy able to incorporate all four types would be a *maximal Christian theodicy*. Anderson, "Evil and the God of Narrative," 149–50. I would argue that the Great Controversy theodicy incorporates all four types and qualifies as a *maximal Christian theodicy*.

Conclusion

The quest of this study has been to understand how the idea of the Great Controversy responds to the most pressing modern challenge to theism—the evidential problem of evil. The guiding question asks how the narrative of Great Controversy resolves the evidential argument and functions as a theodicy. It is now time to venture an answer to the thesis question and offer a conclusion. In summary, this study suggests the Great Controversy functions as a theodicy by *fulfilling the free will defense*.[1] The word "fulfilling" is used here to mean the completing and enabling of the free will defense to succeed as a theodicy.[2] More exactly this idea of fulfilling or completing the free will defense is accomplished by an interlocking process of *reframing, freeing,* and *furthering* the free will defense. Once properly fulfilled in a larger cosmic conflict framework, the foundational idea of free will presents a theodicy that more adequately corresponds to the observable evidential reality of evil while maintaining consistent conceptual coherence (theologically and ethically).

REFRAMING

The main way the Great Controversy theodicy fulfills the free will defense is by reframing the context for free will. The free will defense is placed within the new framework of a theodicy based in cosmic warfare which

---

1. Here by "free will defense" I do not mean specifically and restrictively Alvin Plantinga's version but rather the basic or generic idea of free will common to free will theologies and theodicies.

2. This does not mean no other theodicy may function in a similar manner, only that this is how the Great Controversy theodicy does. Gregory Boyd's TWT attempts to do the same, although my study suggests the Great Controversy theodicy does so more satisfactorily. See Duah, "A Study of Warfare Theodicy."

itself is placed within a metanarrative of controverted love called the Great Controversy.[3] The initial effect of the reframing is to move a defense (free will defense), that is adequate to the logical problem of evil but ineffective against the evidential version, into a theodicy. A theodicy is more equipped to offer reasons for God's permission of gratuitous evil, something defense does not do.

The more significant effect of this reframing is the resulting three explanatory layers of 1) free will, 2) cosmic warfare and 3) Great controversy. The free will defense then only needs to account for more limited dimensions of evil (e.g., evil's origins). Free will introduces the idea of the risk of evil as a potential but non-necessitated by-product of God's decision to make a free creation capable of love. The second layer of cosmic war allows for a cosmic-sized expansion of the free will defense's explanatory ability. Together free will and cosmic war are able to argue that the extreme degree of evil in the world reflects the fact that the world is a cosmic war zone. Gratuitous evil is not unnatural in a cosmic war zone. This cosmic scaling of moral evil to include Lucifer/Satan, in addition to Adam, also enables free will to account for natural evil, something that is often considered a weakness of the free will defense. These two layers give a more satisfactory account of evil's origins, its vast scale, and ongoing continuation than just the free will defense alone.

The third layer of Great Controversy encapsulates the initial layers of free will and cosmic war within itself but goes beyond them and even transforms them with its more extensive narrative framework. The Great Controversy allows for a cosmic-historical-political layer of explanation for many of the elements of evil. This strategically reduces the need to appeal to metaphysical explanations to account for challenges that metaphysics is ill-equipped to deal with. The Great Controversy theodicy is not necessarily anti-metaphysical; in fact, one of its central ideas is a metaphysical one. This is its idea of the "mystery of evil" which claims that original evil is inexplicable and unjustifiable, and due to this it is also inherently confounding to creaturely reason. The entire Great Controversy theodicy narrative rests and arises on this presupposition. Building on it, and inseparable from it, is the narrative idea of Satan's "mystification of evil" where he attempts to justify and rationalize evil. This results in a cosmic-moral-political-ideological war which can only be answered by an extensive divine process that exposes all dimensions of evil, its architect and his mystifications, and responds with a redemptive counter-demonstration vindicating the divine character,

---

3. Boyd likewise argues that his TWT is all about reframing the problem of evil from the idea of God controlling evil to the idea of God fighting evil. Boyd, *God at War*, 291.

government, and law. This supplies non-metaphysical reasons for evil's long but circumscribed continuation. It also makes clear how evil can be ended.[4]

This reframing ultimately rejects as inappropriate the way the evidential problem of evil frames the question of evil. The evidential argument is not neutral. The Great Controversy theodicy accepts the evidential argument's factual premise that gratuitous evil exists. But in contrast to traditional theodicy, it rejects the theological premise of the evidential argument that theism necessarily affirms meticulous providence.[5] It also rejects the unwarranted way the evidential problem and greater good theodicies assume ethical consequentialism. Therefore, the Great Controversy theodicy affirms the strongest element of the evidential argument (the factual premise) but reframes it in a different theistic context where it no longer serves as an argument against God. This requires skeptics and traditional theists alike to engage in a very significant paradigm shift.

FREEING

Reframing free will in this larger cosmic framework frees it from a number of self-defeating contexts and strategies. Examples of self-defeating contexts include Augustine's theological determinism, which nullifies any utility free will may have for theodicy and process theology's finite god who is incapable of ever ending evil.[6] As referred to earlier the denial of gratuitous evil or the factual premise of the evidential problem of evil is another self-sabotaging strategy. This denial of something people experience as axiomatic puts traditional theodicy at a fatal disadvantage. An alternative theodicy capable of integrating gratuitous evil has both removed a significant objection to theism and commended its plausibility. Interrelated to this is the ubiquitous but deeply problematic use by theists of a full greater good defense to cover all evil. These greater goods necessitate evil and make God dependent on what is morally reprehensible to him in order for him to accomplish his goals. A theodicy unburdened by this unworkable expectation is truly free and more feasible. These problems are connected to a doctrine of meticulous providence which intimately links an all-powerful or omni-controlling God

---

4. Once the issues in the cosmic controversy are perfectly clear then evil can be ended. Truth and demonstration instead of coercion overcome accusation and deception. Metanarrative rather than metaphysics is the key.

5. It also rejects "restricted standard theism."

6. Other examples could be added. Origen placed free will within a theological context with a number of unorthodox, speculative, and even heretical features. We could also add Gregory Boyd's Open theist rejection of full divine foreknowledge which exasperates the risk of risk as seen in chapter 4.

with every occurrence of evil. It is hard to avoid a sense of divine culpability. In contrast, a God of general but careful providence who fights, overturns, or even repurposes evil, rather than ordaining and willing it, is on a more defensible side of the moral ledger.

Underlying all of this reasoning in the evidential argument is an assumed ethical consequentialism (unchallenged by traditional theodicy) that directly conflicts with the deontological ethics of Christian theism. This internal theoretical incoherence is devastating and makes theodicy unworkable. The burden to find greater goods for extreme evil has proven unachievable, as has justifying God for instrumentally ordaining evil as a means to the greater good. To be free of ethical consequentialism allows the Great Controversy theodicy to affirm an ethics, theology, and theodicy which are harmoniously deontological and without contradiction. This deontological consistency is revealed in its compatibility with the Doctrine of Double effect.

Instead of acquiescing to the flawed assumptions of the evidential argument, the Great Controversy theodicy uses a Michael Peterson-style partial-greater good understanding of freedom. The great good of freedom is not subsequent to nor dependent upon a necessary prior evil. Instead, evil is an unnecessary, unjustified intruder that abused an antecedent greater good and catalyzed cosmic war. This abuse of free will is foreseen, planned for, and fought against but not foreordained or willed. God is justified in making the original good which he also rescues and restores.

The Great Controversy theodicy reframing also frees its eschatology from tilting in one of two theodicy-undermining theological extremes. On the one hand are distortions of divine mercy that compromise God's justice. Greater good theodicies require eschatology to provide overbalancing good ends to justify God's use of evil as a means to these goals. This often leads to innovations that are highly speculative or lacking in biblical support (examples include post-mortem salvation opportunities, purgatory, and universalism). On the other hand is the "problem of (an eternal) hell" with its merciless justice. Hell is the most egregious example of divinely ordained suffering and evil. When combined with end-justifies-the-means reasoning[7] it is a most extreme and insoluble form of the problem of evil.[8] The Great Controversy theodicy avoids both extremes by opting for a deontologically based annihilationist perspective. In the cosmic controversy, God mercifully holds off eradicating evil and evil-doers until the justice of doing so is

---

7. Or even worse still add double predestination.
8. Hell arguably eternalizes evil in time and internalizes evil in God's will.

seen and conceded by all, including evil-doers themselves. This eschatology balances well the justice and mercy of God.

Lastly, the idea of the "mystery of evil" has a very practical outcome in that it frees theological and philosophical reason from the dangers of self-deception and self-sabotaging because it enables reason to humbly recognize the inherently confounding nature of evil as well as the artificial confounding based in Satan's "mystification of evil."

FURTHERING

This reframing and freeing results in furthering or extending the explanatory power of free will within the Great Controversy theodicy. This study identified that the Great Controversy theodicy requires a move from standard libertarian freedom to soft or virtue libertarianism. This move resolves the "win it" problem of how evil will end if the freedom to choose good or evil is permanent. Free will has the goal of virtuous character, and when it has been solidified into the right moral state, it is free from the possibility of evil (or conversely freedom is justly eliminated if virtue is irredeemably rejected). This new theodicy, therefore, avoids Boyd's equivocation between incompatible models of freedom.

The reframing of the free will defense within the Great Controversy theodicy means it is no longer vulnerable to the criticisms of anti-theodicy that (traditional) theodicy is unethical. The Great Controversy Theodicy, like anti-theodicy, both rejects ethical consequentialism and shifts the problem of evil from a sterile theoretical-metaphysical issue to a practical one. This new theodicy is not a metaphysical response but a narrative articulation of God's activity in fighting evil through atonement—a fight we are invited to join.[9]

This metanarrative approach produces an authentically Jesus-centered theodicy. This is very significant. Philosophical and theoretical approaches are notorious for radically marginalizing Jesus as inconsequential to the actual theodicy and instead make natural law, soul-making, process philosophy, or even free will central.[10] The placement of free will within the Great Controversy context produces a new Jesus and trinitarian-centered set of justificatory patterns. These are the Redeemed Good Defense which

---

9. In line with anti-theodicy the Great Controversy theodicy also exhibits a cruciform theodicy.

10. Jesus does play a significant role in felix culpa (and to a lesser extent the divine glory defense). This role is compromised by various self-defeating contexts (e.g., consequentialist ethics or theological determinism).

is based in a *Felix Soter* theodicy. The Redeemed Good Defense shows that the original greater goods by God (i.e., the making of a good, loving, but free creation) are not created as a means to an end but are good ends that are redeemable. Because these great goods necessarily come with risk, they are only actualized by God because they are redemptive guaranteed goods. God covenants himself to his creation as its blessed savior or *Felix Soter*. Creation is a risk to itself, but God foreknows and embraces that risk as his own. We are not a means to God's end; God is the self-guaranteed means to our (inclusive of God and creation) end.

ANSWERING SCOTT'S FIVE QUESTIONS ESSENTIAL TO THEODICY

Taken together, this reframing, freeing, and furthering by the Great Controversy metanarrative fulfills the potential of the free will defense and provides new and substantial responses to the five theodicy questions of Mark Scott.

In response to Scott's first question of how evil originates and who is responsible, the Great Controversy answers that this cannot be understood abstractly or generically but only in relation to evil's actual history. While the idea of free will is crucial, it is the free will of a particular being that originates evil. This being is the rebel angel Lucifer who willingly falls into evil's mysterious irrationality and aggressively justifies himself with a deceptive mystification of evil as a "liberating" alternative to the divine rule.

The Great Controversy answers Scott's second question about the ontology of evil and how it exists by affirming evil as ultimately inexplicable and confounding. Not understanding this point confounds human reason and further contributes to evil's dangerous effects. Metaphysically evil is privative but perversely and parasitically so. A created being misuses God's good creation. Evil is essentially and unavoidably a moral and personal conflict. No metaphysically account of evil is adequate. Evil entails a free self, justifying the unjustifiable rejection of God's character, law, love, and government. There is no accurate non-confounding understanding of evil without this cosmic controversy perspective.

Scott's third question about how evil poses a problem to theodicy is for the Great Controversy theodicy the problem of freedom's risk to creation itself. The actualization of this risk takes the form of evil as cosmic war and cosmic controversy. That is the real "problem of evil." The classical problem of evil trilemma is a secondary problem resulting from the epistemic limitations of finite creatures and aggravated by their fallen condition.

Scott's fourth question asks what is God's morally sufficient reason for permitting evil. The Great Controversy theodicy responds that evil itself has no reason. However, the divine act of making a good creation with free will is justified even if subsequently it is tragically and unjustifiably abused by that creation. This is because God is willing to be the guarantor and redeemer of creation in order that the risk of evil does not veto the eternal good of his creatures being able to exist by grace. God takes our risk as his own. The unjustified embrace of evil by some of creation does not prevent or prohibit the divine right to create a good creation which will be sustained in its original goodness or restored by redemptive divine sacrifice to its original goodness.

Scott's fifth and final question is about how God will end evil. In response, the Great Controversy theodicy claims that evil's end is brought about by the comprehensive extensive way God deals with evil's mystery, mystification, and multiplication via the manner he conducts himself in the cosmic conflict culminating in his own work of atonement (the mystery of godliness). This is articulated in a "Redeemed Good Defense" based in a *Felix Soter* theodicy. The additional use of virtue libertarianism as a model of freedom shows how the freedom that makes evil possible is no impediment to evil subsequently becoming "impossible."

AREAS FOR FURTHER STUDY

The Great Controversy is understudied as a theodicy at an academic level. There are many areas for further study. For instance, more work could be done on exactly how the Great Controversy theodicy relates the question of natural evil to moral evil and cosmic conflict. The nature of love and law is crucial for the Great Controversy theodicy but more study could be conducted on the various theological models of love and law and their relationship to the idea of cosmic conflict. Exegetical and biblical-theological work needs to be done in the area of cosmic warfare and to what degree the various elements of cosmic controversy can be discerned in Scripture. Finally, a deeper study of ethical theory in theodicy is needed.

Bibliography

Adams, Roy. *The Sanctuary: Understanding the Heart of Adventist Theology*. Hagerstown, MD: Review and Herald, 1993.

Alexander, David E., and Daniel M. Johnson, eds. "Introduction." In *Calvinism and the Problem of Evil*, 1–18. Eugene, OR: Pickwick, 2016.

Alston, William P. "The Inductive Argument From Evil and the Human Cognitive Condition." In *Philosophy of Religion*, 5:29–67. Philosophical Perspectives. Ridgeview: Atascadero, 1991.

Anderson, A. K. "Evil and the God of Narrative: Four Types of Contemporary Christian Theodicy." Graduate Theological Union, 2006.

Aquinas, Thomas. *On Evil*. Edited by Brian Davies, translated by Richard Regan. Oxford: Oxford University Press, 2003.

Asscherick, David. *God in Pain: Another Look at Evil, Suffering and the Cross*. Berrien Springs, MI: Pan De Vida Productions, 2009.

Augustine. "The Confessions of St. Augustin." *The Confessions and Letters of St. Augustin with a Sketch of His Life and Work*. Edited by Philip Schaff. Translated by J. G. Pikington. Vol. I. The Nicene and Post-Nicene Fathers of the Christian Church. Buffalo, NY: Christian Literature Company, 1886.

———. "Against the Epistle of Manichæus Called Fundamental." *St. Augustin: The Writings against the Manichaeans and against the Donatists*. Edited by Philip Schaff. Translated by R Stothert. Vol. VI. The Nicene and Post-Nicene Fathers of the Christian Church. Buffalo, NY: Christian Literature Company, 1887.

———. "The City of God." *St. Augustin's City of God and Christian Doctrine*. Edited by Philip Schaff. Translated by Marcus Dods. Vol. II. The Nicene and Post-Nicene Fathers of the Christian Church. Buffalo, NY: Christian Literature Company, 1887.

———. "The Enchiridion." *St. Augustin: On the Holy Trinity, Doctrinal Treatises, Moral Treatises*. Edited by Philip Schaff. Translated by J. F. Shaw. Vol. III. The Nicene and Post-Nicene Fathers of the Christian Church. Buffalo, NY: Christian Literature Company, 1887.

———. "A Treatise on Rebuke and Grace." *Saint Augustin: Anti-Pelagian Writings*. Edited by Philip Schaff. Translated by Robert Ernest Wallis. Vol. V. The Nicene and Post-Nicene Fathers of the Christian Church. Buffalo, NY: Christian Literature Company, 1887.

Barth, Karl. *Church Dogmatics: The Doctrine of Creation*. Edited by G. W. Bromiley and T. F. Torrance. Translated by G. W. Bromiley, G. T. Thomson, and Harold Knight. Vol. III/3, §50. London: T & T Clark, 2009.

Basinger, David. "Evil as Evidence against God's Existence." In *The Problem of Evil: Selected Readings*, edited by Michael L Peterson. Notre Dame, IN: University of Notre Dame Press, 1992.

Bauckham, Richard. *The Theology of Jürgen Moltmann*. Edinburgh: T & T Clark, 1995.

Beilby, James K., and Paul R Eddy, eds. *Divine Foreknowledge: Four Views*. Downers Grove, IL: InterVarsity, 2001.

———. *The Nature of the Atonement: Four Views*. Downers Grove, IL: InterVarsity, 2006.

Beilby, James K., and Paul Rhodes Eddy, eds. *Understanding Spiritual Warfare: Four Views*. Grand Rapids, MI: Baker Academic, 2012.

Bergmann, Michael, and Daniel Howard-Snyder. "Grounds for Belief in God Aside, Does Evil Make Atheism More Reasonable than Theism?" In *God and the Problem of Evil*, edited by William L. Rowe, 140–55. Malden, MA: Blackwell, 2001.

Bertoluci, Jose M. "The Son of the Morning and the Guardian Cherub in the Context of the Controversy between Good and Evil." Th.D., Andrews University, 1985.

Betenson, Toby. "The Problem of Evil as a Moral Objection to Theism." Ph.D Thesis, University of Birmingham, 2014.

———. "Anti-Theodicy." *Philosophical Compass* 11 (2016): 56–65.

Block, Daniel. *The Book of Ezekiel*. New International Commentary on the Old Testament. Grand Rapids, MI: Eerdmans, 1998.

Bloesch, Donald G. *God the Almighty: Power, Wisdom, Holiness, Love*. Downers Grove, IL: InterVarsity, 1995.

Boyd, Gregory A. *God at War: The Bible & Spiritual Conflict*. Downers Grove, IL: InterVarsity, 1997.

———. "Trouble With Angels: Recovering the Warfare Theodicy of the Early Post-Apostolic Church." 1–32. 49th Conference of the Evangelical Theological Society. Santa Clara, CA, 1997.

———. *God of the Possible: A Biblical Introduction to the Open View of God*. Grand Rapids, MI: Baker, 2000.

———. *Satan and the Problem of Evil: Constructing a Trinitarian Warfare Theodicy*. Downers Grove, IL: InterVarsity, 2001.

———. "The Open-Theism View." In *Divine Foreknowledge: Four Views*, edited by James K. Beilby and Paul R Eddy, 11–47. Downers Grove, IL: InterVarsity, 2001.

———. "Christian Love and Academic Dialogue: A Reply to Bruce Ware." *Journal of the Evangelical Theological Society* 45 (2002): 233–43.

———. *Is God to Blame? Moving Beyond Pat Answers to the Problem of Evil*. Downers Grove, IL: InterVarsity, 2003.

———. "Neo-Molinism and the Infinite Intelligence of God." *Philosophia Christi* 5, no. 1 (2003): 187–204.

———. "Unbounded Love and the Openness of the Future: An Exploration and Critique of Pinnock's Theological Pilgrimage." In *Semper Reformandum: Studies in Honour of Clark H Pinnock*, edited by Stanley E. Porter and Anthony R. Cross. Carlisle, UK: Paternoster, 2003.

———. "Christus Victor View." In *The Nature of the Atonement: Four Views*, edited by James K. Beilby and Paul R Eddy, 23–49. Downers Grove, IL: InterVarsity, 2006.

———. *The Myth of a Christian Nation: How the Quest For Political Power Is Destroying the Church*. Grand Rapids, MI: Zondervan, 2006.

———. "Six Theses of the Warfare Worldview." December 29, 2007. http://reknew.org/2007/12/six-thesis-of-the-warfare-worldview/.

———. "What Happens to Babies That Die." *ReKnew* December 29, 2007. http://reknew.org/2007/12/what-happens-to-babies-who-die/.

———. "What's Your View of the Tribulation Period and the Rapture?" *ReKnew* December 29, 2007. http://reknew.org/2007/12/when-will-jesus-return/.

———. "Are You an Annihilationist, and If So, Why?" *ReKnew* January 19, 2008. http://reknew.org/2008/01/are-you-an-annihilationist-and-if-so-why/.

———. "The Case for Annihilationism." *ReKnew* January 19, 2008. http://reknew.org/2008/01/the-case-for-annihilationism/.

———. "The Kingdom as a Political-Spiritual Revolution." *Criswell Theological Review* 6 (2008): 23–41.

———."Advancing the Cruciform Revolution: A Kingdom Perspective on Evangelism." *Word & World* 29, no. 4 (2009): 407–17.

———. "Evolution as Cosmic Warfare: A Biblical Perspective on Satan and 'Natural Evil.'" In *Creation Made Free: Open Theology Engaging Science*, edited by Thomas Jay Oord, 125–148. Eugene, OR: Pickwick, 2009.

———. *The Myth of a Christian Religion: Losing Your Religion for the Beauty of a Revolution*. Grand Rapids, MI: Zondervan, 2009.

———. "Purgatory and the Judgment Seat of Christ." *ReKnew* March 17, 2009. http://reknew.org/2009/03/purgatory-and-the-judgment-seat-of-christ/.

———. "What about the Thief on the Cross?" *ReKnew* February 3, 2009. http://reknew.org/2009/02/what-about-the-thief-on-the-cross/.

———. "God Limits His Control." In *Four Views on Divine Providence*, edited by Dennis W. Jowers, 183–208. Grand Rapids, MI: Zondervan, 2010.

———. "Response to Paul Kjoss Helseth." In *Four Views on Divine Providence*, edited by Dennis W. Jowers. Grand Rapids, MI: Zondervan, 2010.

———. "Baby Universalism and Reasonable Infanticide." *ReKnew* February 9, 2011. http://reknew.org/2011/02/baby-universalism-and-reasonable-infanticide/.

———. "The Ground-Level Deliverance Model." In *Understanding Spiritual Warfare: Four Views*, edited by James K. Beilby and Paul Rhodes Eddy, 129–57. Grand Rapids, MI: Baker Academic, 2012.

———. "Review of Proof of Heaven (Eben Alexander)." *ReKnew* October 30, 2012. http://reknew.org/2012/10/review-of-proof-of-heaven-eben-alexander/.

———. "Satan and the Corruption of Nature: Seven Arguments." *Reknew* July 29, 2019. http://reknew.org/2008/01/satan-and-the-corruption-of-nature-seven-arguments/.

Boyd, Gregory, and Edward K. Boyd. *Letters From a Skeptic*. Colorado Springs: Cook, 1994.

Bychkov, Oleg V. *Aesthetic Revelation: Reading Ancient and Medieval Texts After Hans Urs Von Balthasar*. Washington, DC: The Catholic University of America Press, 2010.

Byrne, Peter. "Helm's God and the Authorship of Sin." In *Reason, Faith, History: Philosophical Essay's for Paul Helm*, edited by Martin Stone, 193–204. Farnham, UK: Ashgate, 2008.

Cairus, Aecio E. "The Doctrine of Man." In *Handbook of Seventh-day Adventist Theology*, edited by Raoul Dederen, 12:205–32. SDA Bible Commentary. Hagerstown, MD: Review and Herald, 2000.

Bibliography

Canale, Fernando Luis. *A Criticism of Theological Reason: Time and Timelessness as Primordial Presuppositions*. Andrews University Seminary Doctrinal Dissertation Series 10. Berrien Springs, MI: Andrews University Press, 1987.

Chappell, T. D. J. "Why God Is Not a Consequentialist." *Religious Studies* 29, no. 2 (1993): 239–43.

Coady, C. A. J. *Morality and Political Violence*. Cambridge: Cambridge University Press, 2007.

Craig, William Lane, and J. P. Moreland. *Philosophical Foundations for a Christian Worldview*. Downers Grove, IL: IVP Academic, 2003.

Davidson, Bruce W. "Glorious Damnation: Hell as an Essential Element in the Theology of Jonathan Edwards." *Journal of the Evangelical Theological Society* 54, no. 4 (2011): 809–22.

Davidson, Richard M. "Sanctuary Typology." In *Symposium on Revelation—Book I: Introductory and Exegetical Studies*, edited by Frank B. Holbrook. Vol. 6. Daniel and Revelation Series. Silver Spring, MD: Biblical Research Institute, 1992.

———. "The Chiastic Literary Structure of the Book of Ezekiel." In *To Understand the Scriptures: Essays in Honor of William Shea*, edited by David Merling, 71–94. Berrien Springs, MI: Institute of Archaeology/Horn Archaeological Museum, 2000.

———. "Cosmic Metanarrative for the Coming Millennium." *Journal of the Adventist Theological Society* 11 (2000): 102–19.

———. "The Divine Covenant Lawsuit Motif in Canonical Perspective." *Journal of the Adventist Theological Society* 21 (2010): 45–84.

Davis, Stephen T., ed. *Encountering Evil: Live Options in Theodicy*. 2nd edition. Louisville, KY: Westminster John Knox, 2001.

———. "Free Will and Evil." In *Encountering Evil: Live Options in Theodicy*, edited by Stephen T. Davis. 2nd edition. Louisville, KY: Westminster John Knox, 2001.

Dederen, Raoul. "Christ: His Person and Work." In *Handbook of Seventh-day Adventist Theology*, edited by Raoul Dederen, 12:160–204. SDA Bible Commentary. Hagerstown, MD: Review and Herald, 2000.

Diller, Kevin. "Are Sin and Evil Necessary for a Really Good World? Questions for Alvin Plantinga's Felix Culpa Theodicy." *Faith and Philosophy* 25 (2008): 87–101.

Douglas, Herbert E. "The Great Controversy Theme: What It Means to Adventism." *Ministry* (2000): 5–7.

Duah, Martha. "A Study of Warfare Theodicy in the Writings of Ellen G. White and Gregory A. Boyd." PhD dissertation, Andrews University, 2012.

Erickson, Millard J. *Christian Theology*. 2nd edition. Grand Rapids, MI: Baker, 1998.

Erlandson, Doug. "A New Perspective on the Problem of Evil." *Antithesis* June 1991. http://reformed.org/webfiles/antithesis/index.html?mainframe=/webfiles.antithesis/v2n2/ant_v2n2_evil.html.

Evans, G.R. *Augustine on Evil*. Cambridge: Cambridge University Press, 1994.

Evans, Jeremy A. *The Problem of Evil: The Challenge to Essential Christian Beliefs*. B & H Studies in Christian Apologetics. Nashville, TN: Broadman & Holman, 2013.

Feinberg, John S. "God Limits His Power (Bruce Reichenbach): John Feinberg's Response." In *Predestination and Free Will*, edited by Basinger, David and Randall Basinger. Downers Grove, IL: InterVarsity, 1986.

———. *The Many Faces of Evil: Theological Systems and the Problem of Evil*. Revised and Expanded Edition. Wheaton: Crossway, 2004.

Forsyth, P. T. *The Justification of God: Lectures for War-Time on a Christian Theodicy.* London: Duckworth, 1916.
Fowler, John M. "Sin." In *Handbook of Seventh-day Adventist Theology*, edited by Raoul Dederen, 12:233–70. SDA Bible Commentary. Hagerstown, MD: Review and Herald, 2000.
Ganssle, Gregory E., and Yena Lee. "Evidential Problems of Evil." In *God and Evil: The Case for God in a World Filled with Pain*, edited by Chad Meister and James K. Dew. Downers Grove, IL: InterVarsity, 2013.
Goldstein, Clifford. "The Inexplicable Unexplained: Another Look at Evil." *Ministry* 77, no. 11 (2005): 9–11.
Graham, Gordon. *Evil and Christian Ethics*. New Studies in Christian Ethics. Cambridge: Cambridge University Press, 2001.
Green, Christopher R. "A Compatibicalvinist Demonstrative-Goods Defense." In *Calvinism and the Problem of Evil*, edited by David E. Alexander and Daniel M. Johnson, 233–47. Eugene, OR: Pickwick, 2016.
Green, Joel B., and Mark D. Baker, eds. *Recovering the Scandal of the Cross: Atonement in New Testament and Contemporary Contexts*. Downers Grove, IL: InterVarsity, 2000.
Griffin, David Ray. *God, Power and Evil: A Process Theodicy*. Philadelphia: Westminster, 1976.
———. "Creation out of Chaos and the Problem of Evil." In *Encountering Evil: Live Options in Theodicy*, edited by Stephen T. Davis. 1st edition. Edinburgh: T & T Clark, 1981.
———. *Evil Revisited: Responses and Reconsiderations*. Albany, NY: State University of New York Press, 1991.
———. "Process Theology and the Christian Good News: A Response to Classical Free Will Theism." In *Searching for an Adequate God: A Dialogue Between Process and Free Will Theists*, edited by John B. Cobb, Clark H. Pinnock, and David Ray Griffin. Grand Rapids, MI: Eerdmans, 2000.
———. "Creation out of Nothing, Creation out of Chaos, and the Problem of Evil." In *Encountering Evil: Live Options in Theodicy*, edited by Stephen T. Davis. 2nd edition. Louisville: KY: Westminster John Knox, 2001.
Griffith-Dickson, Gwen. *The Philosophy of Religion*. London: SCM, 2005.
Gulley, Norman R. "The Cosmic Controversy: World View for Theology and Life." *Journal of the Adventist Theological Society* 7 (1996): 82–124.
———. *Systematic Theology: Prolegomena*. Berrien Springs, MI: Andrews University Press, 2003.
———. *Systematic Theology: Creation, Christ, Salvation*. Berrien Springs, MI: Andrews University Press, 2012.
Hart, Matthew J. "Calvinism and the Problem of Hell." In *Calvinism and the Problem of Evil*, edited by David E. Alexander and Daniel M. Johnson, 248–72. Eugene, OR: Pickwick, 2016.
Hasker, William. "Must God Do His Best?" *International Journal for Philosophy of Religion* 16 (1984): 213–23.
———. "Does God Take Risks in Governing the World? God Takes Risks." In *Contemporary Debates in Philosophy of Religion*, edited by Michael L Peterson and Raymond J. Vanarragon, 218–28; 240, 241. Oxford: Blackwell, 2004.
———. *Providence, Evil, and the Openness of God*. New York: Routledge, 2004.

———. *The Triumph of God over Evil: Theodicy for a World of Suffering*. Downers Grove, IL: InterVarsity, 2008.

———. "All Too Skeptical Theism." *Journal for Philosophy of Religion* 68, no. 1 (2010): 15–29.

Helm, Paul. "Does God Take Risks in Governing the World? God Does Not Take Risks." In *Contemporary Debates in Philosophy of Religion*, edited by Michael L Peterson and Raymond J. Vanarragon, 228–38; 240, 241. Oxford: Blackwell, 2004.

Helseth, Paul Kjoss. "The Trustworthiness of God and the Foundations of Hope." In *Beyond the Bounds: Open Theism and the Understanding of Biblical Christianity*, edited by Piper John, Taylor Justin, and Paul Kjoss Helseth. Wheaton, Il: Crossway, 2003.

———. "On Divine Ambivalence: Open Theism and the Problem of Particular Evils." *Journal of the Evangelical Theological Society* 44, no. 3 (2001) 493–511.

———. "God Causes All Things." In *Four Views on Divine Providence*, edited by Dennis W. Jowers, 25–52. Grand Rapids, MI: Zondervan, 2010.

Hick, John. *Evil and the God of Love*. 2nd edition. Basingstoke & London: Macmillian, 1977.

———. *A John Hick Reader*. Edited by Paul Badham. London: Macmillian, 1990.

———. *The Fifth Dimension: An Exploration of the Spiritual Realm*. Oxford: Oneworld, 1999.

Hoffman, Tobias. "Theories of Angelic Sin from Aquinas to Ockham." In *A Companion to Angels in Medieval Philosophy*, edited by Tobias Hoffman, 283–317. Leiden, Netherlands: Brill, 2012.

Holbrook, Frank B. *The Atoning Priesthood of Jesus Christ*. Berrien Springs, MI: Adventist Theological Society, 1996.

Hume, David. *Dialogues Concerning Natural Religion*, Edited by Nelson Pike. New York: Macmillian, 1985.

Inwagen, Peter van. "The Argument from Evil." In *Christian Faith and the Problem of Evil*, edited by Peter van Inwagen, 55–73. Grand Rapids, MI: Eerdmans, 2004.

Johnson, Daniel M. "Calvinism and the Problem of Evil: A Map of the Territory." In *Calvinism and the Problem of Evil*, edited by David E. Alexander and Daniel M. Johnson, 19–55. Eugene, OR: Pickwick, 2016.

Jowers, Dennis W., ed. *Four Views on Divine Providence*. Grand Rapids, MI: Zondervan, 2010.

Kamm, Francis. "The Doctrine of Triple Effect and Why a Rational Agent Need Not Intend the Means to His End." *Proceedings of the Aristotelian Society, Supplementary Volumes* 74 (2000): 21–39.

Kärkkäinen, Veli-Matti. *The Doctrine of God: A Global Introduction*. Grand Rapids, MI: Baker Academic, 2004.

Keathley, Kenneth. *Salvation and Sovereignty: A Molinist Approach*. Nashville, TN: Baker Academic, 2010.

King, Peter. "Augustine and Anselm on Angelic Sin." In *A Companion to Angels in Medieval Philosophy*, edited by Tobias Hoffman, 261–81. Leiden, Netherlands: Brill, 2012.

Kis, Miroslav M. "Christian Lifestyle and Behavior." In *Handbook of Seventh-day Adventist Theology*, edited by Raoul Dederen, 12:675–723. SDA Bible Commentary. Hagerstown, MD: Review and Herald, 2000.

Knight, George R. *The Cross of Christ: God's Work for Us.* Hagerstown, MD: Review and Herald, 2008.

Kreiner, Armin. *Gott Im Leid: Zur Stichhaltigkeit Der Theodizee-Argumente.* Freiburg im Breisgau: Herder, 2005.

Lactantius. "A Treatise on the Anger of God." In *The Ante-Nicene Fathers: Translations of the Writings of the Fathers down to A.D. 325*, edited by Alexander Roberts, James Donaldson, and A. Cleveland Coxe. Vol. 7. Edinburgh: T & T Clark, 1886.

Ladd, George Eldon. *The Presence of the Future: The Eschatology of Biblical Realism.* Grand Rapids, MI: Eerdmans, 1974.

Leibniz, Gottfried Wilhelm. *Theodicy: Essays on the Goodness of God, the Freedom of Man, and the Origin of Evil.* Translated by E. M. Huggard. La Salle: IL: Open Court, 1988.

Little, Bruce A. *A Creation-Order Theodicy: God and Gratuitous Evil.* Lanham, MD: University Press of America, 2005.

MacGregor, Kirk R. "The Existence and Irrelevance of Gratuitous Evil." *Philosophi Christi* 14, no. 1 (2012): 165–80.

Mackie, J.L. "Evil and Omnipotence." *Mind* 64, no. 254 (1955): 200–212.

———. *The Miracle of Theism: Arguments for and against the Existence of God.* Oxford: Clarendon, 1982.

MacPherson, Anthony. "Theodicy and Contrasting Eschatological Visions: The Investigative Judgment and the Problem of Evil." *Eschatology from an Adventist Perspective: Proceedings of the Fourth International Bible Conference: Rome, June 11–20, 2018*, edited by Elias Brasil de Souza, A. Rahel Wells, Laszlo Gallusz, and Denis Kaiser. Silver Spring, MD: Biblical Research Institute, 2021. 457–476.

Madden, Edward, and Peter Hare. *Evil and the Concept of God.* Springfield, IL: Charles C. Thomas, 1968.

McBrayer, Justin P. "Skeptical Theism." *Philosophy Compass* 5, no. 7 (2010): 611–23.

———. "Are Skeptical Theists Really Skeptics? Sometimes Yes and Sometimes No." *International Journal for Philosophy of Religion* 72, no. 1 (2012): 3–16.

McCabe, Herbert. *God and Evil: In the Theology of St Thomas Aquinas.* London: Continuum, 2010.

McIntyre, Alison. "Doctrine of Double Effect." In *The Stanford Encyclopedia of Philosophy,* edited by Edward N. Zalta. 2014. https://plato.stanford.edu/archives/win2014/entries/double-effect/.

McIntyre, John. *The Shape of Soteriology: Studies in the Doctrine of the Death of Christ.* Edinburgh: T & T Clark, 1992.

McNaughton, David. "Is God (almost) a Consequentialist? Swinburne's Moral Theory." *Religious Studies* 38, no. 2 (2002): 265–81.

Middleton, J. Richard. "Why the 'Greater Good' Isn't a Defense: Classical Theodicy in Light of the Biblical Genre of Lament." *Koinonia* 9 (1997): 81–113.

Ministerial Association of the General Conference of Seventh-day Adventists. *Seventh-day Adventists Believe: An Exposition of the Fundamental Beliefs of the Seventh-day Adventist Church.* 2nd edition. Boise, ID: Pacific, 2005.

Moltmann, Jürgen. *The Trinity and the Kingdom of God.* Translated by Margaret Kohl. San Francisco: Harper & Row, 1981.

Moskala, Jiri. "Toward a Biblical Theology of God's Judgment: A Celebration of the Cross in Seven Phases of Divine Universal Judgment (An Overview of a Theocentric-

Christocentric Approach)," *Journal of the Adventist Theological Society* 15, no. 1 (2004): 138–165.

Mosser, Carl. "Evil, Mormonism, and the Impossibility of Perfection Ab Initio: An Irenaean Defense." *Southern Baptist Journal of Theology* 9, no. 2 (2005) 56–69.

———. "Exaltation and Gods Who Can Fall: Some Problems for Mormon Theodicies." *Element* 3, no. 1 & 2 (2007): 45–67.

Murphy, Nancey, and George F. R. Ellis. *On the Moral Nature of the Universe: Theology, Cosmology, and Ethics*. Minneapolis, MN: Fortress, 1996.

Nash, Ronald. *Faith and Reason: Searching for a Rational Faith*. Grand Rapids, MI: Zondervan, 1988.

Nichols, Aidan. *The Shape of Catholic Theology: An Introduction to Its Sources, Principles and History*. Collegeville, MN: Liturgical Press, 1991.

Oderberg, David S. "The Doctrine of Double Effect." In *A Companion to the Philosophy of Action*, edited by T. O'Connor and C. Sandis, 324–30. Oxford: Wiley-Blackwell, 2010.

Oliver, Simon. "Foreword." In *The Wonder of the Cross: The God Who Uses Evil and Suffering to Destroy Evil and Suffering*, by Richard A. Shenk, ix—xi. Eugene, OR: Pickwick, 2013.

Olson, Roger. *Arminian Theology: Myths and Realities*. Downers Grove, IL: InterVarsity, 2006.

Ormerod, Neil, *A Public God: Natural Theology Reconsidered*. Minneapolis, MN: Fortress, 2015.

Oswalt, John N. *The Book of Isaiah 1–39*, New International Commentary on the Old Testament. Grand Rapids. Grand Rapids, MI: Eerdmans, 1986.

Patrick, Anne E. "Is Theodicy an Evil? Response to The Evils of Theodicy by Terrence W. Tilley." In *Evil and Hope*, 201–4. New York: Catholic Theological Society of America, 1995.

Peckham, John C. "The Concept of Divine Love in the Context of the God-World Relationship." PhD Thesis. Andrews University, 2012.

———. *The Love of God: A Canonical Model*. Downers Grove, IL: InterVarsity, 2015.

———. *Theodicy of Love: Cosmic Conflict and the Problem of Evil*. Grand Rapids, MI: Baker Academic, 2018.

Peterson, Michael, et al. *Reason and Religious Belief: An Introduction to the Philosophy of Religion*. Oxford: Oxford University Press, 1991.

Peterson, Michael L. *Evil and the Christian God*. Grand Rapids, MI: Baker, 1982.

———. *God and Evil: An Introduction to the Issues*. Boulder, CO: Westview, 1998.

———. "Religious Diversity, Evil, and a Variety of Theodicies." In *The Oxford Handbook of Religious Diversity*, edited by Chad Meister. Oxford: Oxford University Press, 2011.

———. "Christian Theism and the Evidential Argument from Evil." In *Philosophy and the Christian Worldview: Analysis, Assessment and Development*, edited by David Werther and Mark D. Linville, 175–95. London: Bloomsbury, 2012.

Phan, Peter C. "The Lesser Evil of Theodicy." In *Evil and Hope*, 192–200. New York: Catholic Theological Society of America, 1995.

Pini, Giorgio. "What Lucifer Wanted: Anselm, Aquinas, and Scotus on the Object of the First Evil Choice." In *Cornell Summer Colloquium in Medieval Philosophy*, 1–26, 2012.

Pinnock, Sarah K. *Beyond Theodicy: Jewish and Christian Continental Thinkers Respond to the Holocaust*. Albany, NY: State University of New York Press, 2002.
Piper, John. "Is God Less Glorious Because He Ordained That Evil Be?" *Desiring God* 1998. http://www.desiringgod.org/messages/is-god-less-glorious-because-he-ordained-that-evil-be.
Piper, Mark. "Why Theists Cannot Accept Skeptical Theism." *Sophia* 47, no. 2 (2008): 129–48.
Plantinga, Alvin. *The Nature of Necessity*. Oxford: Clarendon, 1974.
———. *God, Freedom and Evil*. Grand Rapids, MI: Eerdmans, 1977.
———. "Supralapsarianism, or 'Felix Culpa.'" In *Christian Faith and the Problem of Evil*, edited by Peter van Inwagen, 1–25. Grand Rapids, MI: Eerdmans, 2004.
Porkoli, Jafar Mirzaee, and Mohammad-Javad Haj'jari. "Double-Effect Reasoning in Paradise Lost: An Investigation into Milton's God's Will in Humankind's Fall." *Brno Studies* 42, no. 1 (2016): 1–19.
Potter, R. Dennis. "Finitism and the Problem of Evil." *Dialogue: A Journal of Mormon Thought* 33, no. 4 (2000): 83–95.
Pruss, Alexander R. "The First Sin: A Dilemma for Christian Determinists." In *Calvinism and the Problem of Evil*, edited by David E. Alexander and Daniel M. Johnson, 187–99. Eugene, OR: Pickwick, 2016.
Pyne, Robert A., and David Piske. Review of *Satan and the Problem of Evil: Constructing a Trinitarian Warfare Theodicy*, by Gregory A. Boyd. *Bibliotheca Sacra* 161, no. January-March (2004): 110–13.
Reichenbach, Bruce. *Evil and a Good God*. New York: Fordham University Press, 1982.
Rice, Richard. "The Great Controversy and the Problem of Evil." *Spectrum* 32, no. 1 (2004): 46–55.
———. *Suffering and the Search for Meaning: Contemporary Responses to the Problem of Pain*. Downers Grove, IL: IVP Academic, 2014.
Rodin, R. Scott. *Evil and Theodicy in the Theology of Karl Barth*. Issues in Systematic Theology 3. New York: Peter Lang, 1997.
Roth, John K., ed. "A Theodicy of Protest." In *Encountering Evil: Live Options in Theodicy*. 1st edition. Edinburgh: T & T Clark, 1981.
Rowe, William L. *Philosophy of Religion: An Introduction*. 3rd edition. Belmont: CA: Wadsworth, 2001.
———. "Is Evil Evidence against Belief in God?" In *Contemporary Debates in Philosophy of Religion*, edited by Michael L Peterson and Raymond J. Vanarragon, 3–12; 25–27. Oxford: Blackwell, 2004.
———. *William L. Rowe on Philosophy of Religion: Selected Writings by William L. Rowe*, edited by Nick Trakakis. Farnham, UK: Ashgate, 2007.
Russell, Jeffery Burton. *Satan: The Early Christian Tradition*. London: Cornel University Press, 1981.
Scott, Mark S. M. *Journey Back to God: Origen on the Problem of Evil*. Oxford: Oxford University Press, 2012.
———. *Pathways in Theodicy*. Minneapolis: Fortress, 2015.
Shea, William H. "Biblical Parallels for the Investigative Judgment." In *Selected Studies On Prophetic Interpretation*, 1:1–30. Daniel and Revelation Series. Hagerstown, MD: Review and Herald, 1982.
Shenk, Richard A. *The Wonder of the Cross: The God Who Uses Evil and Suffering to Destroy Evil and Suffering*. Eugene, OR: Pickwick, 2013.

Snapper, John. "Paying the Cost of Skeptical Theism." *International Journal for Philosophy of Religion* 69, no. 1 (2011): 45–56.
Soelle, Dorothee. *Suffering*. London: Darton, Longman & Todd, 1975.
Sproul, R. C. *Chosen by God*. Wheaton: Tyndale House, 1986.
———. *Not a Chance: The Myth of Chance in Modern Science and Cosmology*. Grand Rapids, MI: Baker, 1994.
Stewart, Melville Y. *The Greater-Good Defence: An Essay on the Rationality of Faith*. New York: St Martin's, 1993.
Sulmasy, Daniel P. "The Use and Abuse of the Principle of Double Effect." *Clinical Practice Management* no. 3 (1996): 86–90.
Surin, Kenneth. *Theology and the Problem of Evil*. New York: Blackwell, 1986.
———. "Taking Suffering Seriously." In *The Problem of Evil: Selected Readings*, edited by Michael L Peterson, 339–50. Notre Dame, IN: University of Notre Dame Press, 2009.
Swinburne, Richard. *The Existence of God*. Oxford: Clarendon, 1991.
———. *Providence and the Problem of Evil*. Oxford: Oxford University Press, 1998.
Tiessen, Terrence. *Providence and Prayer: How Does God Work in the World?* Downers Grove, IL: InterVarsity, 2000.
Tilley, Terrence W. *The Evils of Theodicy*. Washington, DC: Georgetown University Press, 1991.
Timpe, Kevin. *Free Will: Sourcehood and its Alternatives*. London: Bloomsbury, 2012.
———. *Free Will in Philosophical Theology*. London: Bloomsbury, 2013.
———. "The Arbitariness of the Primal Sin." In *Oxford Studies in Philosophy of Religion*, edited by Jonathan L. Kvanvig, 5:234–57. Oxford: Oxford University Press, 2014.
———. "The Best Thing in Life Is Free: The Compatibility of God's Freedom and His Essential Moral Perfection," *Free Will and Classical Theism: The Significance of Freedom in Perfect Being Theology*, edited by Hugh McCann, 133–151. Oxford: Oxford University Press, 2017.
Timpe, Kevin, and Audra Jenson. "Free Will and the Stages of Theological Anthropology." In *The Ashgate Research Companion to Theological Anthropology*, edited by Joshua R. Farris and Charles Taliaferro. New York: Routledge, 2016.
Timpe, Kevin, and Timothy Pawl. "Incompatibilism, Sin, and Free Will in Heaven." *Faith and Philosophy* 26 (2009): 396–417.
Timpe, Kevin, and Daniel Speak, eds. "Introduction." In *Free Will and Theism: Connections, Contingencies, and Concerns*, 1–26. Oxford: Oxford University Press, 2016.
Tonstad, Sigve K. *Saving God's Reputation: The Theological Function of Pistis Iesou in the Cosmic Narratives of Revelation*. Library of New Testament Studies 337. London: T & T Clark International, 2006.
Trakakis, Nick. *The God Beyond Belief: In Defence of William Rowe's Evidential Argument from Evil*. Dordrecht: Springer, 2007.
———. *The End of Philosophy of Religion*. London: Continuum, 2008.
Trakakis, Nick, and Yujin Nagasawa. "Skeptical Theism and Moral Skepticism: A Reply to Almeida and Oppy." *Ars Disputandi* 4 (2004). http://www.arsdisputandi.org/.
Von Stosch, Klaus. *Theodizee*. Vol. Grundwissen Theologie. 3867 vols. Paderborn, Germany: Ferdinand Schoningh GmbH & Co, 2013.
Wallenkampf, A.V., and W.R. Lesher, eds. *The Sanctuary and the Atonement: Biblical, Historical, and Theological Studies*. Hagerstown, MD: Review and Herald, 1981.

Warburton, Nigel. *Philosophy: The Basics.* 5th edition. New York: Routledge, 2013.
Ware, Bruce A. *God's Lesser Glory.* Leicester: Apollos, 2000.
———. "Defining Evangelicalism's Boundaries Theologically: Is Open Theism Evangelical?" *Journal of the Evangelical Theological Society* 45 (2002): 193–212.
———. "Rejoinder to Replies by Clark H. Pinnock, John Sanders, and Gregory A. Boyd." *Journal of the Evangelical Theological Society* 45 (2002) 245–56.
———. *God's Greater Glory.* Wheaton, IL: Crossway, 2004.
Webster, Eric Claude. "The Millennium." In *Handbook of Seventh-day Adventist Theology,* edited by Raoul Dederen, 12:927–46. SDA Bible Commentary. Hagerstown, MD: Review and Herald, 2000.
Wetzel, James. "Can Theodicy Be Avoided? The Claim of Unredeemed Evil." In *The Problem of Evil: Selected Readings,* edited by Michael L Peterson. Notre Dame, IN: University of Notre Dame Press, 2009.
Whidden, Woodrow W. *Ellen White on the Humanity of Christ.* Hagerstown, MD: Review and Herald, 1997.
———. "God Is Love—Trinitarian Love!" *Journal of the Adventist Theological Society* 17, no. 1 (2006) 98–124.
White, Ellen G.
———. *Spiritual Gifts.* Vol. 3. 3 volumes. Battle Creek, MI: Seventh-day Adventist Publishing Association, 1858.
———. "Last Talk with the Disciples." *The Signs of the Times,* January 24, 1878.
———. *Early Writings.* Washington, DC: Review and Herald, 1882.
———. "Young Men as Missionary Workers." *The Advent Review and Sabbath Herald,* July 17, 1883.
———. "In What Shall We Glory?" *The Advent Review and Sabbath Herald,* March 15, 1887.
———. *The Sanctified Life.* Washington, DC: Review and Herald, 1889.
———. "Compassion for the Erring." *The Advent Review and Sabbath Herald,* July 16, 1889.
———. "What Was Secured by the Death of Christ." *The Signs of the Times,* December 30, 1889.
———. *Patriarchs and Prophets.* Washington, DC: Review and Herald, 1890.
———. "The Plan of Salvation." *The Signs of the Times,* February 13, 1893.
———. "The Weapon against Satan's Delusion." *The Signs of the Times,* September 18, 1893.
———. "The Treasure of Truth Rejected." *The Advent Review and Sabbath Herald,* April 3, 1894.
———. "The Cross Incontrovertible Evidence." *The Signs of the Times,* March 7, 1895.
———. "Humanity the Lost Pearl." *The Youth's Instructor,* October 17, 1895.
———. *Steps to Christ.* Hagerstown, MD: Review and Herald, 1896.
———. *Thoughts from the Mount of Blessing.* Mountain View, CA: Pacific, 1896.
———. "Christ Represents the Beneficence of the Law." *The Advent Review and Sabbath Herald,* March 9, 1897.
———. "The Mystery of God." *The Signs of the Times,* March 25, 1897.
———. *The Desire of Ages.* Mountain View, CA: Pacific, 1898.
———. "Christ's Attitude to the Law." *The Advent Review and Sabbath Herald,* November 15, 1898.
———. "Christ Glorified." *The Signs of the Times,* May 10, 1899.

---. "The Only True Mediator." *The Signs of the Times*, June 28, 1899.

---. "Sacrificed for Us." *The Youth's Instructor*, July 20, 1899.

---. "Against Principalities and Powers." *The Youth's Instructor*, October 26, 1899.

---. "The Cost of Salvation." *The Bible Echo*, November 20, 1899.

---. *Christ's Object Lessons*. Washington, DC: Review and Herald, 1900.

---. "Lessons from the Christ-Life." *The Advent Review and Sabbath Herald*, March 12, 1901.

---. "The Great Standard of Righteousness." *The Advent Review and Sabbath Herald*, April 23, 1901.

---. "Spiritual Growth." *The Signs of the Times*, June 12, 1901.

---. "Obedience the Fruit of Union with Christ." *The Advent Review and Sabbath Herald*, September 3, 1901.

---. "Without Excuse." *The Advent Review and Sabbath Herald*, September 24, 1901.

---. "The Abiding Trust." *The Gospel Herald*, May 14, 1902.

---. "Words of Admonition Elmshaven, St Helena, Cal." *The Workers' Bulletin*, September 9, 1902.

---. *Education*. Washington, DC: Pacific, 1903.

---. *The Ministry of Healing*. Mountain View, CA: Pacific, 1905.

---. *The Acts of the Apostles*. Mountain View, CA: Pacific, 1911.

---. *The Great Controversy between Christ and Satan*. Mountain View, CA: Pacific, 1911.

---. *Counsels to Parents, Teachers, and Students*. Hagerstown, MD: Review and Herald, 1913.

---. "Satan and Our Appetites." *The Signs of the Times*, August 10, 1915.

---. *Prophets and Kings*. Mountain View, CA: Pacific, 1917.

---. *Counsels on Health*. Mountain View, CA: Pacific, 1923.

---. *Testimonies to Ministers and Gospel Workers*. Mountain View, CA: Pacific, 1923.

---. *Fundamentals of Christian Education*. Nashville, TN: Southern, 1923.

---. *Counsels on Stewardship*. Washington, DC: Review and Herald, 1940.

---. *The Story of Redemption*. Hagerstown, MD: Review and Herald, 1947.

---. *Testimonies for the Church*. Vol. 3. 9 volumes. Mountain View, CA: Pacific, 1948.

---. *Testimonies for the Church*. Vol. 2. 9 volumes. Mountain View, CA: Pacific, 1948.

---. *Testimonies for the Church*. Vol. 6. 9 volumes. Mountain View, CA: Pacific, 1948.

---. *Testimonies for the Church*. Vol. 5. 9 volumes. Mountain View, CA: Pacific, 1948.

---. *Testimonies for the Church*. Vol. 8. 9 volumes. Mountain View, CA: Pacific, 1948.

---. *Welfare Ministry*. Washington, DC: Review and Herald, 1952.

---. "Ellen White Comments." In *The Seventh-day Adventist Bible Commentary*, Vol. 1. Washington, DC: Review and Herald, 1953.

---. "Ellen White Comments." In *The Seventh-day Adventist Bible Commentary*, Vol. 3. Washington, DC: Review and Herald, 1954.

---. "Ellen White Comments." In *The Seventh-day Adventist Bible Commentary*, Vol. 4. Washington, DC: Review and Herald, 1955.

---. "Ellen White Comments." In *The Seventh-day Adventist Bible Commentary*, Vol. 5. Washington, DC: Review and Herald, 1956.

---. "Ellen White Comments." In *The Seventh-day Adventist Bible Commentary*, Vol. 6. Washington, DC: Review and Herald, 1956.

---. "Ellen White Comments." In *The Seventh-day Adventist Bible Commentary*, Vol. 7. Washington, DC: Review and Herald, 1957.

———. *Selected Messages*. Vol. 1. 3 volumes. Washington, DC: Review and Herald, 1958.
———. *Selected Messages*. Vol. 2. 3 volumes. Washington, DC: Review and Herald, 1958.
———. *Selected Messages*. Vol. 3. 3 volumes. Washington, DC: Review and Herald, 1958.
———. *Our High Calling*. Hagerstown, MD: Review and Herald, 1961.
———. *Confrontation*. Hagerstown, MD: Review and Herald, 1970.
———. "Ellen White Comments." In *The Seventh-day Adventist Bible Commentary*, Vol. 7A. Washington, DC: Review and Herald, 1970.
———. *This Day with God*. Hagerstown, MD: Review and Herald, 1979.
———. *Manuscript Releases*. 21 volumes. Silver Springs, MD: Ellen G. White Estate, 1981.
———. *The Upward Look*. Washington, DC: Review and Herald, 1982.
———. *The Ellen G. White 1888 Materials*. 4 volumes. Washington, DC: Ellen G. White Estate, 1987.
———. *Christ Triumphant*. Hagerstown, MD: Review and Herald, 1999.
White, Heath. "Theological Determinism and the 'Authoring Sin' Objection." In *Calvinism and the Problem of Evil*, edited by David E. Alexander and Daniel M. Johnson, 78–95. Eugene, OR: Pickwick, 2016.
Whitehead, Alfred. *Adventures of Ideas*. New York: Macmillan, 1933
Whitney, Barry. "Anti-Theodicy: Is Theodicy Itself Evil?" *Studies in Religion* 31 (2002): 472–74.
———. *Theodicy: An Annotated Bibliography on the Problem of Evil, 1960–1991*. Bowling Green, OH: Bowling Green State University Philosophy Documentation Center, 1998.
Woo, B. Hoon. "Is God the Author of Sin? Jonathan Edwards's Theodicy." *Puritan Reformed Journal* 6, no. 1 (2014): 98–123.
Wood, John W. "'All Must Appear': The Investigative Judgment Theme in the Writings of Ellen G. White." In *The Sanctuary and the Atonement: Biblical, Historical, and Theological Studies*, edited by A.V. Wallenkampf and W.R. Lesher, 639–66. Washington, DC: Review and Herald, 1981.
———. "The Mighty Opposites: The Atonement of Christ in the Writings of Ellen G. White, Part 1." In *The Sanctuary and the Atonement: Biblical, Historical, and Theological Studies*, edited by A.V. Wallenkampf and W.R. Lesher, 694–709. Washington, DC: Review and Herald, n.d.
———. "The Mighty Opposites: The Atonement of Christ in the Writings of Ellen G. White, Part 2." In *The Sanctuary and the Atonement: Biblical, Historical, and Theological Studies*, edited by A.V. Wallenkampf and W.R. Lesher, 710–30. Washington, DC: Review and Herald, 1981.
Wykstra, Stephen. "The Humean Obstacle to Evidential Arguments from Suffering: On Avoiding Evils of Appearance." *International Journal for Philosophy of Religion* 16 (1984): 73–93.
Young, Norman H. "Five Charges Against God." *Record* May 6, 2004: 11–12.
Zimmerman, Dean. "An Anti-Molinist Replies." In *Molinism: The Contemporary Debate*, edited by Ken Perszyk, 163–86. Oxford: Oxford University Press, 2012.
Zurcher, J. R. *Touched with Our Feelings: A Historical Survey of Adventist Thought on the Human Nature of Christ*. Hagerstown, MD: Review and Herald, 1999.

www.ingramcontent.com/pod-product-compliance
Lightning Source LLC
Chambersburg PA
CBHW062020220426

43662CB00010B/1404